D0457452

SEX IN AMERICA

SEX IN AMERICA

A DEFINITIVE SURVEY

Robert T. Michael, John H. Gagnon,
Edward O. Laumann, and
Gina Kolata

Little, Brown and Company

Boston   New York   Toronto   London

First Edition

Library of Congress Cataloging-in-Publication Data

Sex in America : a definitive survey / Robert T. Michael . . . [et al.].
— 1st ed.
    p.   cm.
Includes index.
ISBN 0-316-07524-8
    1. Sexual behavior surveys—United States.   2. Sex customs—United
States.   3. Sex customs—United States—Statistics.   4. Sex—United
States.   5. Sex—United States—Statistics.   I. Michael, Robert T.
HQ18.U5S475   1994
306.7'0973—dc20   94-18258

10   9   8   7   6   5   4   3

MV-NY

Published simultaneously in Canada by Little, Brown & Company
(Canada) Limited

Printed in the United States of America

CONTENTS

ACKNOWLEDGMENTS

The authors gratefully acknowledge the support of the following foundations who made possible the National Health and Social Life Survey on which this book is based: The Robert Wood Johnson Foundation, The Henry J. Kaiser Family Foundation of Menlo Park, The Rockefeller Foundation, The Andrew Mellon Foundation, The John D. and Catherine T. MacArthur Foundation, The New York Community Trust, American Foundation for AIDS Research, and The Ford Foundation. The skilled staff and corporate commitment of NORC made this challenging survey project a success, and the dedicated University of Chicago students and staff who have worked with us helped transform that survey data into a coherent body of evidence. None deserves our thanks more than the 3,432 respondents each of whom in an hour-and-a-half interview gave us his or her sexual life history and made the findings in this book more complete.

A COMPANION VOLUME

This book is one of two that report the findings from a national survey of adult sexual behavior. The other book is written for professional social scientists, couselors, and health professionals and has more detailed statistics. Its title is *The Social Organization of Sexuality*, by Edward O. Laumann, John H. Gagnon, Robert T. Michael, and Stuart Michaels, published by the University of Chicago Press, 1994. We have written the two books in tandem and published them at the same time. In *Sex in America* we have selected many highlights from the study and presented them with interpretation in a manner that we hope will reach a wide audience and will help inform many about this important aspect of social behavior, both public and private.

SEX IN AMERICA

I

SEX IN AMERICA

AMERICA has a message about sex, and that message is none too subtle. Anyone who watches a movie, reads a magazine, or turns on the television has seen it. It says that almost everyone but you is having endless, fascinating, varied sex.

But, we have found, the public image of sex in American bears virtually no relationship to the truth. The public image consists of myths, and they are not harmless, for they elicit at best unrealistic and at worst dangerous misconceptions of what people do sexually. The resulting false expectations can badly affect self-esteem, marriages, relationships, even physical health.

This is a book about sex in America, a true story about sex, based on scientifically accurate survey data. It is not an advice manual, nor is it a compendium that feeds out tidbits of sexual trivia. Instead, it is a book that offers the facts about Americans' sexual practices, putting them in a context that helps explain not only what we do but why. And by knowing why, you can consider, in a logical way, whether you want to change aspects of your sexual life and, if so, what it might take to change them.

Nearly everyone has had questions about his or her sex life. And nearly everyone has found that the stories about sex that we tell ourselves and the myths we are told are somehow unsatisfying. The questions have lingered.

As individuals, we may be beset with private difficulties ranging from the search for a loving relationship to the perennial question, for many women, of how to have orgasms. Some questions are specific: As a twenty-nine-year-old single man, with about four partners a year, what are my chances of getting a sexually transmitted disease? As a forty-year-old professional woman who has never married, what are the chances that I will marry eventually? As an unattached young gay man living in New York, how likely am I to find a partner if I take a new job in Rochester, Minnesota? Or, someone else might ask: Is there something perverse about my sexual fantasies? Still other questions are more general: Are most people having sex as seldom as I am? Are other married women faithful to their husbands?

The questions may change as we move through life, going from wondering about how to find a partner or what to do sexually and how soon to have sex with a new partner, to questions about whether to be faithful or whether our partners are faithful to us. And then there are those nagging questions about what sexual frequency is normal.

Each individual's story is unique, but the themes are universal.

Felicia, a middle-aged, upper-middle-class woman, lives with her husband and young son in a luxurious apartment on the Upper East Side of Manhattan. She seems to have it all — a lucrative job, a loving husband, an affluent lifestyle. However, she confessed to writer Anita Shreve, she does not have a very active sex life. "My husband and I are very easy with each other," she said. "But the truth is, I seldom *feel* like doing it. I'm exhausted all the time. So I've got two vibrators? Frankly, I can't remember when the last time I used them was. We make love now, maybe twice a month, if we're lucky. When I fall into bed, I crave sleep, not sex."

She wonders if she's normal. "Sometimes I think I'd like to get at this problem: Do other couples stop making love like us? Is it age? Is it exhaustion? Is it work? Is it temporary? It must be an issue that bothers other women, too. But I have to laugh when I say that. There's *no way* that I could even consider talking with other women about this, sex life or no sex life."

Jim Walsh, a man in his early thirties who reports on rock music, also wonders about his sex life. He considers it to be exceptionally mundane. Other men his age, he believes, are having a wild time.

In thinking about his sex life, Walsh says he is reminded of a make-out party that he went to when he was thirteen, in 1974. It was a party where he tried, but failed, to score. His friends mocked him for weeks afterward, he wrote.

Then Walsh added, "It was no big deal, really. I don't sit around preoccupied with how I was tormented by those kids that first week of 1974. But just as I felt I was on the outside looking in then, I find myself 20 years later sitting on the same sidelines of the so-called new sexual revolution. I don't have toys or tapes or even anything all that out of the ordinary when it comes to a fantasy life.

"What I've got is a wife, the same woman I've been with for 14 years. Mind you, I don't trot this fact out with any holier-than-thou vanity; fact is, sometimes I'm almost embarrassed to admit it." Walsh believes that most of his friends and certainly most celebrities have a sex life that is so totally unlike his that, he said, he sometimes feels inadequate hearing about their exploits. "In my worst moments, the Spur Posse makes me feel like an uptight, hyper-cautious square," he wrote, referring to a gang of high-school athletes who competed to see who could have sex with the most girls.

Felicia grew up in the 1950s and 1960s, Catholic and "extremely sheltered," she says, when sexual behavior was under wraps and left largely to people's vivid imaginations. In Jim Walsh's adolescence and young adulthood, in the 1970s, fantasies of sexual behavior entered the realm of public entertainment, showing up in movies, music, books, magazines, and newspapers. But both Felicia and Jim Walsh have a similar, pressing question: Are they normal? What sort of sex lives do other people have?

Felicia and Jim Walsh are only part of the story. There are endless permutations and combinations of their overarching questions. Some suspect there may be more than a tinge of hype in the stories we tell ourselves about other people's sex lives, but they cannot help feeling a sort of perplexed envy when they look at couples who seem to live the American sexual dream. Others puzzle over the hand they think fate has dealt them.

Mary Lou Weissman, a screenwriter, is leery of the myths, but reacts to them anyway. In a magazine article, she describes the one-upsmanship that she sees at dinner parties, when couples compete to show off their marriages. "Contending couple No. 3 cannot wait to get home. She pops canapés into his waiting mouth. He pats her bottom suggestively. She whispers hoarsely, 'Is it too early to leave yet?' He whispers back, 'Soon.' "

Weissman mulls over her response. "It is the sickening green sense of envy that everybody is having a better marriage than you are," she explains. "It is the same fantasy that tempts people to believe that everyone else's Thanksgiving dinner was catered by Norman Rockwell, and that only you have a father who can't carve, a mother who can't cook, a divorced sister, a daughter who decided to spend Thanksgiving with her boyfriend's family, an uncle who won't shut up about his EST sessions and no dog Spot. It is the same ultimately self-abusing urge that makes people cling to the fantasy — against all contrary evidence — that other people who are thin eat as much as they want. Only you have to diet."

Cesar, a gay man in his forties who eventually died of AIDS, lived a life of quiet compromise, resigned to a sexual life that fell short of what he thought it might have been.

Cesar moved to San Francisco, looking for love and a free and open sexuality. But he found himself settling for periodic impersonal sex. In his memoir *Borrowed Time,* his friend Paul Monette says Cesar "wasn't lucky in matters of the heart. He was still in the closet during his years back east, and the move to San Francisco was an extraordinary rite of passage for him. He always wanted a great love, but the couple of relationships he'd been involved in scarcely left the station. Still, he was very proud and indulged in no self-pity. He learned to accept the limited terms of his once-a-week relations in San Francisco."

Mary Lou Weissman was cynical, but drawn to the romantic dream. Cesar could not understand why it eluded him. Felicia and Jim Walsh thought they knew about sex in America and they felt like outsiders, standing with their noses pressed to the window. Yet none of them had any real knowledge of what the sexual world was like.

The consequences of this sexual ignorance are far more profound than simply leaving people wondering whether they are normal. Myths and misconceptions about sex make it difficult if not impossible for Americans to understand how their sex lives develop and to think realistically about how to change those aspects that they do not like.

With limited information, individuals in their private lives and those who are responsible for social policy about sex are stymied in trying to understand and change the circumstances of our sexual lives. A divorced woman who is trying hard to meet a man does not understand the structure of social relations that limit her prospects in the remarriage market. A man who wants to have more sex with his wife does not understand the processes by which their sexual life has become so limited. Nor does he understand how to reverse those processes. The parents of a teenager who want their son to refrain from sex gain nothing by relying on simplistic slogans, telling him to "just say no." Government officials attempting to track the AIDS epidemic, or health-care workers designing materials to promote sexual health, are hindered by inadequate knowledge about sexual life.

Despite media mythology, personal anecdotes and gossip, and the opinions of pundits, we have had no way of objectively deciding whether most, or even many, men or boys are like the Spur Posse or the Tailhook military officers, who drunkenly assaulted women at a convention, or whether most of them are quietly watching all of this sex from the sidelines. And despite the example of sexy and aggressive women in movies, Americans have had little objective information about the sexual lives of ordinary women.

While the country lives in the shadow of AIDS, scientists do not have answers to fundamental questions about sex, even though they need those answers to determine whether the epidemic will spread in the general population. To be sure, there has been good research on populations that are especially at risk of being infected with HIV, the virus that causes AIDS, but even then little is asked beyond whether people have changed their behavior or whether they use condoms. And despite the widespread impression that Americans are having more and more sex with more and more partners, beginning at younger and younger ages, this picture is mostly based on studies that are limited in scope and generality, if not methodologically flawed. There has been a dearth of reliable estimates of how much sex Americans have in a week, a month, a year, or a lifetime, and of how many partners Americans really have.

The sex myths fuel the singles clubs and the personal ads, where latter-day lonely hearts tell themselves that the way to find a partner — a sexy, rich, attentive partner — is to explore new vistas. They provide an eternal audience for magazine articles that promise to reveal the secrets of making yourself sexy and the secrets of how to behave in bed to lure your partner like a fly to honey. They offer the scripts for movies and romance novels that show us the world as we wish it was, that tell us that the young and the lovely really can have it all.

Yet, in the absence of reliable information about the sex lives of Americans, how is it that we believe that America has become a nation in which sex is easily available to all, perhaps dangerously out of control?

Even a casual examination of the past reveals that America has undergone a sea change. In the decades since World War II, sex has become ever more publicly represented — in movies, newspapers and magazines, books, and advertisements — and ever more openly discussed. This transformation took place in a piecemeal fashion, in fits and starts, so that it was difficult to notice consciously what was happening. But the alteration is so dramatic that the sexual world as we knew it in the 1950s now seems almost unrecognizable.

This change was reflected in and driven by popular culture. In the past fifty years, America has been remade from a society where sexual matters were covert and unmentionable to one in which sexuality is ever-present.

This escalation of sexual openness in the mass media has created a widespread belief that the American people themselves are more sexual than ever before. If the 1950s appeared to be a time of complete sexual repression, the 1990s are a time of deep anxiety about the new explicitness about sex and where it will lead the nation. Saturated by the images of sexuality — from X- and R-rated movies to tell-it-all talk shows and do-it-all soap operas — many Americans, instead of being liberated from an artificial prudery, are worried that the nation has entered a morally dangerous era of licentiousness.

At the same time, the changed rules have left many people at a loss to know where the boundaries are of acceptable sexual conduct in everyday life. What is polite, mixed-company conversation about our sexual experiences, about our views and beliefs and knowledge about sexual matters? What should we consider acceptable sexual behavior by our political leaders, our prospective judges and child-care providers, our neighbors, our children, our parents?

Increasingly, we cannot as conveniently keep our opinions to ourselves. We find ourselves in discussions where we are expected to reveal much more about our ideas and opinions than we used to. Do you consider it worse for political leaders to have extramarital affairs or to lie about them? Is it a more telling character flaw to have lusted after an acquaintance or to have cut corners in paying taxes?

Religious conservatives seem bent on confronting us, the discomfited majority, with decisions about what they call matters of ethics and morality — we, who have not paid that much attention to these sex questions and who would prefer not to do so now.

At the same time, assertive liberals seem every bit as intent on confronting us with taking stands on the rights of gays or obnoxious speech or embarrassing displays of sexuality. It is not permissible these days to have no opinions about these sexual issues that many people would prefer just stay out of our conversations, off of our airways, and off the pages of mainstream newspapers and magazines that Americans have read for years.

We are left with haunting questions about this profound transformation. Why and how did the changes take place? Who wanted them and who benefits?

It is hard to imagine now what ever happened to the old version of America, the land of the free and sexually innocent. Where did that time go, before X- and R-rated movies and videos, before rap music and MTV, before rock and roll, before *Playboy,* before Kinsey and Masters and Johnson? It is hard even for those who were alive in those days before 1948, when Kinsey's first book on sexual practices was published, to recall how empty was the erotic landscape in American society. And it is equally difficult to pinpoint the pivotal events that eroded our long-held sanctions against sexual images, leading America, by fits and starts, to evolve from a society in which sexual matters were covert and unmentionable to one in which sexuality is ever-present.

Yet something is missing. Although sex is in the open now, the nearly constant babble about it remains highly stylized. There is men's talk and women's talk, but men and women rarely talk to each other except in the oblique language of seduction. There is what parents say and what children and teenagers actually listen to. Complaining, bragging, denying, gossiping, and moralizing characterize most sexual talk in our society. Some parts of people's sex lives, such as whether they masturbate, are almost never mentioned. Perhaps never before in history has there been such a huge disparity between the open display of eroticism in a society and that society's great reluctance to speak about private sexual practices.

We are a nation that is deeply ambivalent about sex. On the one hand, sex is so much a part of the landscape that we almost take it for granted, and the message we get is that everybody else seems to be doing it and we are missing the party if we don't get moving. We should liberate our sexual natures, polish up the hot buttons, follow our hormones, and seek fulfillment somewhere across a crowded room. Sex is the ultimate expression of the American dream of freedom, liberation, and mobility. On the other hand, we hear just how frightening sex can be. Some of that comes from the powerful hold of our Puritan heritage, but with a uniquely modern twist. AIDS, urban anonymity, sexual abuse and assault, all make sex a dangerous pastime. And this dovetails nicely with the old morality that coexists with our alleged libertine behavior.

At one moment, we view sex as potentially redemptive, offering individuals and society a seemingly endless source of pleasure and transcendence. Sex is the ultimate cookie jar that nasty parents keep locked up. At the next, we view sex as a potential disaster area and the source of both individual and collective troubles. Out-of-control sex leads not only to the grave but to damnation after the grave.

It is not difficult to find examples of these crosscurrents at work. For sex-as-the-peak-pleasurable-experience argument, there are the testimonials of proponents of mutual orgasm. These people say that when married couples have shared orgasms during sexual intercourse, they experience the pinnacle of physical pleasure and establish the basis for deep emotional commitment.

For the sex-as-a-sin arguments, there are the outraged cries of people who oppose providing condoms to teenagers in high schools.

These critics often argue that condoms corrupt the morals of young people, sending a message that sex is expected and acceptable. They say that condoms offer an incentive for premarital intercourse.

These conflicting views about sex are so much a part of life in the United States that they often go unnoticed, unremarked, as though they were both natural and compatible. The clashing images intertwine, for example, in the process by which people learn about sex. Young people learn by doing, with limited guidance from adults but with the message that sex is secret and maybe dirty but also irresistible.

As a consequence, boys often believe that they have an uncontrollable sex drive and girls often think they were overcome by desire. Ignorance is combined with an intense interest in sex, producing a heady mixture that retains its ability to confuse well into adulthood. When they have or think about sex, people alternately believe it is powerful and mysterious and dangerous and disgusting. In the absence of the correcting power of honest communication and objective knowledge, this imagery easily leads to a sort of magical thinking.

We are at cross-purposes with ourselves about sex, and we don't know where to turn. There are no end of experts telling us what's going on and what to do, particularly in popular books and magazines. But such experts are often woefully misinformed and captives of the same kind of confused thinking that characterizes those to whom they give advice and counsel.

It may seem hard to understand that the vast majority of the plethora of popular books and magazine articles about sex might have gotten it wrong and have led us further astray. Our problem is that nearly everyone is a prisoner of the belief that sex is all-powerful and all-overcoming; they differ only on whether it is a good or bad thing. Rarely have we stepped back from the representation of sex and turned to the reality.

What is the sexual behavior of everyday Americans actually like? How does it relate to the media visions of sex? Are Americans constantly in a state of sexual activity or sexual frustration? Are Americans overcome by their powerful sex drive? What are the attitudes of Americans about sexuality?

These are questions that cannot be answered without careful research on the sexual behavior of everyday Americans. The answers to these questions cannot be found by watching soap operas or talk shows or reading advice columns. Because we have rarely studied the sexual behavior of the average American with any scientific rigor, we have been left with only myths and half-truths, the laments about sex made by conservatives and the praise of sex offered by liberals. The vacuum of sexual ignorance is filled by fantasy and falsehood.

What, then, are the facts? Why don't we know them? And where can we go to find them?

The history of attempts to study sexual behavior is almost a tragicomedy in its convolutions and raised expectations and dashed hopes. It is a history that has led to some confused ideas of what other people do when they have sex, and it is a history that led our research team to what almost seemed like a fool's mission when we blithely set off on what turned out to be a seven-year quest to study sexual behavior in the same way that other social behaviors have been studied.

For decades, the few researchers who set out to study sex complained that it was all but impossible. Masters and Johnson themselves, writing in the 1960s, were taken aback by the dearth of research on sexuality. They began their book *Human Sexual Response* by decrying what had been called science's "sole timidity" about studying sexuality. Sexuality alone, among all subjects of inquiry, had been ruled out of bounds. Yet, they wrote, sexuality concerns everyone. "Can that one facet of our lives, affecting more people in more ways than any other physiological response other than those necessary to our very existence, be allowed to continue without benefit of objective, scientific analysis?"

Their question is just as pressing today. The consequence of this suppression of science is that the errors of inadequate research have not been corrected and, in some cases, fake research has been encouraged. Even quite simple questions have not had adequate answers: How many sexual partners do contemporary Americans really have? Where do these partners come from? What is the likelihood that a married man or woman will have an extramarital partner? If these easy questions have not been answered, consider the more difficult questions: To what degree is your sex life under your own control, and can it be changed? What can policymakers do to reduce the tide of teen pregnancies or limit the spread of HIV? The answers to these questions are clouded by both a lack of information and an abundance of magical thinking.

One reason why sex was not studied was that the government and private foundations were uninterested in paying for sex research. Since it was believed that everyone shared the same view that most sex was sinful and wrong, what was the point in studying it? Further, there was a palpable fear of what sex researchers might discover and how it might affect moral and religious standards. If they found that everyone had sex before marriage, those who wanted to hold out would feel intense pressure to go along with the majority, this reasoning went. If they learned that homosexuality was common, it might be harder to argue that it was a perversity. Scientific research was treated as the enemy of conventional morality.

A second reason was that many scientists themselves steered clear of the subject, feeling that sex research was somehow tainted or marginal, dirty or potentially dangerous. Senior scientists often warned their students not to engage in sex research because it would be the kiss of death to their careers. Others, who went ahead and did the research, had difficulty publishing their findings in prestigious journals. Many scientists also shared the view that sex research was not very interesting, thinking that all that needed to be understood was the strength of the sex drive and the ways it could be controlled.

Even though these attitudes of funders and scientists had nothing to do with science, the result was that sex research became a tattered orphan of social science, poorly supported and disdained.

In the late 1960s and early 1970s, federal agencies that investigate and promote health made a few limited forays into the study of sexuality, asking about sexual practices of young people and about homosexuality. But, for the most part, the government has studiously avoided supporting research on sexuality. And the private foundations, frightened by intensely negative reactions to Alfred Kinsey's work in the 1940s and early 1950s, largely avoided supporting investigations of sexual issues, even when they were directly related to the foundations' concerns, like population control and reproductive health.

There have been many sex surveys over the past few decades, of course, but the problem is that until very recently virtually all were methodologically flawed, making their data unreliable, uninterpretable, and impossible to use to understand sexual behavior. *The Hite Report*, the *Redbook* survey, the *Playboy* survey, *The Janus Report* —

all are so flawed and unreliable as to be useless. And although there were several fine studies conducted in the second half of the 1980s, these studies were limited in scope and did not gain the public attention of the widely known, but useless, studies.

In a sense, having the results of these bad surveys is worse than having nothing because they lead to a widespread belief that we know at least some of the answers and that we know what the answers mean.

To know what sex in America is like, we need findings that go beyond anecdotes and flawed interviews. The research needs to include reliable information on the wide variety of Americans — the middle-aged as well as the young, people with high-school educations as well as those with college degrees, Americans with religious affiliations that span the spectrum, including conservative evangelical Christians as well as atheists. We need data that reveal the sexual experiences of Americans of different races and ethnicities — blacks, Hispanics, and Asians, as well as whites. And we need data that show the sexual behavior of people who live in different social worlds — farmers, Wall Street bankers, and nurses. Data like these can come only from well-conducted and reliable surveys whose results are replicable and can be trusted.

To know how sex in America compares to sex in other countries, we need equally well-conducted studies from those other countries. And, to make sense of the data, we need theories that frame the facts and put them in context.

Now, for the first time, we have such a survey. We have conducted a scientifically accurate survey of sex in America that represents nearly all adult American men and women, and includes questions on a wide range of sexual behavior. In our view, such a survey can help clear up much of the confusion and misinformation about what is going on in the sex lives of Americans. Our findings, from this national study, are corroborated by research from other surveys here and abroad that looked at pieces of the general picture.

When we designed our study, we had no agenda, no preconceived notions of what the data would show or what sexual behavior ought to be. We were open to surprises and we expected to be surprised by what we found. But, as social scientists, we did have a goal and a particular philosophical approach.

Our goal was to give people a different way to think about sexuality, to reveal the social forces that affect sexual behavior, just as they affect every other sort of human behavior. We suspected that there would be social constraints on such things as who our sexual partners are, how we find them, how often we have sex, and what we do when we have sex.

Our philosophy was that there was nothing magical about sex. It was a behavior that could be understood in the same way that social scientists have come to understand other behaviors, such as how people vote or how they choose the neighborhoods they live in. We studied and analyzed sex with the same reliable and well-accepted methods that social scientists use to study more mundane aspects of life, such as choosing a college or finding a job.

Our findings, however, are anything but mundane. They explode many myths about sex and show a society that is, at heart, very different from the tales we tell ourselves.

We tell ourselves that sex is just an animal instinct, a biological imperative that is generated only by our own drives, controlled only by our own willpower.

"The way I think about it is that anybody can have sex with anything," says Roseanne Arnold. "You're the one that's sexual. The person you're having it with doesn't do anything to make you one way or the other."

We believe that love knows no social rules, that we can fall in love with anyone, of any background or social class. We believe in Cinderella and we believe in Romeo and Juliet. Likes do not have to marry likes, we think.

We devour movies, like *Pretty Woman,* that tell us that anything is possible for those in love.

We tell ourselves that marriage may be a necessary social institution but that it is deadly to a sex life. If you want to have a lot of sex with a partner, you must be unattached, on the loose, ready to seize opportunities when they come your way.

We tell ourselves that everybody is having lots of sex, and that those who are not are probably frustrated and miserable.

We think that most Americans have lusty sexual appetites, enjoying a wide variety of partners and practices.

We strongly suspect that most married people have been unfaithful. We believe there is a seven-year itch or a midlife crisis when even rock-steady faithful men tend to stray.

We believe that masturbation is an inferior substitute for sex with a partner. We see it as a practice of the partnerless, the unhappy, frustrated people who have gone too long without satisfying their sexual drives with a partner.

We think that 10 percent of the population is homosexual.

We believe that the AIDS epidemic must spread inexorably through the heterosexual population. Everyone who is sexually active is substantially at risk, we say.

All of these beliefs, suspicions, and tales are wrong.

Although these individual findings are intriguing, we tried to get beyond the lists of such factlets as how many partners an average person has, what the incidence of marital infidelity is, and how many adults are virgins. In our analysis of the data, we try to answer questions of people like Jim Walsh and Felicia, who wonder if they're normal, but we also try to reveal why Walsh and so many others have had those questions in the first place.

We also focused on how social forces determine our social behavior and attitudes, how they shape our reactions to the make-out parties of adolescence and to the faithful marriages and all the myriad variations in between. And we analyzed the darker sides of sex, asking how the data can help us understand the spread of AIDS and other sexually transmitted infections.

In the end, we hope that a door has been opened and that this study will be just a beginning, a first step forward in the long struggle to, at last, include scientific studies of sexual behavior as a legitimate research topic in social science.

2

THE SEX SURVEY

O<small>F</small> all the studies that purport to
tell about sex in America, the vast majority are unreliable; many
are worse than useless. As social scientists, we found that the well-
established survey methods that can so accurately describe the nation's voting patterns or the vicissitudes of the labor force rarely were
used to study sexuality. And the methods that were used in many of
the popular studies had flaws so deep and so profound that they ren-
der the data and their interpretations meaningless.

In fact, the field is so impoverished that experts still find themselves
citing data gathered by Alfred Kinsey during the late 1930s and into
the early 1950s, a time when America was very different than it is
today.* It also was a time when the sort of study that we conducted,
using reliable and valid scientific methods, was impossible, both because the methodology was not well developed and because people

---

*Alfred C. Kinsey, Wardell B. Pomeroy, and Clyde E. Martin, *Sexual Behavior in the Hu-
man Male* (Philadelphia: W. B. Saunders Co., 1948); Alfred C. Kinsey, Wardell B. Pomeroy,
Clyde E. Martin, and Paul H. Gebhard, *Sexual Behavior in the Human Female* (Philadelphia:
W. B. Saunders Co., 1953).

thought that no one could conduct a sex survey in the same way they might ask people what foods they liked to eat or what cars they like to drive.

Many of the popularized studies that came after Kinsey, like *The Hite Report* or the *Redbook* survey, are even worse. Although the science of survey research was much better established when these studies were conducted, the studies ignored what social scientists had learned and used methods guaranteed to yield worthless results.

The problems with sexuality research go beyond abstract theorizing and arcane academic arguments over how best to design a survey. They go to the very heart of the questions of what we do sexually, and why.

Most Americans believe that the factors that determine their sex lives lie mostly or solely within themselves. Their sexual drives, their hormones, their individual desires, are all that matter. This is in large part a legacy of the long history of attempts to study and control sexuality, dating back to studies in the past century that focused on "deviants" and sex criminals. Those studies segued into psychological studies by Sigmund Freud and others that sought to explain sex as a basic drive, something we are born with and that obeys its own rules. Freud used the image of a riderless horse galloping out of control.

The long history of attempts to study sexuality had as a dominant theme this idea that sexuality comes from within, that it is a feature of the individual, and that to understand sexual behavior we have to understand the individual's sex drives and hormonal surges and even genetic predispositions. As a consequence, the popular explanations of sexual behavior, the belief that the individual is the sole actor on the sexual stage, are an echo and a legacy of these previous sex studies.

Our viewpoint is very different. We are convinced, and our data bear us out, that sexual behavior is shaped by our social surroundings. We behave the way we do, we even desire what we do, under the strong influence of the particular social groups we belong to. We do not have all the latitude we may imagine when we look for a partner, nor do we have all the choices in the world when we decide what to do in bed. The choices we make about our sex lives are dramatically affected by our social circumstances.

So if old and deeply flawed research gives us a false picture of the driving forces that underlie our sexual behavior, the problems with these studies transcend what may sound like pedantic nit-picking over their design.

The era of large sex surveys began with the Kinsey reports. And the story of those reports illustrates what has gone wrong with attempts to study sex in America.

Alfred Kinsey felt that standard sample survey methods were a practical impossibility when it came to the subject of sex, so he compromised. And when he published his results, Kinsey shocked the nation with his findings and evoked a public response so strong that most social scientists decided to steer clear of this area of research.

An evolutionary biologist from Indiana University, Kinsey had never studied human behavior. He was a professor of zoology, an expert on gall wasps, who never thought to study human sexuality until 1938, when he was asked to teach the sexuality section of a course on marriage. In preparing his lectures, he discovered that there was almost no information on the subject. As a consequence, he decided to conduct what he called a taxonomic investigation of human sexuality.

Using the methods he was most comfortable with, Kinsey began his study by first giving a questionnaire about sexual practices to the students in his classes. Finding this method unsatisfactory, he turned to face-to-face interviews and then began reaching out to different social groups. Eventually, he and his three associates interviewed nearly eighteen thousand people. It was a long and arduous task. Kinsey said it took him six months to persuade the first sixty-two people to be interviewed, but that as he got better at interviewing it became easier to recruit respondents. The problem was not who he interviewed but how he found them.

Kinsey knew that the ideal situation would be to select people at random. That way it would be guaranteed that those he interviewed represented the general population. But Kinsey just did not think it was possible to coax a randomly selected group of Americans to answer truthfully when he asked them deeply personal questions about their sex lives.

"Unfortunately, human subjects cannot be regimented as easily as cards in a deck," Kinsey wrote. "Neither is it feasible to stand on a street corner, tap every tenth individual on the shoulder, and command him to contribute a full and frank sex history. Theoretically less satisfactory but more practical means of sampling human material must be accepted as the best that can be done."

Kinsey's compromise was to take his subjects where he could find them. He and his associates went to college sororities and fraternities, college classes and student groups, rooming houses, prisons, mental hospitals, social organizations of many kinds, and friendship groups in which one interview might lead to others. For a fourteen-year period, he even collared hitchhikers in town.

To make his data more credible, Kinsey often attempted to interview 100 percent of the members of his groups. He'd try to get every single student in a classroom or every single boarder in a rooming house to answer his questions.

It sounds impressive. After all, if he interviewed eighteen thousand people and if he got anywhere near 100 percent of the groups he approached, why would his data be unreliable?

One looming problem was that the people Kinsey interviewed could not stand in for all Americans. A fraternity here, a college class there, a PTA from a third place, and a group of homosexual men from somewhere else do not, taken together, reflect the population of the United States.

Instead of studying randomly selected members of the population, Kinsey interviewed what is called a sample of convenience, a sample that consisted of volunteers that he recruited or who came to him. This introduced two problems. First, the people he interviewed could not be thought of as representative of anyone in the population other than themselves. They got into the sample because they were relatively convenient for Kinsey to find and persuade to participate, or because they offered to participate on their own. Consequently, while they may have told the truth about their own sex lives, neither Kinsey nor anyone else can know how to generalize from these people to say anything useful or accurate about the whole population or about any particular subset of the population.

It's like interviewing people near the train station at 8:45 in the morning to ask how they usually get to work. If 80 percent of them say they take the train, no one would use that fact to generalize that

80 percent of the people who commute to work in that city take the train.

The second problem was that many of Kinsey's respondents volunteered to be in the study. For a sex survey, it seems likely that those who do volunteer and those who do not have different behavior, different experiences, and different attitudes about sex. If so, the data that are collected from volunteers will give an inaccurate picture of the whole population. By including the sexual histories of those who especially want to be counted in the survey, that survey gives a biased picture. This is true for any survey, not just one on sexual behavior. Many studies have suggested that people who volunteer for surveys are not like people who do not volunteer,* and there is some evidence that people who volunteer for sex surveys have wider sexual experience than those who do not. In addition, there is evidence that people who engage in highly stigmatized behaviors, such as incest, may refuse to be interviewed or would not volunteer to do so.

So, since Kinsey did not select his respondents in a way that permitted generalization, the data he obtained are at best interesting facts about the people he interviewed but are not useful for making statements about the population at large.

Yet though the study was flawed, even by the standards of the time, Kinsey's data shocked the nation and became enshrined as the nation's report card on sexual behavior.

It's not as though Kinsey's two books made lively reading. Despite their racy subject matter, the books were filled with tables and charts of enormous length. It is doubtful that many people read them from cover to cover. As a biologist trained to record reams of data, Kinsey made dense tables of his often shocking observations, but said he was deliberately avoiding interpretation. In his book on the human male, for example, he wrote: "The present study, then, represents an attempt to accumulate an objectively determined body of fact about sex which strictly avoids social or moral interpretations of the fact."

But the subtext of his books, and what particularly outraged many of his critics, was Kinsey's view that a wide variety of sexual practices

*Norman M. Bradburn and Seymour Sudman, *Polls and Surveys: Understanding What They Tell Us* (San Francisco: Jossey-Bass Publishers, 1988).

were normal and biologically based, part of the animal world as well as part of human society.

Kinsey wrote, for example: "In many instances, variant types of behavior represent the basic mammalian patterns which have been so effectively suppressed by human culture that they persist and reappear only among those few individuals who ignore custom and deliberately follow their preferences in sexual techniques. In some instances sexual behavior which is outside the socially accepted pattern is the more natural behavior because it is less affected by social restraints."

He shocked the majority of Americans who thought virginity among unmarried women was the norm by reporting that half the women who married after World War I were not virgins on their wedding day. He went even further, pointing out that there was nothing in biology that supported the idea that virginity before marriage was natural.

Many Americans were outraged when Kinsey reported that half the husbands in American had had extramarital sex and when he reported on marriages that had been improved by extramarital sex. For example, he wrote, "Some women who had difficulty in reaching orgasm with their husbands, find the novelty of the situation with another male stimulating to their first orgasm; and with this as a background they make better adjustments with their husbands."

Kinsey's data on homosexuality were most troubling for a society that was convinced that sex between men was rare. He reported that one man in three had a sexual experience with another man at some time in his life. Ten percent of the men that Kinsey interviewed had had sex exclusively with other men for at least three years. It is this figure that may be the basis for the widely quoted "one person in ten in the United States is gay."

The critics' greatest fear about Kinsey's data was that they would break down the moral order. If a man learned that half of all married men are unfaithful, might he not use that as an argument to have extramarital sex? If a young woman learned that half of all women have sex before they marry, might she not decide that virginity was a throwback to the Victorian age? Evangelist Billy Graham voiced the nightmares of many when he denounced the book *Sexual Behavior in the Human Female* by saying that "It is impossible to estimate the damage this book will do to the already deteriorating morals of America." Of course, with no way of knowing what Americans really did sexually and no way of continually taking the pulse of the nation, we do not know whether Kinsey's findings had any effect.

In the spirit of this negative reaction, the *New York Times* did not review Kinsey's book on men and refused to advertise it. And when the book on women came out during the Korean war, it upset members of Congress, who felt that Kinsey's statement that a quarter of all women had extramarital sex was unpatriotic. It would lower the morale of our fighting men, these congressmen said, if they heard data like that.

Although some statisticians pointed out that Kinsey's methods of sampling were bound to lead to unreliable data, skewed toward an exaggeration of Americans' sexual activities, his data were all we had and their inadequacies went little noticed in the sea of criticism over what they would do to the moral fabric.

Even as Kinsey's studies shocked and fascinated the nation, they also elicited strong criticism from people who thought that sexuality should not be studied by scientists with questionnaires. The blistering attacks on Kinsey were so effective that surveys of sexuality were not only born with Kinsey — they almost died with him too. After the extreme negative reactions to Kinsey's work, few scientists and fewer funders wished to conduct similar studies that would have improved on his findings.

Kinsey's study was followed, a decade later, by a new type of sex study, initiated by William Masters, who was a gynecologist, and Virginia Johnson, who was his research associate at Washington University in St. Louis. Like Kinsey, Masters and Johnson thought that sex was a natural biological process and that if people were not having a satisfying sex life, the answer was to fix the organism, unleash the individual's potential. Social circumstances had little to do with it.

So Masters and Johnson watched and described the sex act, performed in the laboratory by subjects that they paid. Coming from the medical profession, they adopted an approach that was clinical. To a doctor, one liver is pretty much like another liver, and to Masters and Johnson, human sexual responses, although they varied, could be seen as part of an inborn expression of a genetic program for sexual plea-

sure. They conceded that their sample was by no means a representative group of Americans but, they wrote, "even admittedly preju-
diced information is of inordinate value in the study of human sexual
behavior."*

Their book, *Human Sexual Response,* was an instant bestseller,
even as it disturbed many Americans. The very idea that people would
agree to be volunteers in their studies (and be paid for it!) was shocking to many, who viewed the transactions as a form of prostitution.
Masters and Johnson, moreover, were forthright about their subjects,
explaining that many liked both the sex and the money. They described "Subject A," a twenty-six-year-old unmarried woman who
"represents the two reasons for joining the program most frequently
vocalized by these subjects — financial demand and sexual tension."

Still, demands for facts about sexual life in America continued un-
abated. Not only were people curious — Am I normal? — but they
often worried, against their better judgment, about whether others
were having more fun.

In the absence of systematic, scientific studies of the American
population, a series of popular "reports" on sexual practices prolif-
erated to fill the void. There was the *Playboy* report, the *Redbook*
report, *The Hite Report,* and, most recently, *The Janus Report.* All of
these reports found as much, if not more, sex than Kinsey. They reinforced the notion that most Americans have high rates of all kinds of
sexual activities. But the flaws in these subsequent studies were even
more profound than those that plagued the studies by Kinsey.

In all these studies, only people who volunteered to complete the
survey were included. But the people who were asked to volunteer
were by no means representative of all Americans. The five million
readers of *Playboy* are already a heavily selected population — they
tend to be young, white men, richer than the average American, and
men who are interested in sex. The nearly five million readers of *Redbook* are mostly white women in their late twenties to late thirties,
married, and more affluent than the average American woman. If you
asked readers of a different sort of magazine, like *Christian Century*
or *Reader's Digest,* to fill out a questionnaire, you'd expect to get very
different answers.

*William H. Masters and Virginia E. Johnson, *Human Sexual Response* (Boston: Little,
Brown, 1966).

Shere Hite sent out surveys to women whose names she got from chapters of the National Organization for Women, abortion rights groups, university women's centers, and university newsletters. She also put notices in the *Village Voice,* in three magazines (*Mademoiselle, Brides,* and *Ms.*), and in church newsletters, asking readers to send to her for questionnaires. She, too, was concentrating on highly selected members of the population.

But suppose you don't care about the behavior of people not included in these surveys. Wouldn't a survey of *Playboy* readers at least tell you about sex among young, affluent white men? The problem is that very few of even those invited to answer the surveys chose to do so, which raises the question of just who these respondents are. Only 1.3 percent of the five million *Playboy* readers returned the questionnaire. In the *Redbook* survey, the issue of *Redbook* magazine containing the questionnaires sold 4,700,000 copies. Barely 2 percent of the *Redbook* readers filled out and returned the survey. And of those 100,000 replies, the magazine analyzed only 2,278.* Shere Hite, in her book *The Hite Report: A Nationwide Study of Female Sexuality,* said she distributed 100,000 questionnaires and got 3,000 back, a 3 percent response rate.†

Even though both magazines and Shere Hite trumpeted the sheer numbers of responses, large numbers in themselves do not mean anything. If too many people decline to answer your questions, you start to worry about the ones who opted out. Were they significantly different from those who participated? If, as in the *Playboy* survey, 1.3 percent of the target population answers your questions, you should be very suspicious that the people who answered are atypical for some reason and that their replies do not represent the sexual practices even of the population that received the survey.

It may sound paradoxical, but the percentage of replies is far more meaningful than the absolute number of them. If you ask 1,200 people to answer your questions, and 1,000 agree to do so, you can generalize to the target group with more accuracy than you can in 50,000 replies from a group of 1,000,000 who were asked. In the first case, 83 percent of those you asked answered your questions. In the

---

*Carol Tavris and Susan Sadd, *The Redbook Report on Female Sexuality* (New York: Delacorte, 1975).

†Shere Hite, *The Hite Report* (New York: Dell, 1976).

second case, only 5 percent of those you asked replied to you, which leaves you wondering how they differed from those who did not reply.

The most recent of these "reports," *The Janus Report,* by Samuel S. Janus and Cynthia L. Janus, was slightly different. The Januses said they distributed 4,550 surveys and got back 2,795 that were "satisfactorily completed."* They argued that their data were credible because their respondents reflected the U.S. population. The way they got this so-called match, however, was by looking at census data on key variables, such as age, marital status, and religion, and then seeking respondents who would match the proportions found in the general population.

For example, the census said that 19 percent of the population was between eighteen and twenty-six, so the Januses sought out enough volunteers in that age group to fill in 19 percent of the slots for respondents in their survey. But it's not how many respondents are of a particular age that's so important — it's how you find them.

The Januses wanted to get enough older Americans to make their survey sample resemble the census data. So they went to sex therapy clinics and looked for older people. Does it matter where they found the old people? We have no way of knowing who these older people were, but the fact that they were at a sex therapy clinic makes it probable that they have sex partners, unlike many older Americans, and that they want to have sex. In fact, the Januses report that over 70 percent of Americans age sixty-five and older have sex once a week. A reputable national survey (the General Social Survey), which did not preselect people, found that just 7 percent of older Americans have sex that often.

Many of these sex reports also had an additional problem — that of knowing who *had* responded. Fraudulent responses — from people who filled out the questionnaires as a lark, making up sexual adventures or pretending not to have had them — would be counted just like anyone else's. A man might have pretended to be a woman and filled in a *Redbook* questionnaire, or a woman might have said she was a man and answered the *Playboy* questions. One busy man could have filled out many questionnaires for *Playboy.*

---

*Samuel S. Janus and Cynthia L. Janus, *The Janus Report on Sexual Behavior* (New York: John Wiley and Sons, 1993).

The surveys, however, fed Americans' thirst for information on sexual practices and their results were often cited uncritically. In fact, however, we have no way of knowing what the data mean; they are simply uninterpretable.

Yet these pseudo-studies provided a picture of a very sexually active nation. And because these studies have been so widely publicized and are cited so often, many Americans walk around thinking they are among the few who do not have a lot of sex partners, thinking that even if they are satisfied, they must be missing something.

The true picture of sex in America, now emerging from our work and from several other important and useful studies, is vastly unlike what these studies have shown. An entirely different image is materializing from a series of studies that looked at specific aspects of sexuality and from our newly completed study that is a comprehensive look at the sex lives of the diverse American population.

Our study, called the National Health and Social Life Survey, or NHSLS, has findings that often directly contradict what has become the conventional wisdom about sex. They are counterrevolutionary findings, showing a country with very diverse sexual practices but one that, on the whole, is much less sexually active than we have come to believe.

There are good reasons, however, to believe that our new data more accurately reflect the behavior of the adult American population. In addition, they fit into an emerging view of sexuality that shows what forces really determine whom we have sex with, when, and why.

Our survey, in contrast to the "reports" that preceded it, was a truly scientific endeavor, using advanced and sophisticated methods of social science research. Although these methods had been developed and used in the past for investigations of such things as political opinions, labor force participation and hours of work, expenditure patterns, or migration behavior, they work equally well in studying sexual behavior. Like studies of less emotionally charged subjects, studies of sex can succeed if respondents are convinced that there is a legitimate reason for doing the research, that their answers will be treated nonjudgmentally, and that their confidentiality will be protected.

In addition to the advantage our study gained from the use of current developments in survey research, the results were strengthened by comparisons to several other recent studies in the United States and abroad. These surveys, which also were methodologically sound, have findings very much like ours.

Our study was completed only after a long and difficult struggle that shows, if nothing else, why it has been so enormously difficult for any social scientists to get any reliable data on sexual practices. The fact that it succeeded in the end was more a matter of our research team's stubbornness and determination than it was a mandate for this information to emerge.

The survey was conceived in 1987, as a response to the AIDS crisis. The human immunodeficiency virus, which causes AIDS, had been identified in 1984. By 1987, it was abundantly clear that it was not going to be easy or quick to find a vaccine or a cure for the disease. As the AIDS epidemic spread across the land, medical scientists began to focus on how to prevent the disease, and which groups of people were most at risk. The disease was infectious, scientists realized, and one of the ways it was spread was through sex. This understanding immediately gave rise to three questions: How quickly was the disease going to spread? Who was most at risk for getting AIDS through sexual contact? How can people be persuaded to change risky behaviors?

But to answer those questions and to contain the epidemic, scientists needed to know about sexual practices in America and they needed to know about people's attitudes toward sex. Yet after years during which sexual research was treated as somehow beyond the pale, public health officials and some policy workers realized that they had almost no data that would enable them to answer these pressing questions. They were left with the forty-year-old Kinsey data, which everyone recognized to be highly problematical. Those findings were out of date and, moreover, were not even an accurate reflection of the population of Kinsey's era. Although it seemed useless to rely on Kinsey to try to analyze the spread of HIV and staunch the epidemic, in the absence of other data, scientists had to turn to his data to estimate, for example, the numbers of men who had sex with men.

Faced with the national emergency of the AIDS epidemic and the dearth of needed data, scientists and administrators at several agencies of the federal government, including the National Institute of Child Health and Human Development, the Centers for Disease Control and Prevention, the National Institute on Aging, and the National Institute of Mental Health, supported the idea of doing a national survey of sexual practices. Leading scientists in these agencies had wanted more general studies of sexuality to examine such issues as teen pregnancy, sexual dysfunction, and child abuse, and they realized that the AIDS crisis finally made such a study politically feasible as well as crucially important.

After scientific blue-ribbon panels, such as one established by the Institute of Medicine, spoke out strongly in favor of a national sex study, the government took the first step toward conducting one. In July of 1987, the National Institute of Child Health and Human Development invited researchers to apply for a grant to design such a study, with the understanding that the best design would be used to conduct the survey. The institute also asked for proposals for designs of a parallel study on adolescent sexual practices.

But our national squeamishness about asking questions about sex and our collective ambivalence about knowing the answers surfaced right away. Even the name of the request for proposals — "Social and Behavioral Aspects of Fertility Related Behavior" — illustrated this simultaneous inching forward and pulling back. Nowhere in that title was there any hint that this was supposed to be a sex survey. And even though such a survey was intended, the original funding was to be only for a year, to determine whether the survey was feasible. Then, after a design was established, the government would issue another request for proposals on actually carrying out the study.

Our team, working through the National Opinion Research Center, a survey research firm associated with the University of Chicago, was awarded the contract to design the study. But even with this support from the federal health establishment, there was still much resistance to such a study elsewhere in the government. In the months that followed, there was a constant pressure to compromise, to pare down a sex survey into an AIDS study.

Many government officials wanted to steer clear of topics that might be important to an understanding of sex but that were not obviously related to the spread of AIDS. For example, they did not want the survey to ask about masturbation, reasoning that masturbation was a private matter and unlikely to have anything to do with the transmission of the AIDS virus. As researchers, facing the problem of limited knowledge, we wished to cast our net widely. Nothing was known about masturbation in relation to sexual practices. Do people masturbate as a substitute for sexual intercourse? Is it used to enhance sexual arousal? Do men use it to prevent premature ejaculation?

Another consequence of the focus on disease and health problems was an argument that if a couple was monogamous, the questioning should cease then and there. The attitude was that we should not be asking these sex questions of "respectable" Americans. In short, some officials assumed they already knew what the answers would be and they knew what behaviors were acceptable and innocuous and which people to leave alone.

Eventually, even this narrow inventory of AIDS-related questions turned out to be too controversial for the government. In September 1991, Senator Jesse Helms introduced an amendment to a bill on funding for the National Institutes of Health that specifically prohibited the government from paying for such a study. The amendment passed, by a vote of 66 to 34, dooming the effort.

Nonetheless, we had been able to work on interview questions and methodology during the period when it looked as if the government might go ahead with the project. Part of the feasibility study that we conducted allowed us to test questions, conduct focus groups, do pilot interviews, and to design the sample. This work laid the groundwork for a full-scale study of sexuality.

When the Senate refused funding to continue the study, we turned to private philanthropic organizations for support.* Freed of political constraints, we decided to make this a sex survey that would go far beyond the original purpose of helping to fight AIDS. We would treat sexual behavior like any other social behavior, using established methods to study it. Our hope was to glean data that would help not only with the fight against AIDS, sexually transmitted diseases, and un-

*We were supported by the Robert Wood Johnson Foundation, the Henry J. Kaiser Family Foundation of Menlo Park, the Rockefeller Foundation, the John D. and Catherine T. MacArthur Foundation, the Andrew W. Mellon Foundation, the New York Community Trust, the American Foundation for AIDS Research, and for the analysis of the data, the Ford Foundation.

wanted pregnancies, but that also would help us understand what enabled some sexual partners to stay together for years while others break apart after only one or a few encounters. We also hoped to learn what were the key features of sexual relationships that were both emotionally and physically satisfying.

It was by no means certain that such a survey could succeed. Many social scientists agreed with Kinsey that one could not expect randomly selected people to reveal the details of their sex lives with complete candor. And there was a widespread belief among social scientists that people would decline to participate in a detailed survey on sex.

In our original study design we wanted a sample size of 20,000, which would enable us to analyze separately data from people who are members of small subpopulations. For example, if 4 percent of the population were gay, a sample size of 20,000 men and women would yield about 400 homosexual men and 400 homosexual women, enough for us to analyze their responses separately.

In the process of designing our survey, it was clear that we would not be able to achieve this sample size with the limited resources of the private sector. We received enough money from private foundations to study nearly 3,500 adults, enough to be extremely confident about the accuracy of the data as a whole, but the sample would not be large enough for detailed analyses of small minority groups (most political polls, for example, have a sample size of 1,000 to 1,500, which gives them sampling errors of no more than 3 percent).

We knew, because we used established statistical sampling techniques, that our respondents represented the general population. In addition, we purposely included slightly more blacks and Hispanics so that we would have enough members of these minority groups to enable us to analyze their responses separately, with confidence that they made statistical sense.

We would have liked to have done the same for homosexuals, including more gay men and lesbians so that we could analyze their replies separately. However, homosexuals are not so easily identified, and for good reason, because their preferences for a partner of the same gender should be private if they want them to be. But that means we could not so easily find an expanded representative sample of ho-

mosexuals as we could find blacks or Hispanics. And that means that
we could not analyze homosexual behavior separately, asking, for example, how many partners gay men and lesbians have in their lifetimes or where they met their partners. But we included homosexual
sex as part of sex in general, so when we ask a question such as, "How
often do you have sex?" we do not distinguish between homosexuals
and heterosexuals.

The most important part of our study was the way we selected the
people to be interviewed. It can be tricky, and subtle, to pick out a
group that represents all Americans. For example, you might say you
will go to every neighborhood and knock on the door of the corner
house on each block. But that would not give you a representative
sample because people who live in corner houses are different from
other people — as a rule, they are richer than their neighbors on the
block because corner houses tend to cost more. Or you might say
you'll find married couples by taking every couple that got married in
June. But then you would end up with too few Jews because there is a
proscription in Judaism against marrying in certain weeks that often
fall in June.

Of course, the most obvious way might be to randomly select
individuals from households across the country. But finding and interviewing people scattered across the United States can be very expensive, so social scientists have found a cheaper, but equally valid, way
of identifying a representative sample. Essentially, we choose at random geographic areas of the country, using the statistical equivalent
of a coin toss to select them. Within these geographic regions, we randomly select cities, towns, and rural areas. Within those cities and
towns we randomly select neighborhoods. Within those neighborhoods, we randomly select households.

This method gave us 9,004 addresses. Naturally, since the addresses were generated by a computer, many of the addresses either
did not have a residence on them or had a residence on them that was
empty. Others had a household but no one who lived there was eligible for our survey — they were not between the ages of eighteen and
fifty-nine or did not speak English. We determined that 4,635 of the
original 9,004 household addresses were ineligible for one of those
reasons, so that left us with 4,369 households that did have someone

living in them who was eligible to participate in the study. Although it may sccm that our sample shrank quite a bit from the original 9,004 addresses, that is normal and to be expected. We did not say we wanted a random sample of addresses for our survey. We wanted a representative sample of Americans who were aged eighteen to fifty-nine and who spoke English.

We selected the individual in a household to interview by a random process. In effect, if there were two people living in a household who were in our age range, we flipped a coin to select which one to interview. If there were three people in the household, we did the equivalent of flipping a three-sided coin to select one of them to interview.

The difference between this method and the method used by, say, *Playboy* magazine, is profound. In the *Playboy* survey, anyone who wanted to be interviewed could be. In our survey, we did not let anyone be interviewed unless we selected them. If we selected a man who offered his wife in his stead, saying he was too busy to be interviewed, we declined to interview her. And if he adamantly refused to be interviewed, his refusal counted against us. He is a nonrespondent, even though his wife might have been eager to fill in for him.

Our method is neither unusual nor remarkable. But our method is right. There is universal agreement among all social scientists: this is the way you do it.

A much trickier problem arose when we wrote our questionnaire. We had to decide how, and with what language, to ask people about their sex lives. We did not want to confuse people by using technical language. Even words like *vaginal* and *heterosexual* were not well understood by many people, we found. Yet we did not want subtly to make the interview itself sexy or provocative or offensive by using slang terms. We wanted to create a neutral, nonjudgmental atmosphere in which people would feel comfortable telling us about one of the most private aspects of their lives.

We also needed to make the questions flow naturally from one topic to another and without prejudicing people's replies because of the order of the questions. We began by asking people about their backgrounds, their race, education, and religion, for example, and moved on to marriages and fertility. Then we gradually moved on to ask about sex. We asked for many details about recent sexual events and we asked for fewer specifics about events further in the past, reasoning that inability to recall details from long ago could result in erroneous, if well-intentioned, answers.

We decided to administer the questions during face-to-face interviews, which lasted an average of an hour and a half. By asking people directly, we could be sure that the respondents understood the questions and that the person who was supposed to be answering really did answer. These were to be questions that would gently lead people through their entire sexual history without making them anxious or bored, and without antagonizing them. At the same time, we wanted the questions to be neutral, so that there was no "right " answer. And we wanted a certain covert redundancy that would allow us to check answers for consistency.

Once we had the questions, we needed trained and experienced interviewers who could put people at their ease and gain their trust. To help us select interviewers whom people would talk to, we used focus groups, asking people of different races and backgrounds whom they would feel most comfortable with. To our surprise, almost everyone, including blacks, Hispanics, and men, preferred middle-aged white women. In the end, we selected 220 interviewers, mainly women in their thirties and forties. These interviewers were for the most part veterans of several other survey projects and all had a professional attitude and commitment to working on this particular survey under the careful management of the National Opinion Research Center.

After selecting the interviewers, we flew them to Chicago for further training, instructing them about how to conduct our survey and suggesting the kinds of difficulties they might encounter. For example, they might hear vernacular terms that might, in ordinary circumstances, embarrass them. As professionals, they could not let their own reactions become apparent to the respondents. We also encouraged the interviewers to tell us their own ideas about how to interview people about sexuality. The interviewers had a very high morale because they saw this study as stretching the limits of what is possible in a scientific survey. It was a professional challenge for them to make this study a success, and they had a shared sense of collective purpose.

In order to be sure that people who were identified as part of the study would agree to participate, the interviewers used all their powers of persuasion, returning again and again to the homes of people who declined, in some cases even paying the most recalcitrant to encourage them to agree to be interviewed. The participants were guaranteed anonymity. We have destroyed all identifiers from our completed interviews; thus, we could not name or find these people again if we wanted to. We also checked our data and found those reluctant respondents answered no differently than the others.

The interviewers began work on Valentine's Day, February 14, 1992, and continued until September of that year, which enabled them to spend as long as seven months in their attempts to find people and persuade them to participate in the study. In most surveys, interviewers spend two to three months tracking down and questioning respondents.

The survey was an expensive proposition, far different from mailing out questionnaires and tallying those that came back, as others have done. But we could be assured that the designated person answered our questions and not someone else. Each interview cost, in the end, an average of about $450, including the interviewer training, the several trips to the residence when necessary to do the interview, and entering the data into a computer for analysis.

Of all the eligible households, our interviewers completed 3,432 interviews, so we have the remarkable outcome that nearly four out of every five persons we wanted to interview, across the nation, were willing to sit down and answer a ninety-minute questionnaire about their sexual behavior and other aspects of their sex lives. This response rate is even more remarkable because it includes as nonresponders people who simply could not be found to be interviewed.

We ourselves were astonished and reassured by the response. It is to the credit of the professional field staff of the National Opinion Research Center — their persistence, their persuasiveness, their reassurances — that they were so successful in persuading such a large portion of the eligible population to participate in the survey. It is equally to the credit of the American public that when they were asked by professional interviewers to help us as a nation to understand our sexual behavior, they willingly did so.

No other fact in this book is as important as the fact that four out of five randomly selected adults were willing to give an interview and to give us honest responses, judged by all the ways we can think of to check their veracity. We had a variety of checks and cross-checks to test the honesty of the responses and, as we will discuss later, the respondents passed with flying colors.

Our interviewers clearly persuaded the prospective respondents of two key things. First, that the information they gave would be of value in understanding sexual behavior in America and in informing public health officials, counselors, and policymakers about the sexual matters we were addressing. And second, that the information they provided would be obtained in privacy, held in confidence, and not be associated with them personally. The success of this survey is a testament to the skill of the professional interviewers and the goodwill of the public.

The first question, of course, is: Were the respondents telling us the truth about their sex lives? Why should we believe that anyone, sitting in a face-to-face interview with a stranger, would answer honestly when questioned about his or her most intimate, personal behavior, including behavior that might be embarrassing to admit?

Survey researchers have several ways to check on the veracity of their data, and we used many of them. First, we had several questions that were redundant, but because they were asked in different ways at different times in the long interview, it would be difficult for a subject to dissemble convincingly. For example, we asked people twice how many sex partners they had had. The first time was as a simple question early in the interview, and the respondent was asked to write down the answer privately and place it into an envelope that was then sealed; the interviewer sent this envelope into the office without opening it. The second time was about an hour later, when the respondent was reviewing a lifetime sexual history. In this case, the number of partners was summed over various periods in the respondent's life. We found that the numbers came out essentially the same both ways, increasing our confidence that people were telling the truth.

We also inserted eleven sex questions from another survey into our survey to see if our respondents gave replies that corresponded to the results of that survey. That other survey, the General Social Survey (also conducted by NORC), did not mention to the respondents when the interview began that there were any sex questions and the sex questions only constituted about two minutes of a ninety-minute interview. Our survey, in contrast, stressed that sexual behavior was the primary focus of the whole study. So this comparison lets us see if the emphasis on sex had any influence on the type of people who answered our questions or on the type of answers they gave. This is one of the only ways we know of to see if there is any indication that our respondents did not tell us the truth about their sex lives or did not have sexual histories that were similar to those of the population at large. The comparison of our results to those of the 1991 General Social Survey is displayed in the table below.

Table I
Comparison of Sex Partner Data in NHSLS and GSS

Q: "How many sex partners have you had in the past twelve months?"

	Men		Women	
Response	GSS	NHSLS	GSS	NHSLS
0	11.6%	11.1%	13.4%	13.7%
1	69.4	67.6	76.4	75.5
2	9.2	9.6	6.7	6.3
3	2.4	4.8	3.6*	4.5*
4	2.4	2.8	—	—
5–10	3.9	3.1	—	—
11+	1.2	1.0	—	—
	100%	100%	100%	100%

*Three or more partners

Q: "Have your sex partners in the past twelve months been exclusively male, both male and female, or exclusively female?"

	Men		Women	
Response	GSS	NHSLS	GSS	NHSLS
Exclusively male	2.8%	2.6%	99.4%	98.3%
Both male and female	0.6	1.0	0.2	0.5
Exclusively female	96.6	96.3	0.4	1.2
	100%	100%	100%	100%

The table shows our respondents' replies to two of the eleven questions as compared to the replies of respondents in the General Social Survey. The answers were remarkably similar. For example, about 11 percent of the men in both surveys said they had no sex partner within the past twelve months, while 68 percent or 69 percent said they had one sex partner in the past twelve months. The women's replies were just as similar in the two studies. The match between the responses in both surveys was extraordinary. We could not expect to get more corroboration or similarity if we asked about any other behavior.

The top panel of the table assures us of an important fact: that our respondents appear to have taken the interview seriously and responded honestly. Or, at least, they responded with remarkable consistency with those in that other survey conducted in quite a different context. There is no indication in the distribution of the number of sex partners in the past twelve months that people thought the question was a joke and wrote down some funny numbers. There may well be some error in our data, as in all measurements, but the respondents here seem to be trying to answer the questions we asked.

The lower panel of the table is one of several pieces of information we have about homosexuality in the population, a topic we discuss at length in chapter 9. Looking at the information here, it is striking how similar the answers are in the two surveys: a little more than 2.5 percent of the men in both samples who had sex partners in the previous twelve months said their partners were exclusively men during that period and another 0.5 percent to 1 percent said they had sex with both men and women. This leaves 96 percent of men who had sexual intercourse in the past year reporting that they had sex only with women during that time. For women, around 1 percent said they had sex exclusively with other women, another half of 1 percent or less said they had sex with both men and women. This leaves nearly 99 percent of women reporting that they had sex exclusively with men in the past twelve months.

Finally, we checked our data on sexual behavior against several other very recent and well-conducted studies that each looked at a part of the general picture we were assembling. Our study, and all of these others, came to the same basic conclusions, greatly strengthening the argument that our data can be trusted.

Even data from western Europe came out the same way. The cultural stereotypes say that the French are sexier and the English less sexy than Americans. But we might have expected sexual behavior in Europe to look like it does in America because our society is not so different from European societies. In fact, many of our results are quite similar to results from recent studies conducted in France and England. For example, we and the British and French researchers found that about 10 percent of men and 15 percent of women report having no sex partner within the past year and about 3 percent report that they never in their life had a sex partner.

A final reason we trusted our data was the reports of our seasoned interviewers. They reported back to us that the participants enjoyed the interview, that they found it a rewarding and often illuminating experience to be gently led through their sex lives and attitudes about sex. In fact, they said it was an affirming event to talk about their sexuality and their sexual history in a nonjudgmental way. The interviewers reported that they had the sense that the respondents were telling the truth.

Once we had the data, we asked whether the 3,432 respondents, as a group, were representative of the population of those aged eighteen to fifty-nine in the United States. We could not do this in advance because, unlike the Januses, we were not looking for people to fit into the census niches. Instead, we were selecting people at random, with no way of knowing ahead of time what their age, sex, race, religion, or education was.

In fact, our sample turned out to be exactly like other highly reputable and scientifically valid national samples. We compared our group to those of the Current Population Survey, the General Social Survey, and the National Survey of Families and Households, looking at such characteristics as marital status, ages, educational levels, race, and ethnicity. We found no evidence suggesting that our sample was not fully representative of the population aged eighteen to fifty-nine.

Table 2 (on page 38) shows a few of the comparisons we made, using our unweighted sample that excludes the extra blacks and Hispanics that we added on purpose. We compared our group to the Census Bureau's Current Population Survey of over 140,000 people for 1991 as the benchmark. It is the best information that demographers can get about the characteristics of the population.

Table 2
Comparison of Social Characteristics
in NHSLS and U.S. Population

	U.S. Population	NHSLS
GENDER		
Men	49.7%	44.6%
Women	50.3	55.4
	100%	100%
AGE		
18–24	18.2%	15.9%
25–29	14.3	14.5
30–39	29.5	31.3
40–49	22.7	22.9
50–59	15.3	15.3
	100%	100%
EDUCATION		
Less than high school	15.8%	13.9%
High school or equivalent	64.0	62.2
Any college	13.9	16.6
Advanced	6.3	7.3
	100%	100%
MARITAL STATUS		
Never married	27.7%	28.2%
Currently married	58.3	53.3
Divorced, separated	12.4	16.2
Widowed	1.6	2.3
	100%	100%
RACE/ETHNICITY		
White	75.9%	76.5%
Black	11.7	12.7
Hispanic	9.0	7.5
Other	3.3	3.3
	100%	100%

Notes: NHSLS unweighted cross-section sample of 3,159.

   Gender: Bureau of the Census, Current Population Survey, 1991.

   Age, Race/Ethnicity: Bureau of the Census, Current Population Survey, 1991.

   Education: Bureau of the Census, Current Population Survey, 1990.

   Marital Status: Bureau of the Census, Current Population Survey, 1992.

The similarities between our sample and the Current Population Survey of the Census Bureau extend to age, education level, and marital status, as the table illustrates. This extraordinary similarity of our sample to the U.S. population, from which we randomly selected our respondents, provides assurance that the respondents who were interviewed were representative of the population of all Americans aged eighteen to fifty-nine.

We also looked at the proportions of men and women who answered our questions. We knew from the census data that 49.7 percent of Americans aged eighteen to fifty-nine are men. Among our respondents, 44.6 percent are men. Other surveys that are of high quality, like the General Social Survey and the National Survey of Family and Households, had virtually the same percentages of men and women as we have. The General Social Survey has 43.8 percent men and the National Survey of Families and Households had 43.0 percent men. So we can say with confidence that the people who agreed to participate in our survey of sexual behavior were just like the population at large in their gender. We were not disproportionately interviewing — or failing to interview — either men or women.

Now there are many people in the nation who are not represented in our survey. We can speak with confidence about the behavior of the noninstitutionalized, currently housed population aged eighteen to fifty-nine. We can say nothing about those who currently live in institutions like hospitals or jails or about the homeless or about those who are under age eighteen or older than fifty-nine. Our sample did not include those groups. But 97.1 percent of American adults aged eighteen to fifty-nine in the nation are represented, and this is the first large-scale study of the broad and inclusive dimensions of the sexual patterns and experiences of this large majority of Americans. All this checking of our data has convinced us that this sample is an excellent one from which we can make generalizations about sex in America and we do so with confidence.

Our study, of course, has limitations that are inherent to all survey research. It is a snapshot of the American population, with all of its diversity and all of its similarities. It is not precise, like the calculations of space scientists who guided the shuttle, nor is it as precise as a chemical experiment.

Instead, the survey provides broad outlines of group behavior. It can tell you, for example, what proportion of thirty-five-year-old white women like oral sex. But it cannot tell you that a thirty-five-year-old divorced woman will have sex twice a week with a man she is dating and will remarry by age forty. It also cannot always capture the behavior of people whose behavior is uncommon, but not necessarily abnormal or unexpected. There may be, somewhere in America, a grandmother who married three times after she reached the age of fifty and who has sex every day. We may not describe her in our sample because there are so few women like her that none happened to turn up in our randomly selected sample, but that does not mean her experiences are impossible or, on the other hand, that because no one like her appears in our survey that the study is wrong.

Because the American population is so large, even uncommon sexual behavior can involve substantial numbers of people. For example, we reported in Table 1 that 1.2 percent of the women in our survey said they had sex exclusively with other women in the past twelve months. While that is a small percentage, there are about 72 million women aged eighteen to fifty-nine in the United States, so 1.2 percent of them is about 860,000 women.

Survey data reflect the characteristics of the population at the time the survey was taken. In this way they differ, once again, from other sorts of scientific data. If you measure the charge of an electron today it will be exactly the same as it was ten thousand years ago. But human beings change over the years and what we find this year may not be the same as what others will find twenty years from now. In fact, even during the lifetimes of our respondents, sexual behavior changed markedly. For example, we find that within the past few decades, a form of sexual behavior, cohabitation, has gone from being almost unheard of to being a very common form of sexual partnership.

But now, with an understanding of what the data can and cannot tell us, and with reliable data in hand, we can begin to understand how society shapes our sexual behavior. We can describe the ways in which social understandings, incentives, and networks combine to elicit the sexual behaviors that usually were attributed to untamed instincts or impulses. We can see and understand how sexual behavior has changed over the decades.

The end result of our work is a huge and complex data set that can shed light on some of the most pressing social questions in America today. Why do we choose our sexual partners? Why do we have so few partners? Where is the AIDS epidemic going and who is at risk of being infected? With data we can trust, we can get beyond the myths and paradoxes and can start having an informed discussion.

3

WHO ARE OUR SEX PARTNERS?

DAVID Copperfield, the magician, says he found the perfect woman for him, supermodel Claudia Schiffer, when he was performing in Berlin on October 10, 1993. Copperfield says that he picked her out from among the 1,400 or so people in the audience. "It was her eyes," he said. "There was a connection, a comfortable feeling."

Copperfield and Schiffer went out together after the show. They danced to a Lionel Ritchie song and mouthed the lyrics, "Hello, is it me you're looking for?" Copperfield's father was there and saw the whole thing. "You know how you get vibes?" he said. "I told David, 'Hey, latch onto this feeling — hold tight. Don't let it go.'" A few months later they were engaged to be married.

It was the perfect romantic story. David Copperfield, né David Kotkin, the son of a haberdasher, who grew up in Metuchen, New Jersey, who said that in high school girls often ignored him, found the blond, beautiful German Claudia Schiffer in a crowd and successfully wooed her. It is the kind of story that has beneath its surface all the glittery tales we tell ourselves. And it is oh so fitting that it appeared in *Esquire* magazine, as a cover story.

We'd like to think that we have the world to choose from when we search for someone to have sex with. We'd like to think that there's almost a physical spark, something magical that tells us that a certain person is meant for us and we are meant for him or her. And that spark knows nothing of social class or social boundaries. It's animal magnetism we are talking about here.

We also might suppose that who we have sex with depends solely on what we want to come of the relationship. We'd choose one type of partner when we are casually dating and another type when we are looking for someone to live with or to marry.

But whom do we have sex with? It's one of the most important social questions that face individuals and society. Its ramifications show up in everyday debates over such things as whether there is a man shortage for educated women in their thirties or older. The answer lies in understanding who chooses whom, and why. It is the question that underlies our wondering what it is that causes one couple to stay together for decades and another to break up after a year or so. It is a question that bears on the search for a partner. Do you go to personal ads or do you ask your friends and family to find a date for you?

The question also is crucial to understanding the transmission of sexual diseases. Many people have become terrified that they risk getting herpes or gonorrhea or, worst of all, the AIDS virus when they have sex with a new partner. The only way to estimate true risks is to know the answer to two questions. First, of course, is the biological question — how likely is it that you will be infected if you have sex with someone who is infected? But equally important is the social question — how likely is it that you will meet and have sex with someone who is infected? The answer to the social question requires knowing how people choose their partners and how many partners they choose.

We asked, for the first time in a national study, whether either, or both, of the myths about sex partners are true. In particular, we asked how similar we are to the people we date and have sex with, as well as to those we marry.

The answer is that the romantic myth of infinite possibilities is just that — a myth — and the perception that we change our sights when we are ready to settle down also is inaccurate. Instead, we usually have sex with people who are remarkably like ourselves — in age, race or ethnicity, and education. Our freedom to find whomever we wish is an illusion. Sparks may fly when we see someone we desire. But we only see a preselected group of people.

Some people do, of course, meet partners who are nothing like themselves, sometimes for a short sexual liaison and other times for a relationship that lasts for years or decades. But when we look at the totality of sexual relationships in America, these are in the definite minority.

We find, in fact, that sexual behavior is very much like other sorts of social behavior. Without consciously thinking about it, we play by the rules when we choose someone to have sex with.

These rules are central to everything else we have to say about sex in America. The rules, in fact, underlie all of our sexual behavior. As we'll show in subsequent chapters, they explain how we find partners, how many partners we have, how often we have sex, what we do when we have sex, what the risks are of getting AIDS or another sexually transmitted disease, and what the chances are that a partner will force you to do something sexual. They provide a guidebook for understanding behavior that can seem random or capricious or as if it is determined by fate. They provide a blueprint for making rational decisions to change behavior that might have seemed beyond an individual's ability to influence. Asking who our sexual partners are opens a window into these social rules.

There were too few homosexuals in our study to analyze their choices of partners separately, but we believe that gay men in stable relationships usually have partners who are similar to themselves, and that the same holds true for lesbians.

One way to see these social rules in action is to look at the sexual partners of unmarried people. This is a population that is dating, so might be experimenting with a variety of partners they find attractive. Some might have no intention of staying with their sexual partner, whereas others may be moving inexorably toward marriage.

By looking at these people, we avoid potential problems that may arise by considering only the married people in our sample. After all, some of the married people were wed decades ago when the world was a different place. The fifty-nine-year-olds in our study may have felt they could not marry outside their race or religion, but we might question whether such restrictions apply as strongly today.

Another problem with focusing on married people is the likelihood that the marriages that last tend to be between people of similar backgrounds. So if we ask how alike married people are to each other, counting people who have been married over a period of time that spans forty years, we might be inadvertently concentrating on couples who are similar and discounting the marriages that ended in divorce but that involved people unlike each other. In fact, several data sets have shown that long-married people tend to have spouses who are more similar to themselves; that is, divorce rates are higher among couples who are dissimilar.

These difficulties would not occur if we look at short-term sexual partnerships, those that have gone on for a month or less at the time of our interviews, in 1992. So consider Table 3, which shows some of our findings.

The surprise is that dating couples are about as alike as those who are married. Black-white couples are very rare, and even differences in education are unusual. Not one woman in our study who had a graduate degree had a sexual relationship with a man who had not finished high school. Although thousands of highly educated women undoubtedly do have less-educated partners, our study shows that the *percentage* of American women who do is very small. In fact, on every measure except religion, people who are in any stage of a sexual relationship are remarkably similar to each other. And married people are even very likely to have the same religion.

For example, if we could choose anyone we wanted and if a mysterious process of sexual allure were operating, we might expect that there would be a noticeable amount of racial mixing. But, instead, as the table shows, about 90 percent of couples are of the same race or ethnicity and as we describe below blacks and whites seldom choose each other.

Our data also show that nearly 94 percent of sexually active unmarried white men have white women as their sexual partners. Just 0.6 percent have black women as sexual partners, 2.1 percent have sexual relationships with Hispanic women, and 1.9 percent have Asian women as sexual partners.

Sexually active white women similarly have sex with white men.

Table 3
Percentage of Partnerships in Which the Two Partners
Are Similar in Social Characteristics

Type of Similarity	Type of Partnership			
	Marriage	Cohabitation	Long-term non-cohabiting	Short-term non-cohabiting
Racial/Ethnic	93	88	89	91
Age	78	75	76	83
Educational	82	87	83	87
Religious	72	53	56	60

Notes: (1) Observations are partnerships, including all sexually active partnerships in the past twelve months. Excluded are marriages or cohabitations that began more than ten years before the interview date. Respondents with more than one sex partner in the past twelve months are represented more than once (up to a maximum of nine partnerships may be included for any one respondent). Short-term noncohabiting partnerships are those lasting less than one month and where no more than ten sexual episodes occurred. Long-term noncohabiting partnerships include those lasting more than one month and/or involving more than ten sexual episodes. (2) Age similarity is defined as no more than five years between partners' ages. Educational similarity is defined as a difference of no more than one educational category where the categories include: less than high school, high school graduate, some college or vocational training, four-year college, and graduate degree. Race/ethnicity categories include: white, black, Hispanic, and Asian. Religions include: none, mainline Protestant, conservative Protestant, and Catholic.

We find that 89.5 percent of single white women have white men as their sexual partners, 6.4 percent have black men as sexual partners, 1.6 percent have Hispanic men, and 0.7 percent have Asian men as sexual partners.

The pattern continues for other races. For example, 82 percent of black men have black women as sexual partners, 7.6 percent have white women, and 4.6 percent have sexual relationships with Hispanic women. Ninety-seven percent of black women have black men as their sexual partners, 1 percent have white men, and 1 percent have Asian men.

Although white women are more likely to have a black man as a sex partner than white men are to have a black woman, the overwhelming majority of whites have white partners and the overwhelming majority of blacks have blacks as their partners.

But race is just one factor, and since it is so easily observed and so divisive an issue, we might argue that it distorts things to focus on race exclusively. Perhaps it is more revealing to look at another characteristic, such as education. When we do, however, we find that, once again, people choose partners who are remarkably like themselves.

People have sex partners with educations similar to their own. Our study shows that men with less than a high-school education, for example, seldom had sex with women who had gone to college. Seventy-eight percent of them had sex with women with no more than a high-school diploma. Men who had a college degree almost never had sex with women who had much less or much more education than they. Just 2 percent of our respondents with a college degree had sex with a woman who had not finished high school and just 8 percent had sex with women with a graduate degree.

The same pattern held for women. Eighty-one percent of women who did not finish high school chose men with a high-school degree or less. Seventy-one percent of women with graduate degrees chose men who had gone to college or postgraduate schools. None of our respondents with a graduate degree had sex with men who had not finished high school.

Partners also are the same age and the same religion. More than 83 percent of people chose sex partners who were within five years of their own age and almost as many chose partners of the same or a similar religion.

Nearly 68 percent of single Catholic men choose Catholic women as sexual partners. Another 25 percent choose Protestant women. Only 6 percent choose women with no religion at all. The same pattern holds for men who are conservative Protestants, like southern Baptists or evangelical Christians. Sixty-one percent choose conservative Protestant women. Twenty percent choose Catholic women, 9 percent choose women of mainline Protestant affiliations, like Episcopalians.

Women also have partners whose religions are the same or very similar to their own. Seventy-two percent of conservative Protestant women have as sexual partners men who are conservative Protestants. Sixty-seven percent of Catholic women choose Catholic men.

What about the partners that people actually marry? We find that people typically marry someone of the same race, the same education, and the same religion, and that they choose a mate whose age differs from their own by no more than five years.

Our data do not say that individuals who differ have no chance to survive as a couple. Of course there are many couples who are of different educational background, races, and religions who are perfectly happy together. But our study says that these couples are rare, the exceptions and not at all the rule.

This finding has striking implications. It suggests that the factors determining who selects whom for a partner come into play long before a couple marries. It also suggests that few people find a partner unlike themselves for a purely sexual relationship. It means that although it is possible that a highly educated man might, for example, pick up an uneducated woman for a weekend of sex, most men do not. That sort of behavior is actually rare.

Something must be operating to limit the choice of possible partners, and it must limit that choice very early on, by the time that people are picking partners for a sexual relationship that may, or may not, lead to marriage.

This, of course, leads us to the question of why people behave this way. The explanation contradicts the romantic myths, but offers insight that can help us to understand our circumstances, and how to change them if we want to.

The conventional idea is that we, as individuals, driven by sexual instincts, determine our own sexual futures. This fits in well with American culture, with the American dream of a nation of rugged individuals who shape their own lives, for whom the past is merely prologue and who have before them an infinite array of possibilities and choices.

Yet this romantic view of finding a sex partner has not solved our partner problems so much as left people alternating between thinking that everything about their sex lives is completely under their own control and thinking that virtually nothing is. They may feel that they can find a partner any time they want one, or that there is nothing anyone can do to prevent teenagers from having sex. Individuals feel they are totally powerful or that they are total victims.

One New York man expressed this existential despair by explaining that when he was fifteen, he wanted to have sex with every woman in the world. When he was eighteen, he wanted to have sex with every woman in New York. When he was twenty, he wanted every woman on Manhattan's Upper West Side. Then, he decided he would settle for every woman on his block. Now, in his mid-twenties, he just wants to no longer be a virgin.

It's no surprise that many of us believe this myth about the search for sexual partners. It is a story we tell ourselves often and that emerges, for example, in our views of politics and economics. We like to believe that each of us can do anything and that we are therefore responsible for what we become. We see poor black boys in urban ghettos who have decided that they can, and will, become the next Michael Jordan. We see elementary-school children in rich white suburbs who have already decided that they are going to go to Harvard. And we sometimes castigate homeless crack addicts, declaring they have brought their troubles upon themselves.

Of course, everybody knows it is not entirely true that we completely shape our own lives. Not everyone can become president of the United States or a Supreme Court justice or go to an Ivy League university or make millions of dollars playing professional basketball. Success is not just a matter of desire and talent and hard work and self-esteem. How your life turns out also is determined by the social standing that you inherit from your parents and what resources you have and what help you receive. If we did not believe this, we would not have federal programs like Head Start or public television shows like *Sesame Street* or equal opportunity laws.

In the same vein, it is clear that who we have sex with, when and where we have sex with them, what we do when we are having sex, and how we understand the sexual aspects of the world around us are all orchestrated by who we are socially and what society we live in.

People do not live their lives on an empty stage. Instead, our entire life, including our sexual life, is spent in specific social circumstances. We grow up in specific families and in specific neighborhoods and in specific religions that encourage or discourage certain patterns of sexuality. As we grow up, the important people in our lives change, and these people in turn make their marks on what we believe and do about sex.

In our neighborhoods and at work or in college, we will find partners who will be approved of or disapproved of by the important other people in our lives. A woman may be attracted to a man she meets at her gym, for example, but would her friends like him? Could she bring him home to meet her parents? When we chose a long-term partner, the relatives and friends of that partner will also come to influence us. We live our sexual lives embedded in reciprocal social relationships that offer opportunities and constraints. We are not teakettles full of hot sexual steam. We are social beings whose lives are shaped by social circumstances.

But understanding how we are victims of our own taken-for-granted theories of sexuality can be extraordinarily difficult because our entire society is so steeped in them. Every time we think about sex, read a newspaper article about a sexual topic, watch a television show or a movie with sexual content, or engage in a sexual activity, we interpret what is happening through the lenses of our theories. And our beliefs are constantly being reinforced by the explanations we are offered about the sexual world around us.

Over the decades, social science researchers have gradually built up a rich body of evidence showing that even the most ordinary behavior, like a group of guys standing on a corner and commenting on the women who walk by, has a social context, a social script. They have developed theories and hypotheses to put the findings into a framework that can help explain them.

As the science developed, researchers learned that certain combinations of friends, family, and personal beliefs can lead us to behave in ways that may seem autonomous but that actually can be quite predictable. The underpinnings are there for a new understanding of sex.

For example, as long ago as 1965, Edward Laumann showed how social forces determine who are friends with whom. He was studying friendships among 1,000 white men who lived in Detroit, asking how the men found their friends, how they sustained their friendships, and why they were friends with some men but not others. In particular, he wanted to know how the social characteristics of the men influenced who their friends were and what sorts of friendships they formed.

To get at the social underpinnings of friendships, Laumann asked the men about their occupations, education, and ethnicity, and he asked about the occupations, education, and ethnicity of their friends. Then he asked the men how they had selected their friends and what they talked about with them.

He discovered that despite the ideology that says that friendships need not be constrained by the boundary lines of status and class, most of these men had friends who were very similar to themselves. They had the same education, the same religion, were of the same ethnic background, and had similar jobs.

Without consciously thinking about it, the men had chosen what turned out to be the easy road to friendship: selecting friends with social and cultural backgrounds like their own, which gives rise to a common range of interests. There are costs when you choose friends who are not like you.

For example, if a man associates with a man of higher status, someone who can be helpful to him and enhance his own social standing, he has to pay for it with a more tenuous, more cautious relationship. In these unequal friendships, both men have shallower emotional ties and the lower-status man must be careful what he says, making sure he does not offend his higher-status friend. The man of superior social status feels free to say things to his lower-status friend that he would not say to his equals. He has the upper hand and can walk away from the relationship without any loss of social standing. On the other hand, the higher-status man also feels constrained. He may not want to invite his lower-status friend to a dinner at his golf club — how would the other club members view *him* in the company of a low-status man? He may keep parts of his life to himself. (Better not say anything to old Joe about our yachting weekend — he'll be hurt I didn't ask him along, and it *does* sound kind of snobbish.)

Even small differences between friends can exact a price, tempting people to edit carefully what they say. A man who voted Democratic might not tell a Republican friend how he voted or he might dissemble and say he voted Republican. However, if his Republican friend also was a friend of his other friends, who were Democrats and who knew how he voted, he would feel less free to tell this little white lie.

In this case, it is not only the differences between friends that are important but the social networks they share. The less the networks overlap, the more free people are to shape their own versions of events; the greater the overlap, the more pressure they feel to tell the same story to everybody. For ease of friendships, it is best that everyone be pretty much alike and the pretty-much-alikeness among friends tends to squeeze out people who are different.

In the years since Laumann's study, others have found similar patterns in other friendship networks. Religion, race, ethnicity, education, and income all serve as boundaries around the friendship "choices" that people make. Unlike the cherished notions fed by the American dream in which anyone can be a friend of anyone, birds of a feather do seem to flock together.

These studies of social networks and their influence on choices of friends and the content of friendly relationships require a shift in focus. Instead of looking at the individual, sociologists are studying the group, defining the opportunities and constraints that go along with belonging. At one level you might ask: How do people construct their social groups, how do they find friends? And an individual can reply: "I go out and find people I like." But the sociologist who focused on the group would say: "You think you construct your own group of friends, but in fact your choices are extremely limited. Your education, your ethnicity, your religion, all have strong effects on your possible choices."

The analogy to choosing sex partners seems obvious, but because sex has been scrupulously avoided by most social scientists, there has been little exploration of how social constraints affect who is chosen as a partner and why.

The closest that sociologists have come to addressing this social question was in studies undertaken in the 1950s and 1960s of racial and religious intermarriage and dating. The idealistic notion was that America really was a melting pot, a term that came from a play of that name written at the turn of the century. To see the melting pot in action, sociologists looked at second and third generations of immigrant families and reported that these people no longer married only within their own ethnic groups. This was taken to mean that the melting pot was real, that no one in America was limited by ethnic background or social origins. In the extreme, the argument went, in America, anyone would marry anyone else; there were no social distinctions that really mattered.

This research was deeply influenced by the egalitarian and ethnocentric traditions of American democracy. Anyone should be able to get any job, go to any college, hold any political office, regardless of race, religion, gender, or family background as long as they were willing to work hard and commit themselves to being true Americans. It was on this basis that it was believed that any American should be able to marry any other American — at least any other American of the same race — Catholics marrying Jews or the Irish marrying WASPS or the old Princetonian marrying the clerk in the convenience store provided evidence that the ancient prejudices of Europe had been dissolved in the American melting pot.

There were hints, however, that sexual behavior, like friendship choices, also is determined by social networks. For example, when these same sociologists asked college students whom they dated, the researchers carefully noted that women in sororities tended to go out only with men in fraternities instead of with non-Greeks or young men from the college town. Fraternity men, however, often dated non-Greeks and townies as well as sorority women. It was clear that these dates were somehow different from the dates with sorority women, and in some cases, the sociologists noted that the men were more likely to have sex when they went out with women who were not in sororities. Sex was embedded in social status.

In fact, social constraints are everywhere as people choose their partners. We often pretend that social barriers are not true impediments, and books and movies feed on Cinderella stories, retold for our time. In the movie *Working Girl,* the working-class secretary from Staten Island pretends to be her upper-class boss when the boss is away. She not only ends up with the boss's job but gets the boss's man as well. In the movie *Pretty Woman,* the beautiful prostitute gets the rich and handsome man.

But our experiences and the stories of our lives tell us otherwise.

Yet why would anyone care about whom others choose for sex partners and how can these vague social forces be so powerful? Why wouldn't a working-class secretary be just as able to marry her boss as the highly educated woman who works with him?

We suggest two reasons why couples sort into pairs that are so much alike. One is that it is useful to the two people themselves, so it is a strategic move on their part. The second is that it useful to the members of their social network.

Not only do the man and woman in a partnership have sex together, but they share conversations and meals, they decide which movie to see on a Saturday night and which radio station to listen to when they drive there. The more alike the individuals are — the more they have similar intellects and interests, for example — the easier it is to share their lives. If a man and woman also have similar levels of education, are of similar ages and similar social and religious backgrounds, it may be even easier for them to share their lives. So, according to this line of reasoning, there are forceful incentives for individuals to date people like themselves.

Just like the men in the friendship networks, sexual partners who have equal social status are more likely to have roughly equal power in the relationship. If a rich woman has a partner who is poor, she either cannot go to expensive restaurants with her friends or she has to pay for the outings. That means that she and her partner are not equals in this aspect of their lives, and that can exact a price on sexual relationships just as it does on friendships. Others in your social network exert their influence in this arena. Your sexual partner is expected to be part of your crowd, so your partner has to be appropriate, has to fit in, which means that your partner is expected to be much like you, your friends, and your family.

There is also a more private reason to end up with a sexual partner who resembles you: such a choice can facilitate the high stakes game of initiating and maintaining sexual intimacy. Nearly everyone is nervous, almost everyone has doubts as sex enters a relationship. A man may feel that he risks being rejected, risks losing the relationship entirely, if he tries to move toward sexual intimacy too fast. A woman may wonder whether she can initiate sex without leaving an impression that she is not morally upright. The price of a mistake is high. Every gesture can become fraught with meaning. But the more that sexual partners share such characteristics as race, religion, and social class, the more they reduce the uncertainties in this game of coordinating sex. They are more likely to feel they understand each other, they are more sure of themselves if they understand, from the start, what their partner's upbringing was like — because they had the same sort of upbringing. Or they know all about their partner's religious scruples because they share them. Any edge, any slight advantage that sharing a social background can bring to a relationship is magnified through the lens of sexual intimacy.

In fact, as we discuss in a subsequent chapter, our study shows that some sexual preferences, like oral sex, are closely related to a person's race and social class. So, without consciously planning it, people who choose partners of the same race and class have a better chance of feeling they are sexually compatible.

Finally, in selecting sex partners, people are also selecting partners with whom they might have children and with whom they might raise children. As most parents quickly learn, it is easier to bring up children when both parents agree about discipline, guidance, and nurturing. Parents who had similar upbringings, and who share similar educational and cultural backgrounds, more often have the same views about the details of bringing up children. So, here again, likes attract.

Likes attract each other because the partnerships between similar people work best, in ways we suggested. So the social institutions that encourage similar people to form partnerships and make it more likely that we meet people like ourselves both limit the choices we might make and facilitate the selection of a partner who is a good match. But this peer pressure and encouragement to select someone like ourselves is not necessarily a detriment — in fact, it is beneficial and productive.

But we do not act alone in deciding who is a suitable partner. The couple who falls in love must gain the approval of an array of bystanders, whose views of the suitability of the match have an impact on the stability of the relationship. This is how the social network and social scripts exert their silent, but immensely powerful, effects.

Our social networks are maintained by a series of stakeholders, people who have their own reasons for wanting you to choose a partner like yourself. The more serious a relationship gets, the more the stakeholders try to have their way. They may not intervene against — and may not even be aware of — a weekend sex partner who is never seen again. But they almost certainly will exert their influence over a partner who seems likely to remain in the picture. In fact, as we will show in the next chapter, the stakeholders even tend to introduce people to their permanent partners, making sure in this way that the partners are acceptable.

These stakeholders appear at different moments and at various distances from the interaction. Parents are often standing right next to the couple, with both sets of parents making sure that the other person is acceptable to be a member of their family. When young people are dating, their parents may threaten and cajole: "You can't go out with her. She has a bad reputation." "He is not a Catholic." "She is a poor student." "He is not our kind."

As relationships get more serious, the screening process gets more serious and comes to include the parents and the family of the person their child is going to marry. In extended families, aunts, uncles, and cousins can get into the act of encouraging or discouraging the prospective new family member.

Other stakeholders are the man's friends and the woman's friends. Each group, consciously or not, wants to be sure that the choice of mate is like them, that the mate fits in with them socially. They, like the parents, are usually happiest and most accepting of the match if both members of the couple are of the same race, have the same education, are roughly the same age, and are of the same religion and social class.

Farther out in the constellation of stakeholders, but still influential, is an array of professionals with very different interests. There are the appointed safeguards of institutions' good names, like the head of the school board who is worried about the reputation of the school. There are the moral or political entrepreneurs, crusading for one cause or the other. These include feminists and the religious right. There are groups like Planned Parenthood, which try to influence fertility with clinics and lobbying and programs. There are supervisors at work who want to be sure that the man does not prevent the woman from doing her job. There can even be strangers who walk by and make disparaging comments when they see a black man with a white woman, or an older woman holding hands with a younger man, or a gay or lesbian couple.

Some stakeholders have changed in past decades, or have shifted roles. For example, in the 1950s and 1960s, college students lived under a policy called *in loco parentis,* or "in the place of parents." Colleges and universities invested heavily in controlling the sex lives of young women students. Essentially, the colleges had made an implicit promise to parents to keep their daughters marriageable until they got out of school. And keeping them marriageable meant keeping them virgins. It was a time, wrote novelist John Updike in *Trust Me,* when "a large and not laughable sexual territory existed within the borders of virginity, where physical parts were fed to the partner a few at a time, beginning with the lips and the hands."*

The rules were strict. There were curfews for women on week-nights and on weekends. Any woman trying to return to her room after curfew would find the dormitory locked. If she broke the curfew rules she would be grounded, not allowed to go out at all for days or weeks at a time. No young men were allowed in the women's rooms. At some universities, the oversight was so stringent that the dean of students would write a letter to a white woman's parents telling them if she was dating a black man.

These rules disappeared virtually overnight in the late 1960s and early 1970s, falling to the pressures of the newly powerful youth movement. Now, colleges are debating other sorts of rules to control sex practices, such as whether they should prohibit sexual relation-ships between students and faculty.

But even though the stakeholders may change or shift roles, they are ever-present. The couple can never escape a web of outsiders who decide whether the match is suitable. Society can debate whether the boundaries set up by our social networks are an affront to our demo-cratic ideals, whether we want to keep people so forcibly in their places. But the reality is that the boundaries are there, that they have not broken down over the past decades when we have spoken so often about antidiscrimination and egalitarianism, and that there is intense social pressure to keep the boundaries intact.

Some of the most vehement proscriptions are against homosexual couples, and this, as we will discuss in a later chapter, is one reason why homosexuality tends to be hidden.

Almost as forbidden is interracial dating. The pressure to choose someone of your own race can begin as soon as teenagers start to date, and often sustains patterns of overt racism.

That social pressure against interracial dating becomes greater the closer a couple comes to marrying.

A few years ago, Angela Harms, a white beautician in Pennsylva-

---

*John Updike, *Trust Me* (New York: Alfred A. Knopf, 1987).

nia, was set to marry a black army private. But four days before the wedding, the Methodist minister who was supposed to marry them refused to do so: he finally had met the man Harms wanted to marry. "The pastor said I didn't tell him about the situation," Harms told a *New York Times* reporter. The two married anyway, but the minister's message could not have been more blunt.

Those couples that flout the conventions and marry can risk being ostracized. A black New Jersey woman who married a white singer said that his parents refuse to see their own grandchildren and never send the children cards or letters or birthday presents. They have disowned their son and his family.

Teresa Johnson, who is white, is married to a black man, Ralph Johnson. But most of her relatives do not know she is married or that she has children, even though the Johnson children are teenagers. Teresa Johnson said to a *New York Times* reporter that, for years, her parents would not let her children visit them. Now, she added, the children can come, but only at night, so the neighbors can't see.

It's not just whites who often oppose mixed-race couples. Blacks can be just as vehement that the races should not mix. Bebe Moore Campbell, a black novelist who lives in Los Angeles, was enraged when she saw a handsome black actor enter a restaurant with a blond woman. "Before lunch was over, I had a headache, indigestion, and probably elevated blood pressure," Campbell recalled in a magazine column. And, Campbell continued, the black women she was with had the same reaction. "Our forks hit the plates on the first beat. An invisible choir director only we could see raised her hands: All together now. In unison we moaned, we groaned, we rolled our eyes heavenward. We gnashed our teeth in harmony and made ugly faces. The altos sang, Umph! Umph! Umph!, then we all shook our heads as we lamented for the 10,000th time the perfidy of black men and cursed trespassing white women who dared to 'take our men,'" she said.

Brent Staples, an editorial board member of the *New York Times*, and a black man, said he has faced hostility from both blacks and whites when he dated white women. Writing in *New York Woman* magazine, Staples says he explained to a black woman friend that black professional men often date white women because they are living in a white world and that's who they meet. But, his friend retorted, "Every time I see a black man who takes a white woman, I view it as an indictment of me."

Spike Lee, the black movie director, poignantly addressed the problems of black-white couples in his 1991 film, *Jungle Fever*. In the movie, Flipper, a rich and married black man, has an affair with Angie, a working-class Italian woman. Both Flipper's friends and family and Angie's friends and family are outraged; Angie's father beats her when he finds out about Flipper. The couple even have trouble getting served in a restaurant. It's no surprise when their love does not last against the barrage of hate and disapproval. At the end of the movie, Flipper says to Angie, "I give up. It's not worth it. I don't love you and I doubt seriously you ever loved me." In fact, he adds, "Love-can-overcome-everything . . . is only in Walt Disney movies and I've always hated Walt Disney movies."

But race is so divisive in America that it may not be surprising that so very few Americans cross racial lines to date. What is particularly striking is the extent to which stakeholders discourage other sorts of what appears to be mismatched relationships.

Deborah Gimelson, found this out when she fell in love with her personal trainer, a poorly educated working-class man who was fourteen years younger than she was. Her friends were dismayed, but she remained infatuated. "When a friend of mine, a major bankruptcy lawyer, jokingly asked whether my trainer had finished high school or received his equivalency (the latter), his shock at the disparity in our sociocultural contacts and his jokes about bimbos couldn't disrupt my intense connection to my trainer," she wrote. Her psychiatrist said, "in obvious helpless worry, 'Maybe you should put an ad in the personals,'" Gimelson recalled.

Other times the pressures are more subtle. A young woman from Maryland took her boyfriend to meet her favorite aunt, and was puzzled when the aunt, usually warm and friendly, with a ready smile and quick laugh, seemed cold. Her boyfriend did not pick up the signals, but the woman was acutely aware of them. The aunt, it turned out, disapproved of the match because she felt the man looked like a hippie and could not possibly share her family's values.

Whether the pressures are as blunt and obvious as the minister's refusal to perform a marriage or as subtle as a favorite aunt's lack of enthusiasm for a person her niece is dating, they are ever-present and cumulative. As all of these individuals and groups try to exert their influence, the players in this game of controlling who associates with whom (which, as we will show, translates into who has sex with whom) become a clamoring Greek chorus, determined to have their say.

On the other hand, individuals who are looking for sex partners have their own motivations that may, or may not, go along with the motivations of the chorus of stakeholders in the background. The result is a sometimes tangled web of pressures and counterpressures, freedoms and constraints, that can limit or shape choices without people even being consciously aware of how their behavior is being molded.

When you are looking for a partner, you want your stakeholders to approve of your choice. After all, you have something to gain by paying attention to what pleases your family. Just as members of your family want to influence you, so you want to be able to influence your family. That means you will not want recklessly to flout their wishes. On the other hand, you also want to look out for yourself and you may want to find a lover right now, without pondering the long-term consequences and without worrying so much about whether your friends and family would approve.

It's an ancient story, of course — the tension between the rights of the individual and the control of the community. This is the story of *Romeo and Juliet, West Side Story, Abie's Irish Rose, Guess Who's Coming to Dinner,* and the multitude of ethnic romance comedies and tragedies that are part of the history of American life.

The community's rules often win, and for the same reasons that the men in Detroit chose friends like themselves. If you are looking for a long-term partner, someone whom you might marry, the attributes that your friends and families want will also be important to you.

Film critic Molly Haskell told of the pitfalls of marrying someone unlike yourself when she discussed her own marriage to a man of Greek heritage, a man who is "the quintessential urban ethnic: rumpled, swarthy, explosive, chocolate brown patches under chocolate brown eyes giving him the look of a doleful gangster." She described herself in the *New York Times* magazine as "a pale-faced Southern WASP, repressed, poised on the outside, churning on the inside, not as bland as I look."

"Gore Vidal once wrote approvingly of the exoticism of mixed marriages," Haskell said. "In the spirit of the peacock lecturing the chickens, he denounced as boring the habit of marrying one's own kind, and reproducing predictable, ethnically pure versions of oneself. Easy to say from the sidelines. Speaking from within an 'interesting' marriage to which I am totally committed, I should nevertheless argue that there are some good reasons for marrying like and staying within the tribe. One strays from its preserves at one's peril."

Haskell cited seemingly innocuous cultural traditions where she and her husband diverged: the cocktail hour, the expected abilities of a man to carve a roast and drive a car, food preferences, the type of wedding ceremony. She concluded that when people marry others not like themselves, "the success — or failure — of these seemingly odd couples depends to a great extent on the success of both partners in establishing their viable independence. A modicum of 'success' is assumed in advance, but at the first sign of weakness or failure the difference in background can become more exasperating than exotic. Then, the sense of isolation can be frightening. You're on a high wire without a safety net. You've burned your bridges, forfeited the automatic warmth and protection of the tribe."

What it means to marry someone unlike yourself, however, can depend on subtle clues, gradations in social status that can be signaled in the most muted ways but that can make a difference in whether your friends and family embrace your partner or whether they are coolly judgmental. In America, we sometimes tell ourselves that there are no rigid class distinctions, but most of us are expert at putting together even the most fragmentary splinters that tell us where people stand on the social ladder.

Even the car someone drives can hint at her or his status. Ron Rosenbaum, a writer on contemporary culture, told of how he knew how to rank people in his Long Island town: "I know I was not immune to the perverse inculcation of status distinctions," Rosenbaum wrote in the *New York Times* magazine. "I recall in high school being made acutely aware of my family's precise position on the Great Chain of

Car Model Status. The fact that we owned a Chevrolet Bel Air, which in the early 60's was one painful step below the top-of-the-line Impala and one deeply relieved step *above* the bare-boned generic Biscayne, signified more than the ludicrously insignificant threefold variations in exterior chrome trim. They represented three distinct *worlds*.

"While I could see through the shallowness, the falseness of those distinctions, I can't deny that, even so, they got to me: every once in a while I found myself, shamefully, wishing we *had* the damned Impala."

There is more to finding a perfect partner, however, than just picking out someone who is a lot like you and with whom you think you will have great sex. Within the constraints of social networks, another type of restriction comes in — the sexual marketplace. There is keen competition out there, and each person has some real limitations on what he or she has to offer.

The jockeying for partners becomes most intense when everyone in the race puts the same high value on a few features, like intelligence or charm or gentleness or beauty. Then it becomes more and more difficult for an individual to win the heart of someone with those attributes. Virtually every man advertising in the personal section of a local newspaper wants a young, slim, attractive woman. That means that such a woman has her pick of partners. So any man she chooses will have to have some attribute of his own that is highly valued.

The process sounds cold and heartless when it is analyzed by social science and certainly most people are not consciously aware of it. It has a medieval air about it, as if dowries are being exchanged. But the covert bargaining has a powerful influence on who chooses whom.

For example, since physical beauty is highly prized, very good-looking people usually can choose partners as attractive as they are. If they select someone who is less attractive, they can demand some other highly prized attribute to compensate them. That is why most couples are fairly evenly matched. Handsome men tend to date beautiful women and less-attractive men date less-attractive women. In fact, this rule of pairing of people according to their physical attractiveness is so common and so well accepted that when it is breached, it is an occasion for comment.

When you see Ross Perot with his blond wife, it is striking that she is more attractive than he is. The same is true for Henry Kissinger, who married a woman who was not only younger and much better-looking than he, but also taller. The world's gossips whispered and nudged each other when Aristotle Onassis, the squat, unattractive billionaire shipping magnate, married America's paragon of class and beauty, the lovely Jackie Kennedy.

These rule violations involve rich and powerful men who find wives who are far more attractive than they are. The men bring resources to the table, like wealth and power, that are normally viewed as out of bounds. We implicitly believe that a man, in our society, should not say to a future bride, "I am rich and I can make your life very comfortable if you marry me," or "I am very powerful and I can make your life an endless round of dinner parties where you can meet and dazzle important people." We comment because the rules were broken.

Still, most people do not have great wealth or beauty or power or fame, yet almost everyone finds a partner. The only thing that saves us all from being brutally squeezed out by the competition for sexual partners is that there are very few people who are rich, smart, good-looking, charming, and accomplished and there is no real consensus about just what array of more ordinary attributes is the best. So most people, without consciously analyzing their behavior, quickly learn how to adjust their expectations and go after people who are appropriate to their status.

The marketplace appears in its most blatant form in the prostitution of women and men. One New York man said he pays to have sex with call girls regularly, every week or so, because he likes the idea of a young, beautiful woman who is at his command and who does not want anything more from him. He says he can get so much more work done without worrying about a relationship.

But this man is the exception. Our study shows that only about 16 percent of men in our survey ever paid for sex.

The sexual marketplace varies with the product that is sought. For example, it includes the arena in which teenagers face off when they compete for a date or attempt to establish their reputations. It includes the college fraternity party or the big game at Homecoming weekend. Among older people it can be the dinner party at a married couple's house, where two recently divorced friends are invited, along with several married couples.

One feature of the sexual market that distinguishes it from most markets in which people buy and sell is that each of us is both the buyer and the seller of essentially the same product. In other markets, we are either the buyer, looking for a product and willing to pay to get it, or we are the seller, selling labor or services and getting paid in return. Sometimes we barter, as when a grocer gives a car mechanic some food from his store and the mechanic, in turn, fixes the grocer's car. But in the sex market, each person is both offering himself or herself and seeking a lover in return.

Another unique feature of the sexual marketplace is the way it is fractured into hundreds of little submarkets. In the labor market, economists talk of segmenting, where people with certain character-istics are barred from or channeled into one sort of job or another. The segmentation of the labor market, however, pales in comparison to the segmentation of the sexual marketplace. Some pockets of the sexual marketplace are for teenagers and others are for young profes-sionals while others serve the elderly or homosexuals or those seeking a one-night-only experience. The searching and bargaining in the market goes on for partners of all sorts, from those who are looking for a one-night stand to those who hope to meet someone to take home and meet the family.

Not only is the market segmented, but it is subdivided within the segments. The myth is that each person has the whole world to choose from. The reality is that when we finish excluding everyone that we consider unsuitable or unobtainable and when we finish dividing the market into sex for recreation or sex for possible marriage, there are very few people left for each of us to seriously consider.

The selection begins with our own personal preferences. Most people are highly selective about whom they will associate with. Some of these restrictions are thought to be personal — "I don't associate with people like that." But actually many of the restrictions are ones we have learned from our network of other people or from the mass media. We still think of these restrictions as our own and we act upon them.

Who we associate with, then, is determined by a combination of our personal preferences, the preferences of people who are important to us, and the segregation of the population based on income, race, education, and geography.

The market has its dark side, too, making some women extremely vulnerable to degradation or abuse. These are the women at the other end of the continuum from the potential marriage partners, like the townies that fraternity men date, or the working-class waitress who dates the rich young man in the movie *Mystic Pizza*. These are the women who are thought of as suitable only for sex. The young woman whom the man considers outside the pale is also the woman who is probably most susceptible to sexual exploitation or rape.

Other disconcerting features of the market appear after the seemingly perfectly matched couple marries. Some of the attributes that a husband or wife wants in a partner may change or may not be revealed until after the marriage. For example, if the husband or wife turns out to be infertile, the expected attribute of an ability to father a child or the ability to conceive turns out not to exist. Researchers have found that when this happens, the marriage is under enormous strain and many marriages fall apart. The husband of an infertile wife or the wife of an infertile husband may decide he or she can do better with another partner. Alternatively, if a husband turns out after marriage to be unable to hold a job, the wife may decide to leave him for what she feels is a more appropriate mate.

Marriages also are likely to dissolve if the husband or wife suddenly acquires desirable attributes that they did not have when they met their mate. A husband who suddenly starts bringing home an enormous income may decide he can now do better in his choice of a wife. A woman who becomes a wildly successful lawyer and suddenly makes huge amounts of money may divorce her less-successful husband. Or the spouses of the newly successful people, realizing all too well that the balance of attributes has shifted, may withdraw, rejecting the more attractive person as a way of protecting themselves from rejection.

These tales play themselves out in the clichéd stories of the faithful wives who worked to put their husbands through medical school or law school only to find that when the men finally got their degrees, they divorced the wives for younger or more attractive or better-educated women. They are a common theme in women's magazines or magazines like *Weight Watchers,* whose advice columns routinely print plaintive letters from women who worry that their husbands keep trying to sabotage their diets or women who complain that now that they are thin, their husbands no longer seem to love them.

Linda Bird Francke, a nonfiction writer, puzzled over this aspect of the marriage market, asking, "What terrors possess men when their women achieve success on their own?" She told of "Maggi, of whom I am very fond, who got along just fine with her executive husband until, with his support, she went back to work and quickly ascended the corporate ladder. Her husband, although he appeared to be proud of his Galatea in public, was evidently quite the opposite in private and for the last three years of their marriage had not slept with her."

In the end, each person brings to the sexual marketplace all the attributes — good and bad — that make up his or her self: personality, looks and physical attributes, occupation and its earning potential, status, interests, diseases, children from a former marriage, and so on and so on.

The process of making a match is complex, often bewildering, and not infrequently a little frightening. It reflects the marketplace at work, the virtues and foibles of competition at its fiercest. Those with more of the currencies valued in the marketplace command a higher price or get the better catches and those with less to offer or unappealing characteristics find they must settle for a less desirable but still achievable mate.

Although it may sound hard and calculating, this way of viewing the sexual market through the eyes of social science can explain some of the most frustrating and perplexing problems that people face as they search for mates. For example, it sheds new light on the bitterly debated question of whether there is a man shortage, a lack of eligible men, so that many women never will find a man to marry.

We will come back to the man shortage question in the next chapter, on finding a partner, asking whether our data demonstrate that there is a problem and, if so, how big a problem it is. And we will come back to the power of social networks and social forces again and again as we ask how we find partners, how many partners we have, what we do sexually, and who is at risk of sexually transmitted diseases.

4

FINDING A PARTNER

At one time or another, almost everyone has felt excluded from the world of loving couples. Almost everyone has watched young lovers walk hand in hand through a park on a balmy spring afternoon or noticed how many women, young and old, beautiful and not so beautiful, sport wedding rings, or how many men, attractive or not, prominently display pictures of their wife and family in their office. And almost everyone has asked: How do people meet their mates?

We like to believe that we will know immediately when we meet Mr. or Ms. Right. We believe we will fall in love in an irrational way, that falling in love involves physical chemistry, an affair of the heart, an experience that is out of our control. Most Americans abhor the idea of an arranged marriage and take umbrage when well-meaning friends and family members try to butt into their personal lives.

It's an old image: Cupid with his bow. Jane Eyre. Cinderella. Famous lines from centuries past. "No sooner met but they looked; no sooner looked but they loved," Shakespeare wrote in *As You Like It*.

This is the image conveyed by the familiar song from the musical *South Pacific:* "Some enchanted evening, you will see a stranger . . .

across a crowded room." We have the classic books, like Daphne du Maurier's ever-popular *Rebecca,* in which the heroine is a poor girl, working as a paid companion to a rich older woman, when the fabulously rich Max de Winter notices her, immediately marries her, and whisks her away to his mansion. We have the movie *Pretty Woman* in which the rich young man falls in love with the poor prostitute.

Yet when people tell how they met the people they married, their stories can sound almost boring, all too mundane — meeting at school, being introduced by friends. The stories scarcely vary, whether the meetings took place decades ago or last month. Rare indeed are the stories of the alluring and mysterious stranger, so totally different from oneself, found in a chance encounter.

Hillary Rodham Clinton and Bill Clinton met when they both were law students at Yale, two bright students on their way up and very much alike — both white, both Protestant, both ambitious. Francis Collins, a doctor and scientist who directs the Human Genome Project, said he married the first girl he ever kissed, his high-school sweetheart. The two began dating when they were fifteen years old and married when they were nineteen.

Ordinary everyday Americans tell the same sort of stories. Martha Bari, a forty-year-old graduate student in art history at the University of Maryland, was introduced to Mike DiPirro, a physicist at Goddard Space Center, by her friend and fellow graduate student, whose husband was Mike's friend and colleague at work. The two fell in love and married a year later.

Kathy, a music student, met Todd, a rhetoric student, in college in Indiana. Three years later they were both members of a friend's wedding and, after that, they began to date. Their friendship turned to love.

On the night before Labor Day in 1974, Paul Monette, a writer, went to a dinner party in Boston. There he met Roger Horwitz, a lawyer, who became not just his best friend but the love of his life.

We wanted to know how people who married met and, just as important, how people met their sexual partners. Do you meet the people you marry in different ways from those you have sex with, but do not marry? Knowing who chooses whom and why can help individuals to understand how they can find a partner if they are looking for one. And understanding partner selection also can help us understand the spread of AIDS and other sexually transmitted diseases. To be at risk for these diseases, you first have to have a partner who is infectious.

Our hunch was that people's choices of sexual and marriage partners are severely constrained but also greatly facilitated by their social networks. It's not that you never see a stranger across a crowded room and fall instantly in love. It's more that that stranger you notice will look just like you. This stranger will be of your race, educational status, social class, and probably religion, too. The single biggest reason why, of course, is that most of the people in that crowded room are preselected to be alike. The social world is organized so that you will meet people like yourself.

At the same time, we learn to be most open to new relationships when we meet people we think are like us and to be wary of total strangers who come to us with no social context.

Tom Byrne, the chairman of the New Jersey Democratic Party, met his wife, Barbara, at a New York club for people from Ivy League colleges. He really did spot her across a crowded room. Barbara, an investment banker, was "a beautiful classy woman," Byrne says. Later, he asked her: what would she have said if he had approached her on a New York subway with the same pickup line? She would have snubbed him, she replied.

Our data support our suspicions. We find that most couples met in the most conventional ways — they were introduced by family members or friends. They met at work. They met at a party.

Despite the mushrooming business in personal ads and singles bars, despite even the emergence of erotic e-mail, where people sit at their computer terminals and type messages to strangers, social networks reign supreme in bringing couples together. In fact, we find, selecting a sexual partner is actually governed by many of the same factors that govern the ways we choose colleges or jobs or cars. And just as we often choose a college, job, or car after consulting with our families, friends, and other advisers, so we rely on our personal social networks when we choose sexual partners.

Very few people met sexual partners by going outside their networks — through a personal ad in the paper or at a bar or on a Club

Med vacation. Moreover, we find, those couples who did venture outside their network were more likely to have short sexual relationships
that never blossomed into anything more. Those who stayed together,
like Harry and Sally in the movie *When Harry Met Sally . . .* , were
more likely to have gotten to know each other as friends first and then
became lovers.

We also find that one group of Americans can be hard put to find
any sex partners at all, no matter how hard they look. These are the
older women, and for them the partner problem is not just hypotheti-
cal — it is starkly real. Our data combined with another national
sample dramatically show that the older a single woman is, the less
likely it is that she will find a sexual partner.

To capture the social factors that determine who meets whom and
who chooses whom, we analyzed the answers to two questions that
we asked of our respondents: Who introduced you to each of your
sexual partners? Where did you meet? By knowing who introduced
people to their partners, we can see how strongly family and social
networks influence our choices. By knowing where people met, we
can see where and with whom there are opportunities to find a partner. It also shows the successful strategies for finding a partner.

In addition to those who are married and cohabiting, our sample
included 1,743 sexual relationships that took place in the last year
among people who were neither married nor living with a sexual partner. About half of these people had only one sexual partner in the
past year.

Most couples were introduced by families or friends or introduced
themselves, usually in situations where others in the room were already preselected — they were at a party given by a mutual friend or
they were at a social organization or club. And the more stable the
relationship, the more likely people were to have met through their
social networks.

As the pie charts in Figure 1 illustrate, people are most likely to
meet individuals that they will have sex with when they are introduced by someone they know well. In Panel C, for example, 55 percent of the unmarried dating couples who had been together for more
than a month were introduced by someone who knew both of them.
The observation that friends and family members are such important

FIGURE 1:
Who Introduced Partners to Each Other

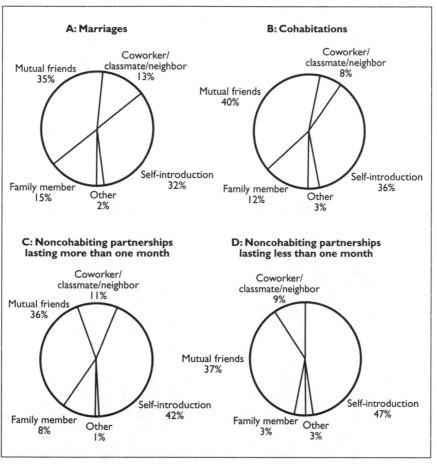

brokers, that they are so likely to introduce us to our sexual partners, shows how and why people end up with partners who are so like themselves.

Married people are even more likely to have been introduced by family and friends, coworkers, classmates, and neighbors. Sixty-three percent of them were introduced in this way, nearly all by family members and friends.

We suspect that many of the self-introductions also took place in circumstances where the potential partners were already chosen to fit in well with the person's social network. Like Tom Byrne's introduction to Barbara, people tend to introduce themselves to people they see at a club for people like themselves or in a classroom. Some people undoubtedly introduced themselves to people they saw in a subway or on the street or at a bar, but, as the next figure shows, this was not a very common way to meet.

These effects of social networks also showed up when we asked where people met their partners. As Figure 2 illustrates, we found that 50 to 60 percent of couples in all four types of partnerships met at school, work, a private party, or church. These are social settings in

FIGURE 2:
Where the Partners First Met

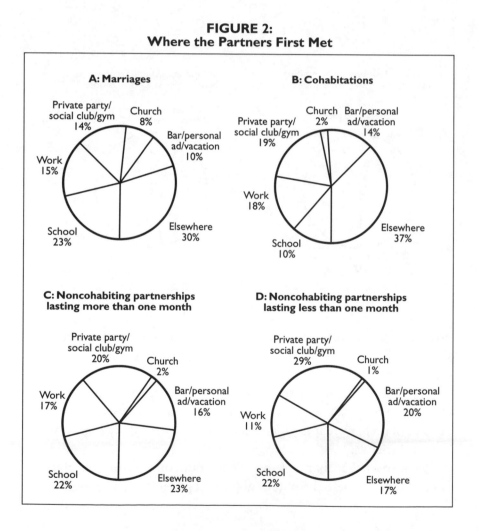

which you are likely to meet someone much like yourself, as contrasted with finding someone through a personal ad or on a vacation.

Those who married were much more likely to meet at church — 8 percent of them did so — than those who had a short-term sexual partnership — just 1 percent of them met at church.

Another way of looking at the data is to ask how often people meet each other in ways that are independent of their social networks. These include, for example, occasions when a man introduces himself to a good-looking woman at a bar, or when a women meets a man through a personal ad. And, we might assume, these are more likely to be relationships that were intended from the start to be short-term, sexual ones. If you just want a passionate partner for the night, why would you want to meet that partner through your social network? Why should your brother or your best friend introduce you to someone you do not intend to see again? It would only lead to misunderstandings and hurt feelings. It might be easier to pick up someone at a bar.

And that is what we find, as Figure 2 shows. Only 10 percent of those who married met in a bar or on vacation or through a personal ad, while 20 percent of those who were short-term, noncohabiting partners met that way.

Of course, just because something is unlikely does not mean it will never happen. A New York doctor in her forties, who had never married and had all but given up on men, finally answered a personal ad, more out of desperation than any expectation that the man would even be presentable. But she met and, within a year, married a college professor who was just as lonely as she was.

The message, however, is that this sort of strategy really is a long shot. And, as our data show, people you meet in these unlikely ways are much more likely to end up as your short-term sexual partners than as your long-term lovers and friends.

The findings suggest that some paths are much more likely than others to lead to a lover. And, they say, there is more to finding someone than trying to lose ten pounds or buying a new wardrobe or frequenting places like a café attached to a bookstore, where you think attractive and unattached people might drift by.

Some people have intuitively grasped this reality. Geri Thoma, a literary agent, offered her friends a prize if they could introduce her to someone she married. Thoma explained her reasoning to a *New York Times* reporter: "It's amazing to me how many single people sit around waiting for the miraculous to happen. They really believe you're going to meet someone in a Laundromat, which means that you're limiting yourself to guys who hang out in Laundromats."

So Thoma proposed her award to her friends at her book club. She says she told them, "The person who sets me up with the greatest number of dates in the next year gets a ten-speed bike, and if you set me up with someone I end up marrying, you get the grand prize. I'll send you on a vacation." Within a few months, however, a friend from outside the book club introduced Thoma to a man she dated, then married. Although the friend did not know of the award, Thoma gave it to him anyway: two tickets to the Caribbean.

Other people thank their matchmakers more subtly. Martha Bari and Mike Di Pirro's matron of honor and best man at their wedding were the friends who introduced them.

The vast popularity of school and work as meeting places is part of the social game, whereby the firm hand of society inevitably guides us toward people that we and our stakeholders would view as acceptable sex partners. One reason why so many people met their partners at school or at work is that most people spend so much time there, going to school for years and then working for decades. The total time spent in school and at work far overshadows the time spent in such places as a bar or on vacation or in a health club.

Another reason, however, is the setting. School and work are far more conducive to meeting someone your friends and family will approve of, someone with interests like yours and a background like yours. They are, in fact, places where your friends and family are likely to introduce you to a partner.

We also can see the importance of social networks in establishing sexual partnerships when we look at the relationship between how a couple met, how long their partnership lasted, and how long they knew each other, as acquaintances or friends, before having sex. People who chose partners within their social network are more likely to have known their partners for some time and to be confident that their partners fit in well with their family and friends. Like Kathy and Todd, a man and woman might first get to know each other at school before starting to date. A gay man may have known another man at work for years before the friendship evolves into love.

The most permanent sexual relationships are marriages, and so, we might expect, people who marry knew their partners longer before having sex with them than people who have short-term sexual relationships. And that is what our data show.

To read Figure 3, look at the upper left-hand set of bar graphs. They show that for the partnerships that are formal marriages, 10 percent of these couples who were introduced by a family member had

FIGURE 3:
Time from First Meeting to First Sex, by Who Introduced Partners

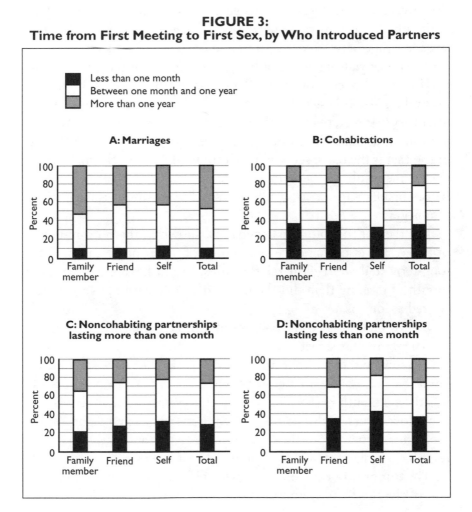

sex less than a month after meeting each other. Once again, this does not necessarily mean that the remaining 90 percent dated for more than a month before having sex — although they might have. It means that they knew each other, as friends, as classmates, as neighbors, as colleagues at work, for more than a month before having sex. About 55 percent of that same group of married couples introduced by a family member knew each other for more than a year before having sex. Each of the bar graphs in this figure can be read in the same way — the black portion showing the percentage of the group who had sex less than a month after meeting, the gray portion at the top showing the percentage who first had sex a year or more after meeting, and the white middle section showing the percentage of the group that had sex some time between one month and one year after meeting.

The upper right-hand set of bar graphs shows the pattern for partnerships that are cohabitations. A much larger portion — 35 percent on average — of these cohabiting couples had sex less than a month after they first met, than was the case for the married couples. You can see that at a glance by noticing the much larger portion of the bar graph that is the black section. Correspondingly, a much smaller portion of these cohabiting couples waited a year or more after they met before first having sex, as seen by the smaller portion of the bar graph that is gray.

For the noncohabiting partnerships, shown in the bottom panels of Figure 3, we see that once again more of these couples, in both the long-term and short-term relationships, began having sex within a month of meeting than did the married couples. And fewer of them waited as long as a year.

Figure 4 tells us how the amount of time before having sex differed by where the couple met.

Those who met in a bar are a lot more likely to have sex quickly. Up to half of those who met in bars and are casual sex partners met less than a month before they first had sex. Apparently, there is also some love at first sight, or more accurately, sex at first sight, on the job, since 41 percent of those who met at work and had only short-term liaisons had sex within a month of first meeting.

The top, gray portion of each bar graph in Figure 4 shows the other end of the spectrum — those who did not have sex within a year of

FIGURE 4:
Time from First Meeting to First Sex, by Where Partners Met

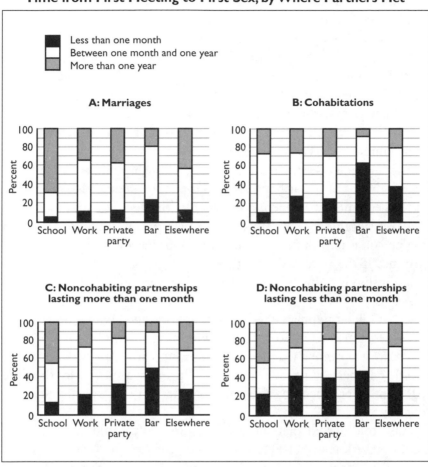

Less than one month
Between one month and one year
More than one year

A: Marriages

B: Cohabitations

C: Noncohabiting partnerships lasting more than one month

D: Noncohabiting partnerships lasting less than one month

having met each other. There we see the mirror image of the story told by the bottom, black portion of each bar graph. Those who met in bars do not typically have sex with each other if they have not done so within a year of first meeting — only one in five do so after so long a time. But then one in five of those who met in bars and subsequently married did know each other for a year before marrying, the table tells us. More than two-thirds of those who met in school and subsequently married did not have sex within the first year of knowing each other. So the classic love story of getting to know your partner gradually, as a friend, going slowly and finally having sex and then marrying is abundantly evident in our data. (For technical reasons, this table, but this table only, has just the married couples who married within the past decade.)

In Figure 3, the type of introduction matters less than the nature of a relationship — like marriage or cohabitation. That is, the different heights of the bar graph in Figure 3 vary more from panel to panel than they vary within a panel. That is not the case for Figure 4, however. There, the location of the meeting — in a bar versus a school, for example — has a much bigger effect on how soon sex occurs after a meeting than does the nature of the relationship that is formed.

We think that what happens is that people often understand, even at the beginning of an encounter, whether the new acquaintance is potentially suitable for marriage. Consciously or not, they judge whether the person is part of their social network or has the same social background. If the potential isn't there for a long-term partnership, the relationship is unlikely to proceed as if it were anything but a causal sexual one.

That's what happened when Lisa, a working-class Italian girl, met Pete, a rich man from Boston, at a swimming pool in Maryland. Their first date was dinner at a modest restaurant, with red-checkered tablecloths and pasta. On their next date, they saw a movie. By the third date, they were spending the night together at Pete's apartment, making love.

Lisa told herself that this relationship really could last, and even though she knew that Pete was all but engaged to Janet, a woman from Pete's social background, back in Boston, she thought that she could lure him away. But Pete never intended to stay with Lisa, and, without ever explicitly saying so or perhaps without ever even admitting it to himself, Pete decided from the start that Lisa was never going to be anything more than a sex partner for the summer. Deeply hurt, Lisa blamed herself when Pete left her to go back to Janet in the fall and thought that she must not be pretty enough or smart enough to keep him.

It's not that Lisa did anything wrong — it's more that she was a victim of the romantic myths we tell ourselves. But because she was not part of Pete's social network, Lisa had a very different relationship with Pete from the start.

If your potential partner shares your social network, you will be cautious about moving too quickly toward sex, because any misunderstandings can have a personal cost to you. If your partner is of the same social background, he or she is unlikely to define the relationship as a short-term sexual one. You also are more likely to know your partner in another context, as a classmate or colleague at work, and you may well be friends already. This means that it will be harder for either of you simply to have sex and then forget the other person.

So before the relationship even gets under way, there are greater investments and greater costs than you would have if you found someone outside your network or social class and dated him or her. This means that we can't simply look at the paltry number of one-night stands that our respondents reported and decide that people just do not want casual sex. The number of one-night stands is also a reflection of the opportunity for such encounters. If you simply want sex, you must find your partners within a context that makes them appropriate for a relationship that is only defined by the desire for sex.

Our survey shows that only 1.4 percent of married couples had sex within the first two days of meeting each other. Nearly ten times as many couples, or 13.7 percent in short-term partnerships of a month or less, had sex so soon after they met. Some of these couples may eventually marry — we got just a snapshot of relationships when we asked about couples who were dating. But we believe that a general pattern is clear.

In fact, even these people who had sex in the first month are unlikely to have sex immediately after meeting, showing, once again, how far from reality is the Hollywood picture of romance, where couples routinely have intercourse within hours after they meet. It also indicates that the Mr. Goodbar type of pickup sex is highly unusual. Moreover, students who met their partners in school are unlikely to have sex within the first month of meeting each other, suggesting that the popular fear that college students are hopping from partner to partner are largely unfounded.

One consequence of the social networks that we use to find partners is that our pool of potential sexual partners is actually very small. We have no way of meeting most Americans, even if we wanted to.

For some people, that is a constant frustration, a slamming shut of the door to a more exciting life. While it has challenged a few to find ways around the barriers of geography and social class, many feel they are trapped by their life circumstances.

One woman, who liked having sex with professional basketball players, said part of the thrill was simply finding a way to meet them. The idea, she said, that a man like Michael Jordan, who seems so unreal, like a god, could actually come to know her was almost unimaginable. These players seemed to inhabit another universe. She quickly realized that her beauty was not enough, nor was dressing provocatively and going to games or to bars after the games. So many other young women had that idea that the odds were against Jordan or any other player noticing her. So she figured out ingenious ways to attract a player's attention, like sending mysterious messages in Federal Express packages to the player she was after. She succeeded in some cases, but her relationships never lasted — which should be no surprise according to the social network theory that we discussed in the previous chapter.

Her story reveals a quiet truth. Unless we do something unusual, like this woman's campaign to meet basketball stars, we simply cannot associate with some people because we do not live near them and they are not in our office or school.

There may be no blacks in a white suburban neighborhood, for example, or no Jews in a small farm town in the Midwest. We cannot know any California girls because we live in New York. We cannot get to know the Rockefellers or the Kennedys because we do not go to the right schools or live in Palm Beach or on Park Avenue.

Even in high schools, where social classes mix, studies have shown that students divide up into homogeneous cliques. The jocks, the intellectuals, the drug users, the Christian right. And these cliques clearly are stratified by social class and race. Classes are segregated according to academic aspirations, which often translate into social class. The college-bound group seldom interacts with the (usually poorer) group of teenagers whose education will end with high school. And, as with any other people looking for sexual partners, teenagers are acutely aware of whom they can bring home to meet their parents.

Teenagers, like adults, are likely to have partners of the same race, not necessarily because they refuse to date people of other races but because they are unlikely to meet many of them. Their parents, for example, may live in the suburbs, so already, deliberately or not, they usually have prescreened their teenager's friends for race.

Although we give lip service to racial equality and although federal fair housing laws might seem to have insured that people can live anywhere they can afford to, many studies have shown that most Americans do not want to live in racially integrated neighborhoods. One way that whites separate themselves from blacks is to live in suburbs. The end result is that Americans live in a segregated society, by any sort of measure of separateness, with blacks and whites in distinct worlds.*

Well before they become sexually active, American adolescents are traveling in social circles with people just like themselves. Adults, too, screen their partners, staying within their social network with organizations like church groups that help newly divorced people find mates who are like themselves. Others find partners because they are part of the same social group. They may be students at the same college or associates in the same law firm or may both be working as trainers at a health club, for example.

Of course, if it were not advantageous for us to pick partners who are like us, we might be less willing to pick partners from within our social networks. And if those social networks were not so well organized, we would not be as successful in finding partners who are so similar to us.

Yet even though we usually restrict our partner search to our own social networks, the system is highly effective in bringing like people together. The problem, however, occurs when people grow older. Many single women have complained that the older they are, the more difficult it can seem to find a man. And older men have said it's not so easy for them, either.

The question of whether there really is a man shortage has prompted countless newspaper and magazine articles, and served as the focus for numerous radio and television talk shows. It became a feminist issue, with some saying that the notion of a man shortage was just a

*Douglas Massey and Nancy Denton, *American Apartheid* (Chicago: University of Chicago Press, 1993).

way to put women in their place, to tell them that if they persisted in delaying marriage to start their careers they would suffer in the end: no man would want them.

One way to decide if there are enough men is simply to divide the number of suitable men for any particular woman by the number of suitable women for these men. If there are 100 single men in a town who wish to marry, regardless of any other of their attributes, and 200 women who wish to marry, again disregarding any other attributes of these women, then the ratio is 1:2. That means that half the women will not find men in this lottery.

We can make the calculation a little more realistic if, as we assume, most people choose marriage partners whose age is within five years of their own. Using data from the *Statistical Abstract of the U.S.*, 1992 edition, we then can determine how many men there are for every woman at various ages. The conclusion, as illustrated in the table below, shows that even if we ignore any other social factors, the age factor alone will force many interested women to be bereft of marital partners.

Age 20–24:	105 men per 100 women
Age 40–44:	98 men per 100 women
Age 60–64:	88 men per 100 women
Age 75+:	55 men per 100 women

As the table illustrates, the only time when there are more men than women is when people are in their twenties, when most people are marrying or living with a partner. But by their forties, men are already starting to die off disproportionately, so that by age forty to forty-four, there are already too few men for the number of women. With every year that passes thereafter, more men than women die. By the time a woman reaches the age of seventy-five or over, there are nearly twice as many women as men her age in the population. The situation for the widowed women in the older age groups is actually worse than the figures suggest because many of the men and the women are, in fact, married, and thus the unmarried women end up with even fewer men to choose from.

So it is no surprise that there is a man shortage for older women.

But a simple proportion is not a sufficient answer. It does not tell who is a suitable partner for whom. More realistically, most people include four criteria in their definition of "suitable." The first is age. Most women want to marry a man who is older than they are, while most men want a woman who is younger. Next is race. Most people want to marry someone of the same race. Then comes marital status. People who are already married usually are not interested in seriously looking for new spouses, and most people who are unmarried do not want to go after a married person. The fourth criterion is education. People tend to marry people with as much education as they have.

People often think of these restrictions, imposed by our culture, as personal preferences, but they are only partially so. The restrictions have become socially structured and they operate to reduce the number of suitable men, especially for women with better educations and women who are older.

The sexual marketplace is entirely different for the single forty-year-old man than it is for the single forty-year-old woman. It turns out that quite conventional men, who do not have great wealth or power to offer, find it much easier to remarry in their later years.

As a newly divorced man in his forties looks around, he discovers that the vast majority of women his own age, race, and education are already spoken for. It can be a sobering experience for him, looking in such a market. Chances are that the last time he was unattached, he was in his twenties and virtually every woman he met was also unattached. Even though the divorce rate is high, these divorces do not all occur at any one age, and at any given moment only a small number of people of any age group are separated, widowed, or divorced. This small number is subdivided into even smaller markets according to such things as race, religion, education, and social class. And the pool of eligible people is constantly shifting as people remarry, with men remarrying much faster than women.

The new marketplace leaves this man with three choices. He can search for one of the few unattached women of his own age, hoping that she will fit in with his social group and that he will be attracted to her. That option leaves the man with very few women to choose from and a slim chance that he will actually end up with a new mate.

A second option is to go after a married woman of his own age.

That choice is fraught with even more severe difficulties. To get a married woman, he has to separate her from her husband and family, a process whose social costs are high. Surveys have consistently shown that nearly 80 percent of Americans strongly disapprove of extramarital sex. It's almost certain that the man's friends and family and the married woman's friends and family will censure any attempt by the man to woo this married woman. In fact, most Americans find marital infidelity so unacceptable that we expect illicit lovers to keep their relationship a secret.

So highly charged are these secrets that one man tried to sue the New York Times Company when one of its papers printed a picture of him walking down the street holding hands with a young woman. The picture was supposed to illustrate love in bloom in the springtime. The problem was that the man and the woman were married — to other people. (He had to drop the suit because the law says that the street is a public place where people do not have to give their permission to be photographed.)

Wary of even getting started with a married woman, many men turn to the third option — to look for a woman where women are still available. That means widening the age range where he looks and even dating younger women, in their twenties, who are not yet spoken for. The older man may have something to offer the young woman — his relative prosperity and lack of encumbrances.

Even a balding, paunchy, sixty-eight-year-old New York taxi driver with bad teeth can find it possible to attract younger women, said Susan Jacoby, a writer who lives in New York. This cabby told Jacoby that he had no trouble finding women in their forties to date.

"I asked him if he ever went out with women his own age," Jacoby wrote. The driver, she added, replied, "Never. You think that's unfair, right? Well, it is unfair, I don't want to go out with women in their sixties. I'll tell you why — their bodies are just as flabby as mine. And, see, I don't have to settle for that. I've got a good pension from twenty-five years in the fire department on top of what I make driving a cab. Gives me something to offer a younger women. Oh, I know they aren't going out with me because I'm so sexy looking. A woman my age is in a tougher spot. See, she looks just as old as I look but most of the time she's got no money and no job. The way I figure it, you've got to have something else to offer when the body starts falling apart."

The story is very different for most older women. A recently divorced woman in her forties looks around her and, like the man her age, finds that there is almost no one available. Almost all the men her age are spoken for, involved in marriages. She faces the same disincentives as the man faces if she tries to pull a man away from an established relationship with another woman. She can look for a younger man, but, unlike the man in his forties, she is likely to have little independent wealth or power to offer. She is likely to have children, an encumbrance the younger man does not want. And she is past her most fertile period, so the younger man cannot look forward to having his own family with her.

Not all relationships between older women and younger men end badly, of course, but older women are at a profound disadvantage when they try to use wealth and power to lure a man because the generally accepted rules of who is suitable for whom virtually guarantee that the match will be disapproved by both the woman's and the man's stakeholders.

The demographic data show that the older men get, within limits, the better their odds because there are more women who are younger, as well as or less educated, single, and of the same race.

A group of demographers have calculated that for every 100 white college-educated women between the ages of thirty-five and thirty-nine, there are only thirty-nine men available who are white, unmarried, as old as or older than the women, and who are also college educated. But white college-educated men aged thirty-five to thirty-nine have the odds in their favor in the sexual marketplace. There are 200 women for every 100 men who fulfill these suitability criteria.

The analysis is actually more complex because there are even more restrictions on the availability of marriage partners; some people are out of the pool of potential partners because they do not want to marry. Others are not interested in sex with people of the opposite gender.

Every problem that white women have is exacerbated for well-educated black women, who are at a much greater disadvantage than white women at every age because fewer black men finish high school and go on to college. Their pool of suitable men is shrunk from the beginning. In contrast, educated black men at every age have a much better chance of finding a suitable partner than do black women.

That's one reason why black women often say they are enraged when they see a professional black man with a white woman.

The following graph shows what happens to a woman's chance of finding a partner as she grows older. The graph combines our data, which go to age fifty-nine, with data from the General Social Survey, which agree with ours up to age fifty-nine but continue to age eighty-nine. By age fifty, women are significantly more likely than men to have no sexual partner in the past year — 22 percent of the women versus 8 percent of the men. But the discrepancies only grow from there. By ages sixty to sixty-four, 45 percent of the women have no partners and 15 percent of the men have no partners. (The respondents in the General Social Survey are noninstutionalized, so they exclude unhealthy elderly who are in hospitals or nursing homes.)

Given data like these, it is no surprise that women have so much trouble finding men.

Of course, men, too, often have problems finding partners as they grow older. Even though they can draw from a larger pool of women,

FIGURE 5:
U.S. Adults with No Sexual Partner in the Past Twelve Months

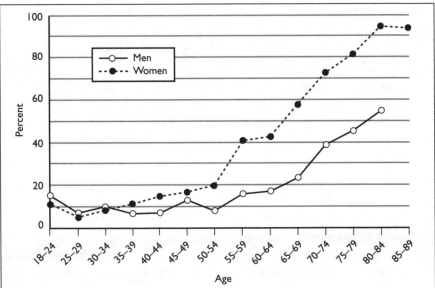

most women in the population still are married or living with a partner, making them essentially inaccessible. And older men, like older
women, often have trouble even finding potential partners since the
extensive social structures, like schools and youth groups, that help
teenagers and young adults are not available to them.

Reflecting the hard time many older people have, male as well as
female writers have poured out tens of thousands of words over the
years on the painful search for someone to share their bed.

Men who divorced and had to look for new mates complained that
it was much harder the second time around. Roderick Thorp, a fiction
writer in Los Angeles, said he found himself alone much of the time,
"and sometimes it's depressing. Other people have told me it's much
the same for them."

Charles Simmons, a novelist, lamented that as an older man, he
has become invisible to women. The grocery store clerks, he said, used
to flirt with him. Now, he wrote, "There comes a time when, like the
boy putting groceries in your cart, she doesn't see you. She sees the
cold cuts and the beer, the half a loaf of bread, and that's all." He
concludes: "You are being screened out."

But the problem for women is deeper and more stubbornly resis-
tant to any obvious solutions. The facts are so bleak that they make
the sort of pat advice dispensed to women look silly. The Saturday
before Valentine's Day in 1994, when every radio show, television
show, and newspaper was casting about for something fresh and new
to say about love, a talk radio show in Philadelphia, "Voices in the
Family," featured a psychologist who said she was an expert on love
and sex between older people. A woman called the show to ask what
an older woman can do if she is unable to find a man. The psychologist replied that women have three options. One is to masturbate. Another is to find a female lover. And the third is to find a younger man.

In fact, there are no easy answers for older women who have not
found a man. The one consolation, as we will discuss later, is that all
of our evidence argues against the theory that a woman without a
partner is a sexually thwarted creature. Instead, we find, women —
and men — who have no partners think less about sex and report
having what often are very happy and fulfilling lives without it.

5

HOW MANY SEXUAL PARTNERS DO WE HAVE?

Sometimes, the myths about sex contain a grain of truth. The common perception is that Americans today have more sexual partners than they did just a decade or two ago. That, it turns out, is correct. A third of Americans who are over age fifty have had five or more sexual partners in their lifetime. But half of all Americans aged thirty to fifty have had five or more partners even though being younger, they had fewer years to accumulate them.

Still, when we ask older or younger people how many partners they had in the past year, the usual reply is zero or one. Something must have changed to make younger people accumulate more partners over a lifetime, yet sustain a pattern of having no partners or only one in any one year. The explanation is linked to one of our most potent social institutions and how it has changed.

That institution is marriage, a social arrangement so powerful that nearly everyone participates. About 90 percent of Americans have married by the time they are thirty and a large majority spends much of their adulthood as part of a wedded couple. And marriage, we find, regulates sexual behavior with remarkable precision. No matter what they did before they wed, no matter how many partners they had, the sexual lives of married people are similar. Despite the popular myth that there is a great deal of adultery in marriage, our data and other reliable studies do not find it. Instead, a vast majority are faithful while the marriage is intact. And, as we will explain, there is a good reason for this.

So, yes, many young people probably are having sexual intercourse with a fair number of partners. But that stops with marriage. The reason that people now have more sexual partners over their lifetimes is that they are spending a longer period sexually active, but unmarried. The period has lengthened from both ends and in the middle. The average age at which people have their first sexual intercourse has crept down and the average age at which people marry for the first time has edged up. And people are more likely to divorce now, which means they have time between marriages when they search for new partners once again.

To draw these conclusions, we looked at our respondents' replies to a variety of questions. First, we asked people when they first had heterosexual intercourse. Then, we asked what happens between the time when people first have intercourse and when they finally marry. How many partners do they have? Do they have more than one partner at any one time or do they have their partners in succession, practicing serial monogamy? We asked how many people divorced and how long they remained unmarried. Finally, we asked how many partners people had in their lifetimes.

In our analyses of the numbers of sex partners, we could not separately analyze patterns for gay men and lesbians. That is because homosexuals are such a small percentage of our sample that we do not have enough people in our survey to draw valid conclusions about this aspect of sexual behavior.

If we are going to look at heterosexual partners from the beginning, from the time that people first lose their virginity, we plunge headfirst into the maelstrom of teenage sex, always a turbulent subject, but especially so now, in the age of AIDS.

While society disputes whether to counsel abstinence from sexual intercourse or to pass out condoms in high schools, it also must grapple with a basic question: Has sexual behavior among teenagers changed? Are more having sexual intercourse and at younger ages, or is the overheated rhetoric a reaction to fears, without facts? The answer is both troubling and reassuring to the majority of adults who prefer teenagers to delay their sexual activity — troubling because most teenagers are having intercourse, but reassuring because sexual intercourse tends to be sporadic during the teen years.

We saw a steadily declining age at which teenagers first had sexual intercourse. Men and women born in the decade 1933–1942 had sex at an average age of about eighteen. Those born twenty to thirty years later have an average age at first intercourse that is about six months younger, as seen in Figure 6. The figure also indicates that the men report having sex at younger ages than the women. It also shows that blacks report a younger age at first intercourse than whites.

Another way to look at the age at first intercourse is illustrated in Figure 7. The figure shows the proportions of teenagers and young adults who experienced sexual intercourse at each age from twelve to twenty-five. To see at what age half the people had intercourse, for

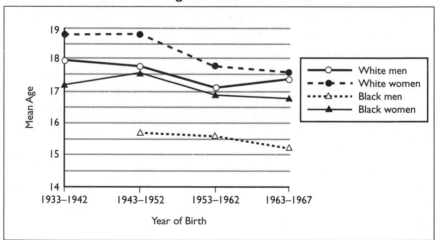

FIGURE 6:
Mean Age at First Intercourse

Note: This includes respondents who had vaginal intercourse no later than age twenty-five and who have reached their twenty-fifth birthday by the date of the interview. Missing line segments indicate insufficient number of cases for a particular category (less than 30). Whites computed from cross-section sample; blacks computed from cross-section and the over-sample.

FIGURE 7:
Cumulative Percentage Who Have Had Intercourse

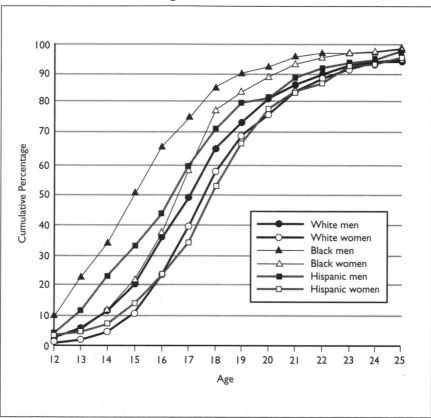

Notes: Cumulative percentage indicates the proportion of respondents of a given group at a given age. This figure only includes respondents who have reached their twenty-fifth birthday by the date of the interview.

example, follow the dotted horizontal line that corresponds to a cumulative frequency of 50 percent. It shows that half of all black men had intercourse by the time they were fifteen, half of all Hispanic men had intercourse by the time they were about sixteen and a half, half of all black women had intercourse by the time they were nearly seventeen, and half the white women and half the Hispanic women had intercourse by the time they were nearly eighteen. By age twenty-two, about 90 percent of each group had intercourse.

The patterns are crystal clear. About half the teenagers of various racial and ethnic groups in the nation have begun having intercourse with a partner in the age range of fifteen to eighteen, and at least four out of five have had intercourse by the time their teenage years are over. Since the average age of marriage is now in the mid-twenties, few Americans wait until they marry to have sex.

Our data, in fact, show that the proportion of women who were either virgins when they turned twenty or had had sexual intercourse with only one person declined from 84 percent, among women born in 1933 to 1942, to about 50 percent for those born after 1953.

It's a change that built up for years, making it sometimes hard to appreciate just how profound it is. Stories of what sex among the unmarried was like decades ago can be startling. Even people who were no longer teenagers, and who were engaged, felt overwhelming social pressure to refrain from intercourse before marriage.

For example, Diana Trilling, a member of the literary and intellectual avant-garde, might have been expected to be most open and unashamed of her sexual activities. Yet she wrote of her own secret sex life with her future husband, Lionel Trilling, around 1930: "It was of the utmost urgency that this violation of the conventions not be known to our families. Even four or five years later, in the mid-30's, when Lionel's mother discovered that a college friend of Lionel's sister, Harriet, had asked Harriet to go to bed with him, she expected Lionel (in her quaint phase) to horsewhip him. Of our friends at the time of our marriage, we knew only one other couple that engaged in so irregular a form of courtship, and I am still convinced that if my father had found us out, he would have — he would have what? There was no talk of sin in my family or, for that matter, of virtue, whether maintained or sacrificed. I was never taught that I would burn in hell for my misdeed. But I had my own scorching hell of the imagination, a terrible unmapped place to which I would be remanded in punishment for any major infringement of family law, and as I thought of my father's discovering that Lionel and I had gone to bed together, I thought I could hear the creaking of its gates."

Although stories like Trilling's may indicate that the reasons why people do — and why they do not — have sexual intercourse before marriage have changed over the decades, we probed that question directly by asking our respondents what led them to have sex the first time. Did they want to? Were they forced? Or did they go along with it to please a partner? This is one way to discern what social factors may have dissuaded some teenagers from having sexual intercourse in earlier years, and what encouraged them to have it now. The results reveal that young men and young women tend to have very different reasons for having sex.

More than 90 percent of the men said they wanted to have sexual intercourse the first time. Fewer than 8 percent said they did not want it but went along with it, and just three in a thousand said they were forced. As seen in Table 4, more than half the men said they were motivated primarily by curiosity and only a quarter of those who wanted sex said they had sexual intercourse out of affection for their partner. In fact, most of the men said they were not in love with their first partner. Of those men who did not want their first experience of intercourse, 29 percent said they felt peer pressure.

The women, in contrast, often said they were in love, and although they too usually wanted to have intercourse, a higher proportion of them said they just went along. About 70 percent of women wanted sex the first time they had it, 24 percent said they only went along

Table 4
Reasons for Having First Sexual Intercourse

Attributed reasons	First intercourse wanted		First intercourse not wanted, but not forced	
	Men	Women	Men	Women
Affection for partner	25%	48%	10%	38%
Peer pressure	4	3	29	25
Curiosity/readiness for sex	51	24	50	25
Wanted to have a baby	0	1	0	1
Physical pleasure	12	3	7	2
Under influence of alcohol/drugs	1	0	3	7
Wedding night	7	21	1	3
	100%	100%	100%	100%

with it, and 4 percent were forced to have intercourse against their will. A quarter said they had intercourse the first time out of curiosity about sex, nearly half those who wanted it the first time said they did it out of affection for their partner (seen in Table 4). For one in five women who wanted their first sex, it occurred on their wedding night. The vast majority said they were in love with their partner the first time they had sex.

Looking in more detail, we can determine that the reasons for having first intercourse have changed over the decades, leading us to believe that peer pressure is now a stronger and more important factor in swaying teenagers than it was in the past. When we contrast women age eighteen to twenty-nine with those age fifty to fifty-nine, and look at only those whose first intercourse was not wanted but not forced, about 37 percent of the younger group said the reason was peer pressure while only 13 percent of the older group gave that reason. About 35 percent of that younger group cited affection for their partner, while 54 percent of the older group gave that reason.

The younger women who had intercourse the first time because they wanted to cited curiosity and affection for their partner as their leading reasons. The older women's main reasons were affection and the fact that it was their wedding night. Virtually *no* women said that they wanted or went along with sex for physical pleasure.

But having had intercourse once is not the same as having it often, with many partners. Lost in the polemics about teen sex are the findings by others that intercourse among teenagers is very episodic and that many younger teenagers do not have any sexual intercourse at all. Those who are sexually experienced may go many months without having intercourse.

One study, based on a national survey of young men conducted in 1988, found that "sexually active" young men age fifteen to nineteen did not have any sexual intercourse in at least six of the previous twelve months. And recent studies hint that teenagers are having less intercourse now than in previous years. For example, a 1978 study found that nineteen-year-old men, the teenage group who had the most sex, had sex an average of four times in the previous four weeks, while in 1988, a comparable group of nineteen-year-old men reported having intercourse an average of three times in the previous four weeks.

With constant talk about the threat of AIDS, many people have hoped that teenagers would be more wary about sex. Chariness might be revealed in a decision to have fewer partners or to delay the age of sexual initiation or to wait until marriage to have sexual intercourse.* We know there was no pronounced tendency to delay the age of sexual initiation or to have fewer partners in the teenage years. But, we asked, was there any other AIDS effect among teenagers?

The answer is that if the shadow of AIDS did encourage teenagers to change their behavior, it did not encourage many and the changes were not profound. We find that a small percentage of young men did abstain from intercourse, but we cannot say whether the effect we saw was due to a desire to avoid the risk of being infected with HIV or whether it had some other, unrelated, cause.

We can calculate, for example, the proportion of men and women who reach age twenty as a virgin. For the successive ten-year birth cohorts, that is, those born in the decades 1933 to 1942, 1943 to 1952, 1953 to 1962, and 1963 to 1972, the percentages of men who were virgins at age twenty rose from 1.0 percent to 1.7 percent to 6.0 percent to 8.3 percent. For women in these four age groups, the percentages who were virgins at age twenty were 4.6 percent, 4.7 percent, 3.6 percent, and 5.8 percent, respectively. But the increase in the number of men who were virgins at age twenty began before the AIDS scare, so we cannot attribute all of that increase to concerns about AIDS.

We are not certain why more twenty-year-old men are virgins now than forty years ago, and can only speculate that perhaps it has become more socially acceptable for a young man to refrain from having intercourse. We found, for example, that the proportion of men whose first sexual intercourse was with a prostitute declined from 7 percent of men who came of age in the 1950s to 1.5 percent of the men who came of age in the late 1980s to early 1990s.

The proportion of women who were virgins has traditionally been somewhat higher than the proportion of men who had had no sexual

*Re 1978 study: Melvin Zelnik and John F. Kantner, *Sex and Pregnancy in Adolescence* (New York: Sage, 1981). Re 1988 study: Leighton Ku, Freya Sonenstein, and Joseph Pleck, "Sexual Behavior in the 90s: Male Youth in the U.S." (mimeo presented at the Population Association of America Meetings, 1992).

intercourse by age twenty, but that gender difference has disappeared. We do not see any marked trend toward increasing proportions of young women who remained virgins until they turned twenty.

In addition to having intercourse at younger ages, many people also are marrying later — a change that is the real legacy of the late 1960s and early 1970s. This period was not, we find, a sexual revolution, a time of frequent sex with many partners for all. Instead, it was the beginning of a profound change in the sexual life course, providing the second reason why Americans have accumulated more partners now than in decades past.

Since the 1960s, the route to the altar is no longer so predictable as it used to be. In the first half of the twentieth century, almost everyone who married followed the same course: dating, love, a little sexual experimentation with one partner, sometimes including intercourse, then marriage and children. It also was a time when there was a clear and accepted double standard — men were much more likely to have had intercourse with several women before marrying than women were to have had intercourse with several men.

At the dawn of the millennium, we are left with a nation that still has this idealized heterosexual life course but whose actual course has fragmented in the crucial years before marriage. Some people still marry at eighteen, others at thirty, leading to very different numbers of sexual partners before marriage. Social class plays a role, with less-educated people marrying earlier than better-educated people. Blacks tend to marry much later than whites, and a large number of blacks do not marry at all.

But a new and increasingly common pattern has emerged: affection or love and sex with a number of partners, followed by affection, love, and cohabitation. This cycles back to the sexual marketplace, if the cohabitation breaks up, or to marriage. Pregnancy can occur at any of these points, but often occurs before either cohabitation or marriage. The result is that the path toward marriage, once so straight and narrow, has begun to meander and to have many side paths, one of which is being trodden into a well-traveled lane.

That path is the pattern of living together before marriage. Like other recent studies, ours shows a marked shift toward living together rather than marriage as the first union of couples. With an increase in cohabitation, the distinctions among having a steady sexual partner, a live-in sexual partner, and a marriage have gotten more fuzzy. This shift began at the same time as talk of a sexual revolution. Our study shows that people who came of age before 1970 almost invariably got married without first living together, while the younger people seldom did. But, we find, the average age at which people first move in with a partner — either by marrying, or living together — has remained nearly constant, around age twenty-two for men and twenty for women. The difference is that now that first union is increasingly likely to be a cohabitation.

In our study, we find that 93 percent of women born between 1933 and 1942 married without ever living with their partner. And 90 percent of these women were either virgins when they married or had premarital intercourse only with the man they wed. In contrast, just 36 percent of women born between 1963 and 1974 got married without living with their spouse first. But among the majority who lived with a man, 60 percent had no other sexual partners or only one other before they moved in with their lover.

With the increase in cohabitation, people are marrying later, on average. The longer they wait, however, the more likely they are to live with a sexual partner in the meantime. Since many couples who live together break up within a short time and seek a new partner, the result has been an increase in the average number of partners that people have before they marry.

Figure 8 (on page 98) shows the pattern of acquiring the first partner for women born in two separate time intervals.

The top portion of the figure shows the pattern of marriage or cohabitation for women born between 1933 and 1942 and the bottom portion shows the comparable pattern for women born between 1963 and 1974.

These data show that in both the younger and the older groups of women, the vast majority formed a live-in partnership. By age 25, about 85 percent of both groups had done so. But, for the younger women, most formed their first partnership by cohabiting. For the older women, cohabiting was all but unheard of; nearly all formed their first partnership by marrying.

The top figure shows that by age eighteen, about 30 percent of these older women were married. By age twenty, 55 percent had married.

The bottom figure shows that by age twenty, only about 20 percent

FIGURE 8:
Age at First Live-in Parnership (Marriage or Cohabitation)

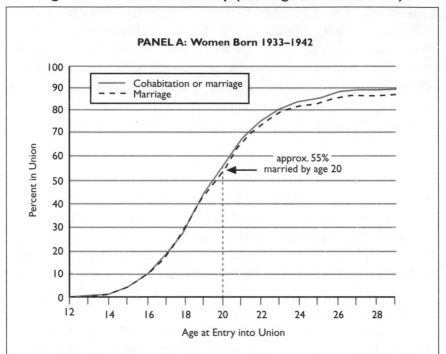

PANEL A: Women Born 1933–1942

Cohabitation or marriage
Marriage

approx. 55% married by age 20

Percent in Union

Age at Entry into Union

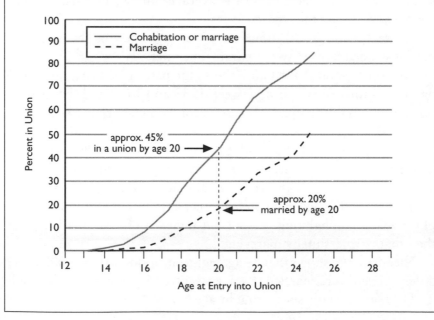

PANEL B: Women Born 1963–1974

Cohabitation or marriage
Marriage

approx. 45% in a union by age 20

approx. 20% married by age 20

Percent in Union

Age at Entry into Union

of the younger women had married — less than half as many as the older women three decades past. But nearly as many had begun living with a man — by cohabiting or marrying. By age twenty, 45 percent of the younger women had either married or begun living with a man. That means that nearly equal numbers of these younger women were living with a man as were married by age twenty.

The vertical distance between the solid and the broken lines in Figure 8 shows the proportion who first entered a cohabitation instead of a formal marriage. In the top figure, the dashed and solid lines are almost on top of each other, which means that practically none of the women in that age group first lived with a sex partner — they almost all married when they entered their first live-in partnership.

The figure also shows that nearly all — 90 percent — of the older women had married by the time they turned twenty-nine. In the younger group, by age twenty-five, nearly 90 percent had formed a partnership. (The younger group had not lived long enough to complete the graph out to age twenty-nine, so it stops at a younger age. But the solid line is approaching 90 percent.) This shows, again, that the younger women are forming partnerships at about the same rate and at about the same age as the older women. It's just that the younger women often live with a man in a cohabitation relationship instead of a marriage.

The graphs for men are nearly identical; we don't show them here.

Another way to look at this trend is illustrated by Table 5. The table shows that 84.5 percent of the men born in the years 1933 to

Table 5
Percentage of First Partnerships
That Were Marriages

Birth Dates	Men	Women
1933–1942	84.5	93.8
1943–1952	66.7	75.7
1953–1962	46.6	57.3
1963–1974	33.9	35.3

1942 and 93.8 percent of the women born in those years married without ever living with their partner first. But just 33.9 percent of the men born in the years 1963 to 1974 married without first living with their partner and just 35.3 percent of the women born in those years married without cohabiting.

Finally, we can look at divorce rates, another key social change that began in the 1960s and that has led to increasing numbers of partners over a lifetime. Our data show this divorce pattern, as do many other data sets in the United States. For example, we can look at how likely it is that a couple will be divorced by the tenth anniversary of their marriage. For people born between 1933 and 1942, the chance was about one in five. For those born between 1943 and 1952, the chance was one in three. For those born between 1953 and 1962, the chance was closer to 38 percent. Divorced people as a group have more sexual partners than people who remain married and they are more likely, as a group, to have intercourse with a partner and live with a partner before they marry again.

These three social trends — earlier first intercourse, later marriage, and more frequent divorce — help explain why people now have more sexual partners over their lifetimes.

To discern the patterns of sexual partnering, we asked respondents how many sexual partners they had. We could imagine several scenarios. People could find one partner and marry. Or they could have sex with several before marrying. Or they could live with their partners first and then marry. Or they could simply have lots of casual sex, never marrying at all or marrying but also having extramarital sex.

Since our respondents varied in age from eighteen to fifty-nine, the older people in the study, who married by their early twenties, would have been married by the time the turbulent 1960s and 1970s came around. Their premarital behavior would be a relic from the past, telling us how much intercourse people had in the days before sex became so public an issue. The younger people in our study can show us whether there is a contrast between the earlier days and the decades after a sexual revolution was proclaimed. We can ask if they have more partners, if they have more than one sexual partner at a time, and if their sexual behavior is markedly different from that of the older generations that preceded them.

Most young people today show no signs of having very large numbers of partners. More than half the men and women in America who were eighteen to twenty-four in 1992 had just one sex partner in the past year and another 11 percent had none in the last year. In addition, studies in Europe show that people in the United Kingdom, France, and Finland have sexual life courses that are virtually the same as the American life course. The picture that emerges is strikingly different from the popular image of sexuality running out of control in our time.

In fact, we find, nearly all Americans have a very modest number of partners, whether we ask them to enumerate their partners over their adult lifetime or in the past year. The number of partners varies little with education, race, or religion. Instead, it is determined by marital status or by whether a couple is living together. Once married, people tend to have one and only one partner, and those who are unmarried and living together are almost as likely to be faithful.

Our data for the United States are displayed in Table 6 (on page 102).

The right-hand portion of Table 6 tells how many sexual partners people had since they turned eighteen. Very few, just 3 percent, had no partners, and few, just 9 percent, had a total of more than twenty partners.

The oldest people in our study, those aged fifty-five to fifty-nine, were most likely to have had just one sexual partner in their lifetimes — 40 percent said they had had only one. This reflects the earlier age of marriage in previous generations and the low rate of divorce among these older couples. Many of the men were married by age twenty-two and the women by age twenty.

The left-hand portion of Table 6 shows the number of sexual partners that people had in the past twelve months. These are the data that show how likely people are to remain faithful to their sexual partner, whether or not they are married. Among married people, 94 percent had one partner in the past year. Couples who were living together were almost as faithful. Seventy-five percent of people who had never married but were living together had one partner in the past year. Eighty percent of people who were previously married and were cohabiting when we questioned them had one partner in the past year. Two-thirds of the single people who were not living with a partner

Table 6
Number of Sex Partners in Past Twelve Months and Since Age Eighteen

	Sex partners past twelve months				Sex partners since age eighteen					
	0	1	2 to 4	5+	0	1	2 to 4	5 to 10	10 to 20	21+
Total	12%	71%	14%	3%	3%	26%	30%	22%	11%	9%
Gender										
Men	10	67	18	5	3	20	21	23	16	17
Women	14	75	10	2	3	31	36	20	6	3
Age										
18–24	11	57	24	9	8	32	34	15	8	3
25–29	6	72	17	6	2	25	31	22	10	9
30–34	9	73	16	2	3	21	29	25	11	10
35–39	10	77	11	2	2	19	30	25	14	11
40–44	11	75	13	1	1	22	28	24	14	12
45–49	15	75	9	1	2	26	24	25	10	14
50–54	15	79	5	0	2	34	28	18	9	9
55–59	32	65	4	0	1	40	28	15	8	7
Marital status										
Never married, noncohabiting	25	38	28	9	12	15	29	21	12	12
Never married, cohabiting	1	75	20	5	0	25	37	16	10	13
Married	2	94	4	1	0	37	28	19	9	7
Divorced, separated, widowed, noncohabiting	31	41	26	3	0	11	33	29	15	12
Divorced, separated, widowed, cohabiting	1	80	15	3	0	0	32	44	12	12
Education										
Less than high school	16	67	15	3	4	27	36	19	9	6
High school graduate or equivalent	11	74	13	3	3	30	29	20	10	7
Some college/ vocational	11	71	14	4	2	24	29	23	12	9

Table 6, *continued*

	Sex partners past twelve months				Sex partners since age eighteen					
	0	1	2 to 4	5+	0	1	2 to 4	5 to 10	10 to 20	21+
Finished college	12	69	15	4	2	24	26	24	11	13
Master's/advanced degree	13	74	10	3	4	25	26	23	10	13
Current Religion										
None	11	68	13	7	3	16	29	20	16	16
Mainline Protestant	11	73	13	2	2	23	31	23	12	8
Conservative Protestant	13	70	14	3	3	30	30	20	10	7
Catholic	12	71	13	3	4	27	29	23	8	9
Jewish	3	75	18	3	0	24	13	30	17	17
Other religion	15	70	12	3	3	42	20	16	8	13
Race/Ethnicity										
White	12	73	12	3	3	26	29	22	11	9
Black	13	60	21	6	2	18	34	24	11	11
Hispanic	11	69	17	2	4	35	27	17	8	9
Asian	15	77	8	0	6	46	25	14	6	3
Native American	12	76	10	2	5	28	35	23	5	5

Row percentages total 100 percent.

had no partners or only one in the past year. Only a few percent of the population had as many as five partners for sexual intercourse in the past year, and many of these were people who were never married and were not living with anyone. They were mostly young and mostly male.

Since most Americans are white and middle class, their experiences will dominate the overall data. So, we asked, does this picture of an essentially monogamous America reflect anything but the experiences of the white middle class? Conventional wisdom says that people of different educational backgrounds or different religions or different races will have different sexual histories. The popular myth is that poor people have many partners, blacks have many partners, and conservative Christians have few.

But when we looked at our respondents' education, race, and religion, these patterns did not emerge. When we looked at education levels, for example, there was no relationship with the number of partners people had in the past year. Table 6 shows the percentages with five or more partners vary with education only 3 to 4 percent; these are not large enough differences to be significant.

There was one notable exception, however. We found that the more educated people were, the more partners they had over their lifetime. In Table 6, we can add together the final two columns and see that as education rose from less than high school to college graduates, for example, the percentage who report having ten or more partners in their lifetime rose from 15 percent to 24 percent. One important reason for this is that people with more education are more likely to postpone marriage while they finish their schooling. The longer they wait, the more time they have to meet, have intercourse with, and, often, live with a succession of partners. It's not that their sex drive is in overdrive. It's rather that they have a greater opportunity to have a succession of sexual partners before they form their monogamous or nearly monogamous marriages.

Blacks were more likely than whites to have had many partners over the past year, but the number of blacks or whites with multiple partners was small. Three percent of whites said they had more than five partners in the past year and 6 percent of blacks had more than five partners. On the other hand, 73 percent of whites and 60 percent of blacks had one partner in the past year and 12 percent of whites and 13 percent of blacks had no partner in the past year. When we look at the number of sexual partners over a lifetime (the right-hand side of Table 6), blacks no longer have more than whites.

One way to imagine the patterns of sexual partners is to think of a graph, with the vertical axis showing numbers of partners and the horizontal axis showing a person's age. The graph will be a series of blips, as the person finds partners, interspersed with flat regions where the person has no partners or when the person has just one steady partner. When the person marries, the line flattens out at a height of one, indicating that the individual has only one partner. If the marriage breaks up, the graph shows a few more blips until the person remarries, and then it flattens out again.

For an individual, the graph is mostly flat, punctuated by a few areas of blips. But if we superimposed everyone's graph on top of each other, we would have a sort of supergraph that looked like it was all blips. That, in essence, is what has led to the widespread impression that everyone is having lots of partners. We see the total picture — lots of sex in the population — without realizing that each individual spends most of his or her life with only one partner.

These findings give no support to the idea of a promiscuous society or of a dramatic sexual revolution reflected in huge numbers of people with multiple casual sex partners. The finding on which our data give strong and quite amazing evidence is not that most people do, in fact, form a partnership, or that most people do, in fact, ultimately get married. That fact also was well documented in many previous studies. Nor is it news that more recent marriages are much less stable than marriages that began thirty years ago. That fact, too, was reported by others before us. But we add a new fact, one that is not only important but that is striking.

Our study clearly shows that no matter how sexually active people are before and between marriages, no matter whether they lived with their sexual partners before marriage or whether they were virgins on their wedding day, marriage is such a powerful social institution that, essentially, married people are nearly all alike — they are faithful to their partners as long as the marriage is intact. It does not matter if the couple were high-school sweethearts who married after graduation day or whether they are in their thirties, marrying after each had lived with several others. Once married, the vast majority have no other sexual partner; their past is essentially erased. Marriage remains the great leveler.

We see this, for example, when we ask about fidelity in marriage. More than 80 percent of women and 65 to 85 percent of men of every age report that they had no partners other than their spouse while they were married. These findings are confirmed by data from the General Social Survey, which reported virtually identical figures for extramarital sex.

The marriage effect is so dramatic that it swamps all other aspects of our data. When we report that more than 80 percent of adult Americans age eighteen to fifty-nine had zero or one sexual partner in the past year, the figure might sound ludicrous to some young people who know that they and their friends have more than one partner in a year. But the figure really reflects the fact that most Americans in that broad age range are married and are faithful. And many of the others are cohabiting, and they too are faithful. Or they are without partners altogether, a situation that is especially likely for older women.

Most adults are married and so when we ask the adult population how many partners they had in the past year, the data, as presented in Table 6, will be dominated by the responses of married people. This is apparent in the raw reporting on married people near the middle of the table. We find only 3 percent of adults had five or more partners in the past year. Half of all adult Americans had three or fewer partners over their lifetimes.

In Europe, similar patterns have emerged. A study in the United Kingdom found, for example, that 73 percent of men had exactly one partner in the past year. In France, 78 percent of men had a single partner in the past year. The number for Finnish men was 78 percent. In our study, 67 percent of men had one partner in the past year.

In the United Kingdom, 79 percent of women had one partner in the past year; in France, 78 percent had only one partner; in Finland, 79 percent had one partner. We found that 75 percent of women in the United States had exactly one partner in the past year.

The extraordinary fidelity in marriage is all the more striking because of the length of time that people spend before, in, and between marriages. They are married for so much longer than they are unmarried that if they were somehow equally at risk of being unfaithful at any time, they should be likely, after years or decades of marriage, to have extramarital partners. On average, the length of time people spend between marriages is four years. The average marriage lasts a quarter century. Yet during that quarter century, most people report that they do not have additional sexual partners.

Nonetheless, the myth of the joys of easy sex with lots of partners has led many a middle-aged man, and some middle-aged women, to wonder whether they missed something by being born too soon for the sexual revolution. We have the persistent myth that men, in particular, get a seven-year itch that makes them look around for a new partner to revive their flagging sex lives. Or, another myth says, the men shed their dull wives and start life anew, leaping headfirst into the new society where sex is abundant and always available.

Instead, it looks as if most people of each generation find a partner, marry in their twenties, and remain sexually faithful unless the marriage breaks up. If a couple divorces, the man usually finds one or more partners; the woman is less likely to find new partners, especially if she is middle-aged or older. For example, about half of the forty- to fifty-nine-year-old men in our study who had been widowed or divorced said they had two or more sexual partners after their first marriage ended. But only 40 percent of the women in that age range found two or more partners after their marriage ended. After a brief period of searching for a new partner, many people marry again and remain faithful.

That is not surprising, for two reasons that have nothing to do with the joys of sex with your spouse. First, once someone marries, there are profound social pressures to stay faithful and to stay married. And as family life and work become more central and take their toll, there is less and less time even to think of finding a partner for extramarital sex, to say nothing of finding time to have that sex.

Another reason why so many people remain married and faithful is that most people realize that finding a new partner and getting married a second time may not be so easy. They sense that the older a person is, the more difficult it is to find a partner. The advice columnist Ann Landers used to reply to women who wrote asking if they should divorce their husbands by telling them to ask themselves: Are you better off with him or without him? It was a question meant to get to the heart of the matter of whether it is easier and more pleasant to remain in a less-than-perfect marriage or try to go it alone, possibly without finding another partner at all.

Lance Compa, a Washington lawyer, said these are the sorts of pressures and complicated emotions that kept him faithful in his marriage even though, he confessed, "I'm not so sure I want to be faithful." Yet, he wrote in the *New York Times Magazine,* "With both of us working, raising kids and running a household, married life takes on a draining routine. Lingering mornings of love play are long gone now; little feet and little stomachaches and quirky faucets and job deadlines see to that, just as they lengthen the intervals between loving nights.

"I know this is a normal, healthy, happy life that I'm intellectually committed to not betraying. But emotionally, it's not easy. In a busy home the relentless demands of keeping things organized bring a hankering for an uncomplicated liaison. This isn't just a male trip, either. My wife feels the same pressures. Will neither of us again know the helpless thrill of a new love? It's an unsettling thought only halfway through life.

"Fortunately, for fidelity, it's not a simple contest of intellectual constancy versus renegade emotion. There's no such thing as an uncomplicated affair. Besides the excitement, I remember the lies, the sneaking and remorse that accompanied extra-relationship affairs when I was single. Even when I wasn't serious about a steady girlfriend, I could barely face her after seeing someone else."

We have shown that a large majority of adults form a partnership — a marriage or cohabitation — during their twenties, and during the length of these partnerships very few adults acquire many sex partners. Nonetheless, as Table 7 shows, the small percentage of adults who do report having many sex partners within the past twelve months or who had twenty-one or more partners within their adult lifetime, are a large number of people. (Table 7 uses weighted data to obtain national estimates, and projecting these rates onto the U.S. population as a whole.) From this table several points emerge.

First, the table shows that men are many times more likely than women to have large numbers of partners. Second, adults seem to accumulate most of their partners while they are in their twenties. This is the conclusion from the figures showing that less than 1 percent of those in their forties had more than five sex partners in the past year and that just 1.9 percent of those in their thirties had that many partners. But 8.1 percent of those aged eighteen to twenty-four had five or more partners in the past year. At the same time, the percentages of those who accumulate more than twenty partners over a lifetime change little after adults reach age thirty. These two observations, taken together, indicate that it is the young who are having multiple partners.

Table 7
Estimated Number of U.S. Adults with Numerous Sex Partners

	Adults with five or more sex partners in past twelve months		Adults with twenty-one or more sex partners since age eighteen	
	Percent estimated from NHSLS	Number in U.S. population	Percent estimated from NHSLS	Number in U.S. population
GENDER				
Men	4.1	2,965,000	15.1	10,920,000
Women	1.6	1,166,000	2.7	1,968,000
AGE				
18–24	8.1	2,155,000	2.9	771,000
25–29	4.4	917,000	8.7	1,813,000
30–39	1.9	813,000	11.5	4,924,000
40–49	0.7	230,000	11.0	3,617,000
50–59	0.3	66,000	7.9	1,743,000
RACE/ETHNICITY				
White	2.5	2,862,000	9.0	10,305,000
Black	5.5	927,000	10.2	1,720,000
Hispanic	2.5	321,000	8.2	1,051,000

Note: NHSLS weighted data

Third, the very sexually active people in the population, who are most at risk of being infected with HIV, did not seem to have been slowed by fears of AIDS. This is seen in Table 7 by considering that 8.7 percent of the people ages twenty-five to twenty-nine had twenty-one or more partners since they turned eighteen and that 11.5 percent of people ages thirty to thirty-nine had that many partners — percentages that are essentially the same for these two age groups. Yet the younger group came of age in the time of AIDS and most in the older group were already age twenty-five or so before the AIDS epidemic began.

Fourth, the small percentages with many partners translate into a large number of people in the population of over 250 million people. These would be the people who are most likely to have been infected with a sexually transmitted disease, because of the sheer number of partners that they had. This subject we discuss at some length in chapter 10.

While our findings include a small percentage who have many partners, and these small percentages imply substantial numbers of people in the population overall, still the general picture is one of relatively few adults who have many partners and relatively many adults who have very few. These findings seem rather tame. The general impression is that there has been an unraveling of the sexual life course in America, yet our data say that most people are not carelessly promiscuous. So why are so many people expressing such grave concerns about the apparently changing mores of society?

Perhaps it is that, in the context of our society, inundated with erotic images, our fears of AIDS, and our prevailing myths about sexuality, we have developed a fundamental misconception of what the sexual life course is and how very likely it is that people will marry and have regular and socially sanctioned sex for as long as they want it. It may be that the images of Woodstock are still playing on our minds.

The old standards of sexual behavior are not so much gone as made more fuzzy, more diffuse, in the time before and between marriages. But there definitely are standards of behavior. And if society's goal is to get people safely married and procreating and faithful to their spouses, the standards have been a roaring success.

In a way, it sounds boring. Where is the bed-hopping that supposedly spiced up the life of Americans and Europeans? But, as we will show in the next chapter, marriage has a surprise benefit that may be one of the best kept sex secrets.

6

HOW OFTEN DO AMERICANS
HAVE SEX?

ANYONE looking at the allusions to sex that surround us every day would have to conclude that sex is an American obsession and that while some people most definitely are the sexual winners, others clearly are the losers. From the sultry young women eyeing a man in a liquor advertisement, to the posters of Marky Mark in his Calvin Klein underwear, muscles bulging on his naked torso, to the women's magazines at the grocery store checkout counter, each with its cover photo of a clear-skinned young model, grinning happily amidst screaming headlines calling out SEX, the message clamors. All the images are of the young and beautiful with perfect teeth, gleaming hair, and hard bodies, glistening with vibrant good health. These are the sexy ones.

Even if, realistically, we dismiss the media bombardment, deep down it is hard to ignore the implications. We see and are told over and over again that all young, healthy Americans are very likely to be having a great deal of sex, and when they are not, they are encouraged to get back into the fray as quickly as possible. And while all attractive Americans are having a good deal of sex, some people are having more sex than others. Blacks are having more sex than other racial groups. Religious conservatives are certainly having less.

Among the sexiest of the sexy, of course, are the young and beautiful — the unmarried, who flit from one partner to another, the youthful divorced people, and those married people having sex with someone other than their spouse. These people form our images of the hot spots of sexual life, the times when men and women have frequent and passionate sex. Their exciting sex lives contrast with the imagined sex lives of the married, where sex is routine, boring, and rare, a dispirited coupling of people trapped in relationships in which the erotic flame has guttered out.

We also have the sad stories of those left out of the sexual banquet. Magazines and many popular books, call-in radio shows and television interview shows tell of sexual troubles, of erections and orgasms not achieved, inhibited sexual desire, partners wanted and partners lost. It is a view primarily aimed at women, but, increasingly, speaking to men as well. It shows a society full of desires that fail to be realized, the sorrow and frustrations of the sexual wonderland gone awry. It shows a vast army of people who linger on the fringes of sexual America, peering in and wondering why they cannot join the party.

Yet these two contrasting images have a common theme — that frequent sex with a partner is overwhelmingly important and desirable, even if it is sometimes difficult to manage.

The truth is far more complex. Americans, we find, are not having much partnered sex at all — at least not much compared to what we are told is a normal or optimal amount. And those people who are supposed to have the most sexual intercourse are having it less often than those who are supposed to be having intercourse the least.

The reality upends all of the conventional stories we tell ourselves about the erotic lives of Americans. No group in society, we find, has anything more than modest amounts of sex with a partner. And the group that has the most sex is not the young and the footloose but the married. Moreover, our data suggest that the rates of sex with partners are similar among all racial and ethnic groups. Finally, the data reveal what anecdotes have suggested — that many older women, in this society that does not value them and their sexuality in the ways it values men, are not having sex at all.

But how often people have partnered sex is only half of the story. We also can ask how much they enjoyed it. Were they thrilled by sex the last time they had it? Or were they bored? Were they satisfied? Or were they frustrated? The two broad questions — how often do you have sex with a partner and how much did you enjoy it — provide a surprising glimpse of sex in America. Although most people don't do it very often, many say they are perfectly happy with the sex when it happens.

The data we will present seem to support an extraordinarily conventional view of love, sex, and marriage, but we do not have any preconceived notions to impose on our findings or our interpretations. Our results could be read to mean that an orthodox view of romance, courtship, and sexuality — your mom's view, perhaps — is the only route to happiness and sexual satisfaction. But that is not what we intend. Instead, we believe that American society is structured to reward those who play by the marriage rules. You are likely to gain the approval of your friends and family and colleagues at work by being happily married by an appropriate age, and you will find yourself part of a group of married couples who are also friends. All the forces of society enhance your satisfaction with marriage. So if in our survey marriage appears as the magical answer to sexual happiness, that should be no surprise. And if you are not happy in your marriage, you are likely to divorce, increasing the chances that, when we look at married people, they tell us how happy they are.

The myths about who has sex, how often, and with whom run deep. Many people whose lives do not fit the common images think that they must be the exception, not the rule. Some unmarried people say they feel there is something wrong with them if they do not have frequent romantic and passionate sex. Others rail against the stereotypes that blind us. So entrenched are the stories about who has partnered sex and how often, that counterexamples, from individuals who looked at their own lives and questioned the conventional wisdom, have had little impact.

Rachel Cline, a writer who lives in Los Angeles, felt trapped by the images of sex in the singles world. She wrote that "among my largely monogamous and/or married peers, single people are like something out of 'Mutual of Omaha's Wild Kingdom': they think that if two of us have dinner together a few times, the beast with two backs is lurking nearby in the underbrush."

With our survey data, we could get beyond the anecdotes and popular psychology and find out how often people really had sex with a partner. And we could ask whether some groups of people have more sex than others.

The first surprise in our data was how little sex with a partner most people had: only one-third of Americans aged eighteen to fifty-nine have sex with a partner as often as twice a week.

We found that Americans fall into three groups. About a third have sex with a partner at least twice a week, a third have sex with a partner a few times a month, and the rest have sex with a partner a few times a year or have no sexual partners at all.

Of course, we have no scientific basis on which to judge what are normal or appropriate rates of sex. Yet the rates we find are so modest, at best, that they confound our expectations. They certainly give the impression that frequent sex is not that important to most Americans. After all, most Americans have a partner — they are married or living with someone. Married sex is morally legitimate and expected. And sex really does not take that long — as we show in chapter 7, most people told us that it takes them less than an hour to have sexual intercourse. So, if people really wanted more sex, they probably could fit it in.

The second surprise was that only three things really mattered to the frequency of partnered sex: how old a person was, whether people were married or cohabiting, and how long the couple had been together. Even though, as we have shown, Americans travel in their own tightly circumscribed social networks and even though they almost always choose their sex partners from within those networks, members of different races and ethnic groups and people of different educations and religions all were having the same amounts of sex with a partner. And even though people in different regions of the country appear to have very different attitudes about sex and correspondingly different behavior, the frequency with which they have sex is determined by these same factors, no matter where they live. A conservative southerner, who has been married for a decade, will probably have sexual intercourse about as often as a West Coast libertarian of the same age who has been married as long.

Table 8 (on pages 116–117) shows the frequency of sex, by gender and several characteristics including age, marital status. From the top row of Panel A, we see that 14 percent of the men in the survey had no sex with a partner last year, and 16 percent had sex with a partner a few times during the year. Nearly 40 percent had partnered sex a few times a month, 26 percent had sex two or three times a week, and 8 percent of the men had it four or more times a week. These proportions are basically the same for women.

The table shows that the youngest and the oldest people in our survey had the least sex with a partner. People in their twenties had the most. But even more striking is the relationship between how often people have sex with a partner and whether they are married or living with a partner. As Table 8 shows, for both men and women, married and cohabiting couples are having the most sex.

The table also shows that the frequency of partnered sex has little to do with people's race, religion, or education. Our data in the previous chapter showed that more educated people had more lifetime sex partners, but, as this table shows, having more partners does not translate into having more frequent sex, at least not within the past twelve months.

Blacks had sex with a partner about as often as whites, although Hispanics had slightly higher rates. Women who never finished high school had sex with a partner as often as people who finished college and went on to get advanced degrees, but noticeably fewer well-educated men had little or no sex. Protestants, Catholics, and people who were not religious had about the same frequencies of sex with a partner. About a third of black men had sex two or three times a week, and so did a third of white men and Hispanic men. About a third of white women had sex with a partner a few times a year or not at all, and so did a third of black women. About a third of Catholic women had sex with a partner two or more times a week, and so did a third of women who had no religion or were Protestants. The data, in fact, are so monotonic that they can look boring. Americans of the same age and marital status are remarkably alike in the frequency with which they have sex.

Why should there be no differences between these groups? The answer seems to be that the variables that play on our fantasies may not work themselves out in the real world. Our prejudices and envies may

Table 8
Frequency of Sex in the Past Twelve Months

	Panel A: By Age, Marital Status, and Gender				
Social characteristics	*Not at all*	*A few times per year*	*A few times per month*	*2 or 3 times a week*	*4 or more times a week*
GENDER					
Men	14%	16%	37%	26%	8%
Women	10	18	36	30	7
AGE					
Men					
18–24	15	21	24	28	12
25–29	7	15	31	36	11
30–39	8	15	37	33	6
40–49	9	18	40	27	6
50–59	11	22	43	20	3
Women					
18–24	11	16	32	29	12
25–29	5	10	38	37	10
30–39	9	16	36	33	6
40–49	15	16	44	20	5
50–59	30	22	35	12	2
MARITAL/RESIDENTIAL STATUS					
Men					
Noncohabiting	23	25	26	19	7
Cohabiting	0	8	36	40	16
Married	1	13	43	36	7
Women					
Noncohabiting	32	23	24	15	5
Cohabiting	1	8	35	42	14
Married	3	12	47	32	7

Panel B: By Education, Religion, and Race/Ethnicity

Social characteristics	Not at all	A few times per year	A few times per month	2 or 3 times a week	4 or more times a week
EDUCATION					
Men					
Less than high school	15	20	28	30	7
High school graduate or equivalent	10	15	34	32	9
Any college	9	18	38	28	7
Women					
Less than high school	19	15	36	23	8
High school graduate or equivalent	11	16	38	30	6
Any college	14	17	37	26	7
RELIGION					
Men					
None	13	25	25	27	11
Mainline Protestant	8	19	38	27	8
Conservative Protestant	11	15	36	32	7
Catholic	8	17	37	31	8
Women					
None	10	19	37	26	9
Mainline Protestant	13	17	40	25	5
Conservative Protestant	15	14	36	26	9
Catholic	14	16	37	28	5
RACE/ETHNICITY					
Men					
White	10	17	36	30	8
Black	8	16	38	30	7
Hispanic	9	15	34	29	14
Women					
White	13	16	38	27	7
Black	17	18	33	25	7
Hispanic	11	10	35	33	10

Note: Percentages in rows total 100 percent.

say that blacks and Jews are more sexual and that the highly religious are less sexual. But these assumptions are wrong because there is nothing about being a member of these groups that translates into more sexual desire or more sexual opportunity.

Age and marital status seem to be the important factors. As the table shows, 36 percent of men age eighteen to twenty-four had no sex with a partner in the past year or had sex just a few times. Twenty-seven percent of women in that age group had sex with a partner that infrequently. Similarly among the oldest people in the study, we see that they have infrequent partnered sex. One-third of men age fifty to fifty-nine and more than half of the women that age had sex with a partner a few times or not at all in the past year.

But although the youngest and oldest were most likely to have little sex, we suggest there are very different reasons for these similar patterns, driven by the availability of a steady partner.

Why, for example, should the rates of sexual activity pick up as people reach their mid to late twenties? We do not think it is simply because they grew older, or, for some biological reason had increased desire. Instead, we think the more likely explanation is that more of them are either married or living with a partner. Young people who are infrequently sexually active tend not to be in stable sexual relationships, but most of them are seeking more or less permanent partners. As they find these partners, their rates of sexual activity go up.

We find that the critical factor that produces the most sexual activity is being part of a couple, whether it is a marriage or a cohabitation. Even though married life is not seen as very erotic, it is actually the social arrangement that produces the highest rate of partnered sexual activity among heterosexuals. What seems to produce the highest rates of partnered sex is an easily accessible partner.

Of course, another factor may also enter in. Marital sex is seen as morally legitimate. It is virtuous sex, the only form of sex that is universally approved.

We also find that more partners do not translate into more partnered sex. People who have extramarital partners or those who are unmarried and who have several partners in a year actually end up having partnered sex less often than people who have only one partner. The sole exceptions were the 5 percent of men who had five or more partners in a year; they had sex slightly more often than people with a single partner. But for most individuals, the most sex with a partner is to be had if you are married or are living with someone or having sex with only one partner. It appears that few people can manage both to have more than one partner and frequent sex.

Table 8 shows that the contrast between the sex lives of the married couples and the people who have no steady partners is dramatic. We found that about 40 percent of married people have sex with their partner two or more times a week and well over half of people who are living together have partnered sex that often. Yet fewer than a quarter of men and women who are not living with a partner have sex that frequently. About half of all married people have sex with their spouses a few times a month. But only a quarter of single people who are not living with a partner have sexual intercourse that often. In fact, fully a quarter of noncohabiting single people have partnered sex just a few times a year, whereas only about one in ten married people has sex so seldom.

The data on marriage and cohabitation show most strongly how profoundly social arrangements affect whether people have partnered sex at all and how often they have sex. Folklore says that the young, the single, and people with multiple partners should have the most frequent sex. But this image is based on a belief that the young, the single, and those with many partners are more interested in having partnered sex and therefore are, in fact, having more. What our data say is that whether or not people with many partners want more sex, they are not having it. Sexual expression is regulated by social structures that determine whether partners are there when we want them.

A more social explanation fits the facts better than the myths about who is the most sexually active. In the United States, regular sex partners who share a common household have solved the problem of access and opportunity by marrying or cohabiting. Those who are looking for a partner or who have partners without easy access to a place to have sex or who are in relationships that have not settled into a routine in which sex is expected or is legitimate are less likely to have high rates of heterosexual activity. They may have more partners, but they will have less sex.

This means that the usual myths about how easy it is to get new partners and the ways in which youth and beauty translate into frequent partnered sex are false.

It takes time and energy to find someone, and even if you do find a person you like, you may not want to have sex with them or they might not want to have sex with you. The more people you try to have sex with, the harder it can become. Just the logistics of having sex with more than one person is time-consuming, even for the youngest, most energetic, and most beautiful people. You have to meet them and attract them and go out with them and, if you are having sex with more than one person at once, you have to juggle your schedule to fit them in and keep them away from each other. The more partners you have, the more time you are going to spend finding and wooing them — time that a married couple could spend having sex.

This finding, that it can be hard to have frequent partnered sex when you are not part of a couple, should not be too surprising to unmarried people who have tried to find partners. For example, a thirty-one-year-old single woman who lives in New York, Johanna Farrand, bemoaned the anxiety she felt when her sex life did not live up to the myths. Farrand's story appeared in *Esquire,* in an article that described her as the answer to the imagined *Esquire* man's dreams: beautiful, with a good job, but not ambitious — domestic, in fact. A woman who likes to sew. Yet even she was confused by what was expected of her. "Sex is all around you. In the ads, in the movies. You start thinking that if you're not having great sex all the time, then there's something wrong with you."

A new pattern of sexual activity starts to emerge when people turn thirty. By this age, three-quarters of Americans are either married or living with someone, so most have a ready sexual partner. Yet, as the table shows, they are starting to have partnered sex less often than couples in their twenties. More are having sex with a partner a few times a month and fewer are having sex a few times a week.

What are we to make of the steadily diminishing amounts of partnered sex as people grow older? Even people who remain married have sex less and less often as they age.

The biological explanation is that the sex drive diminishes with age. It suggests an evolutionary reason why this might happen: the older people get, the less likely they are to have children, which is the ultimate evolutionary purpose of sex.

But we believe that social factors play a dominant role. We cannot rule out the biology-as-destiny argument, but we can say that its effects are amplified, at least, or even overwhelmed by social conditions.

If sex were only a matter of hormones, our data would make little sense. On average, sex hormone levels are not much changed until age fifty, although by age thirty people are already having less frequent partnered sex.

Yet the social factors feeding into this steady diminution of sexual activity are not entirely obvious either. At first glance it would seem that the social situation is ripe for people to have more frequent sex with a partner as they grow older. Most people are married and so have an available partner. And, of course, virtually everyone is bombarded with erotic images on television, in movies, in music, and in advertisements, and these images are widely supposed to elicit a desire for sex. Something must be counteracting these factors to make people have less and less sex as they grow older.

In part, it may be the wear and tear of everyday life, the demands of working and commuting, taking care of children, and all of the problems of managing a complicated life in the modern world. It is hard to find a place for sex in the middle of other demands — here the women's magazines are telling the truth. And there is that other mythology, that passionate sex is for the young and the beautiful and the unmarried. This exotic world of movies, television, and novels may be more of a disincentive than an incentive to sex with a partner. It is more an invitation to dreams than to action. Older people might have less partnered sex and spend less time at it because they think that frequent, time-consuming sex is no longer appropriate for them. They may feel less sexy as they look at their aging bodies and compare them to the trim, youthful bodies of the people they see having sex in movies.

Going along with a general decline in sexual activity as people grow older, we also see another trend. Starting with the frequency of sex at age thirty, are the first outlines of what later becomes a striking pattern — a marked difference between the amount of partnered sex that men have and the amount women have. While most men seem to have sex with partners until old age, more and more women each year are pushed out of a partnered sexual life entirely.

About 7 percent of men between the ages of thirty and forty-five said they had no partnered sex at all in the past year — the same number as men in their mid to late twenties. The percentage of men without sexual partners increases slightly when the men reach their late forties, and the percentage continues to climb as the men grow older and older. But at virtually every age, most men have at least occasional partnered sex. By combining our data, which looked at men only to age fifty-nine, with data from another highly reliable national survey, the General Social Survey, which included people age sixty and older, we found that even in their seventies the majority of men were having sex. Only a third of men in that age group said they were having no partnered sex.

The contrast with women is stark. Starting at age thirty, the number of women without a sexual partner in the past year starts to climb until, eventually, more women are not having partnered sex than are having it. As many as one in five women age fifty to fifty-four said they had no sex with a partner in the past year. More than four in ten age fifty-five to fifty-nine had no sexual partners. An astonishing 70 percent of women in their seventies were no longer having partnered sex (according to the GSS data), twice the number of men of that age who had no sex partner in the past year. More than 90 percent of women age eighty or older had no sex with a partner, whereas less than 60 percent of men in that age group were having no partnered sex.

What is happening to women's sexual prospects? We do not believe that women disproportionately lose interest in sex with a partner. Instead, as we discussed in chapter 4, the dearth of sex among older women reflects the logistics of the marketplace for sexual partners, the higher mortality rate for men, and the value that women place on affection and continuity in sexual relations. It is not desire but opportunity and attitude that make the difference for men and women.

The general picture of sex with a partner in America shows that Americans do not have a secret life of abundant sex. If nothing else, the startlingly modest amounts of partnered sex reveal how much we as a society can deceive ourselves about other people's sex lives. Our imaginations can be so vivid, our suppositions about what other people must be doing can be so strong, that we come to think we know what a normal sex life should be. Probably, in different social circumstances, the frequency with which people have partnered sex could be much higher or much lower but, in our society, with the social constraints that control our sex lives people have settled on these rates. Rates in Europe seem to be about the same, probably reflecting similar patterns in marriage and partner selection.

But then we come to the next question: Are people frustrated and dissatisfied with their sex lives or do they find fulfillment and love even if they only have partnered sex a few times a month? If frequent sex with a partner was truly important to people, we might expect them to complain about their sex lives. And when we asked them to tell us how their sex lives made them feel, we might expect to hear a litany of discontent.

Instead, many people tell us that they are happy, even thrilled with their sex lives, so the low levels of partnered sex in general and the decline in sexual activity as people grow older does not necessarily mean that America is a nation of sexually frustrated, thwarted adults. Many said that sex with their partner made them feel wanted, satisfied, loved, and cared for, which indicates that even if they do not have sex as often as we might have suspected, many couples still enjoy sex when they have it. Moreover, even though most women say they do not always have orgasms, they still seem happy with their sex lives.

Figure 9 (on page 124) illustrates some of our findings.

Considering the enormous emphasis that has been placed on orgasms — how to achieve them, how crucial they are supposed to be to physical satisfaction — our data are unexpected. Despite the fascination with orgasms, despite the popular notion that frequent orgasms are essential to a happy sex life, there was not a strong relationship between having orgasms and having a satisfying sexual life.

Few women, just 29 percent, said they always had orgasms whereas most men, 75 percent, always had them, as the figure shows. Yet the percentage of women and men who were extremely pleased physically with their sex lives and who were extremely emotionally satisfied were about the same — 40 percent. If frequent orgasms were a prerequisite for sexual satisfaction, we would expect to see a closer relationship between orgasm and satisfaction among men and women. We would expect that many more men would be satisfied. Apparently, more is involved in a good sex life than having orgasms, and not everyone who has an orgasm every time has a blissful sex life. This suggests,

FIGURE 9:
Three Measures of Sexual Satisfaction with Primary Partner

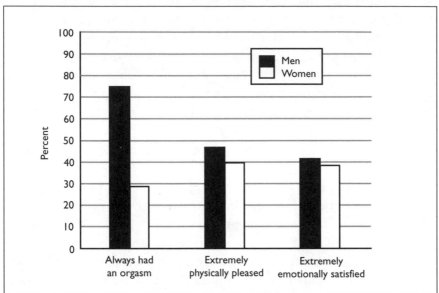

once again, that sex with a partner is more than a matter of sexual technique and that love and affection can matter a great deal.

Once again contradicting the common view of marriage as dull and routine, the people who reported being the most physically pleased and emotionally satisfied were the married couples. More than 50 percent of men who were either married or divorced and now cohabiting said they were extremely physically satisfied by sex with their primary partner. About 40 to 45 percent of married women were extremely physically satisfied, and about 50 percent of married or divorced, but cohabiting, men said they were extremely emotionally satisfied by sex with their partner, and over 40 percent of married or cohabiting women said they were extremely emotionally satisfied. The lowest rates of satisfaction were among men and women who were neither married nor living with someone — the very group thought to be having the hottest sex.

When we include people who said they were either "very" or "extremely" satisfied with their sex lives with their partner, the figures soar to include the vast majority of Americans. The data show (figure not included) that about 88 percent of married people said they received great physical pleasure from their sexual lives and about 85 percent said they received great emotional satisfaction. People who were dating and having sex together also were overwhelmingly physically pleased and emotionally satisfied, but, again, slightly less so than the people who were living together.

Physical and emotional satisfaction started to decline when people had more than one sexual partner. About 59 percent of married people who had a second sex partner in addition to their spouse said they were physically pleased and just 55 percent said they were emotionally satisfied by their sex lives with their primary partner — a spouse, someone they lived with, or a partner they were dating. Of course, a lack of physical or emotional satisfaction may be what led them to find another partner in the first place, so we cannot say which came first, dissatisfaction or infidelity. But we have found that most people are faithful to their sexual partners, and most of them are highly satisfied.

The least satisfied were those who were not married, not living with anyone, and who had at least two sexual partners. Only 54 percent of them reported they were extremely or very physically pleased and only a third said they were extremely or very emotionally satisfied.

Our data also show that married or cohabiting people who have a second partner, like the husband with a lover he sees regularly or the girlfriend who is still seeing her old lover on the side, were less happy with their sex lives. And these people seemed to get more pleasure from sex with their primary partner, their spouse or person they were living with, than they did with their secondary partners. The only exception was that slightly more married people said sex with their secondary partner was physically pleasurable.

We can also look at the flip side of the coin, asking how many people have sexual troubles, and what these problems might be. Figure 10 (on page 126) shows some of these findings.

Figure 10 shows that only a minority of Americans have sexual problems, but, among them, women are much more affected than men. In only two categories — anxiety about performance and climaxing too early — was the percentage of men with the problem

FIGURE 10:
Sexual Difficulties for at Least One of the Past Twelve Months

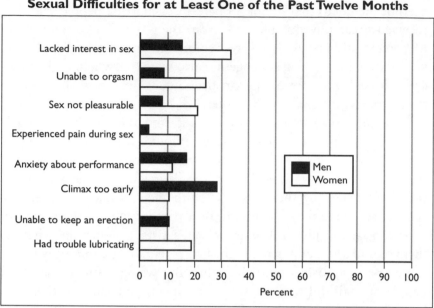

greater than the percentage of women with the problem. One out of three women said they were uninterested in sex, but just one out of six men said they lacked interest. One woman out of five said sex gave her no pleasure, but just one man out of ten said sex was not pleasurable. Yet men were more likely to be anxious about their performance during sex. More than one man out of six said he was anxious, but just a little more than one woman out of ten said this problem plagued her. Ten percent of men reported inability to keep an erection and nearly 20 percent of women reported trouble lubricating.

Since orgasms were a primary concern for many women, in particular, we looked at who is most likely to have orgasms. This information is shown in Table 9 (on pages 128–129).

More than one woman in four, but three men in four, always have an orgasm during sex with their primary partner. At the other end of the spectrum, about 30 percent of women and 5 percent of the men have orgasm "sometimes" or less frequently.

Although age was related to the frequency of having partnered sex, it is not much linked to the likelihood of having orgasms during sex with a partner, as seen in Table 9.

The relationship between being married and having orgasms during sex with a partner was very strong. Married women had much higher rates of usually or always having orgasms — 75 percent — as compared to women who were never married and not cohabiting — 62 percent. The most suggestive number, however (not shown separately in the table), is the fact that the never-married and non-cohabiting women have much higher rates of *never* having orgasms — 11 percent — compared to the rate for all other women — 2 percent. Here the issue may well be the woman's sexual inexperience, or her lover's lack of experience.

Table 9 also shows the orgasm data by race, religion, and education of the respondents, allowing us to see whether people of different races and social groups differed in their likelihood of having frequent orgasms.

As the second half of Table 9 shows, there were very few differences by education, religion, or race or ethnicity. The most educated women were a little less likely to always have orgasms (25 percent as compared to 35 percent of high-school graduates and 30 percent of those women who did not complete high school). The women with no religious affiliation were somewhat less likely to report that they always had an orgasm, while the conservative Protestant women had the highest rates. Also, only 26 percent of white women always had orgasms while 38 percent of black women and 34 percent of Hispanic women reported that they always did. None of these patterns occur in the data on men. About three out of four men, regardless of race or ethnicity, education, or religion, reported that they always had orgasms.

The association for women between religious affiliation and orgasms may seem surprising because conservative religious women are so often portrayed as sexually repressed. Perhaps conservative Protestant women firmly believe in the holiness of marriage and of sexuality as an expression of their love for their husbands. In this sense, the findings are consistent with the other findings on sexual satisfaction.

And despite the popular image of the straitlaced conservative Prot-

Table 9
Frequency of Orgasm During Sex with Primary Partner

Panel A: By Gender, Age, and Marital Status					
Social characteristics	Always	Usually	Sometimes	Rarely	Never
GENDER					
Men	75	20	3	1	1
Women	29	42	21	4	4
AGE					
Men					
18–24	70	22	6	0	2
25–29	73	21	3	2	2
30–39	77	20	2	0	1
40–49	79	18	2	0	0
50–59	72	19	3	2	4
Women					
18–24	22	39	26	5	8
25–29	31	40	21	3	5
30–39	29	41	22	5	4
40–49	34	44	16	4	2
50–59	26	47	20	5	2
MARITAL/RESIDENTIAL STATUS					
Men					
Noncohabiting	74	20	3	1	1
Cohabiting	74	21	1	2	1
Married	75	20	3	0	1
Women					
Noncohabiting	30	32	24	6	8
Cohabiting	24	44	28	2	2
Married	29	46	18	4	2

Panel B: By Education, Religion, and Race/Ethnicity

Social characteristics	Always	Usually	Sometimes	Rarely	Never
EDUCATION					
Men					
Less than high school	77	14	6	1	3
High school graduate					
or equivalent	76	20	3	0	1
Any college	73	21	3	1	1
Women					
Less than high school	30	35	27	6	2
High school graduate					
or equivalent	35	38	18	5	4
Any college	25	45	21	4	5
RELIGION					
Men					
None	75	21	1	1	2
Mainline Protestant	73	21	4	1	1
Conservative Protestant	75	20	3	1	1
Catholic	79	16	3	1	2
Women					
None	22	48	22	4	5
Mainline Protestant	27	44	20	4	5
Conservative Protestant	32	37	23	5	3
Catholic	26	43	20	6	4
RACE/ETHNICITY					
Men					
White	75	21	2	1	1
Black	75	15	7	1	2
Hispanic	84	12	2	0	3
Women					
White	26	44	21	5	4
Black	38	34	21	4	3
Hispanic	34	34	23	5	4

Note: Includes opposite-gender partnerships only. Row percentages total 100 percent.

estants, there is at least circumstantial evidence that the image may be a myth at least as it pertains to sexual intercourse. One conservative Protestant woman, Marabel Morgan, wrote a book that cited Christian doctrine and, at the same time, encouraged women to bring excitement to their marriage by a series of ploys that some critics said bordered on the pornographic. Her book, *The Total Woman,* was a bestseller.

Another surprise about women's orgasms was how unlikely their male partners were to know whether the women experienced them. Although just 29 percent of women said they always had an orgasm, 44 percent of men said that their female partners always had an orgasm. In contrast, women guessed correctly about their male partners.

It may seem obvious that a woman could tell when a man had an orgasm, but men, too, can fake it if they want to. Since a quarter of men are not having orgasms every time they have sex, a substantial number of them would have an opportunity to dissemble. That is one topic we did not ask about.

We find, not surprisingly, that a satisfying sex life requires more than simple marital status or access to a partner. Happiness with partnered sex is linked to happiness with life. We cannot say which comes first — general happiness or a good sex life — but the correlations are clear and striking. And happiness is clearly linked to having just one partner — which may not be too surprising since that is the situation that society smiles upon.

Virtually all the people who were happy in general also said they were happy with their sex lives. And almost all of these happy people had just one partner — most, in fact, were married and faithful to their spouse. These happy people found physical pleasure and emotional satisfaction with their sex lives and, those who reported themselves more happy also reported far more frequent sex — e.g., the percentage of the respondents who had sex at least once a week in the past year were 72 percent of those who were extremely happy, 58 percent of those very happy, 48 percent of those generally satisfied, 35 percent of those sometimes fairly unhappy, and only 27 percent of those unhappy most of the time. (We cannot say which caused which.)

People who are not happy tend to report that they are uninterested in sex, have trouble having orgasms, do not find sex pleasurable, have pain during sex, and are anxious when they have sex.

For example, 20 percent of women who said they were extremely happy in general said they lacked interest in sex, while 75 percent who said they were unhappy most of the time said they lacked interest in sex. Three percent of men who were extremely happy in general found sex not pleasurable, while 35 percent of the unhappy men reported that they did not obtain pleasure from sex.

We are left with a picture that does not fit any of the popular images. Americans are having relatively little sex with partners, compared to what we may have imagined. But many say they are enjoying it, even if they do not have orgasms all the time. Those having the most partnered sex and enjoying it most are the married people. The young single people who flit from partner to partner and seem to be having a sex life that is satisfying beyond most people's dreams are, it seems, mostly a media creation. In real life, the unheralded, seldom discussed world of married sex is actually the one that satisfies people the most.

It may not be an exciting picture of sex in America, but if we look at the social forces that push us toward married life it is an understandable, if not predicted, picture.

7

PRACTICES AND PREFERENCES

OF all the questions we have about sex, one stands out: What do people do when they have sex with each other?

The nation is suffused with a sort of moral uneasiness about specific sexual activities, which is part of the general ambivalence about sexuality in American society. The conventional script for the physical sequence of sex is well known to most adults: it goes from hugging to kissing to bodily caressing and manual stimulation of the genitals to intercourse. But this conventional script does not include all the acts that people have thought about, dreamed about, or enjoyed.

Even with the script so tightly written, many people remain unsure of the rightness or legitimacy of specific sexual practices and feel the need to compare what they do with what others do. Is it normal to want your partner to perform oral sex on you? Do other heterosexuals want anal sex? Does fantasizing about group sex place you outside the pale? What can you actually ask your partner to do? Most of us have wondered, deep down, if everyone likes what we like or whether what we want, or what we'd like to try, is odd or is overly staid and conventional.

Once we depart from the most traditional sexual practices, we find ourselves in badly charted territory where we seem to be in constant need of reassurance.

We don't have to look far to see people questioning what other people do in the privacy of their sexual lives.

Daphne Merkin, a writer, was attending a dinner party when the hostess mentioned that two people the guests knew were now having "kinky" sex lives. "Of course I understood the term, in some purely literal sense, as I assume the other guests did," Merkin wrote in *The New Yorker.* But, she added, "then my mind wandered off in directions peculiar to my history and I felt the draft of separateness in the room. What, I wondered, were the other guests conjuring up to go with the word 'kinky'? Was it anything like the stuff I had in mind?"

Merkin mused that "the one thing that stands out in the haze of confusion that surrounds the subject of sex is that there is no real consensus on what constitutes erotic pleasure."

In a nation in which there are so many conflicted messages about sex, the question "Am I like other people?" becomes more pressing. As writer Sallie Tisdale wrote, "I needed information not about sex but about the sexual parameters, the bounds of normal. I needed reassurance, and blessing. I needed permission."

Of course, a survey cannot tell us what is normal, only what is frequent. It cannot tell us what is erotic, only what practices people say they would enjoy, and whether or not they actually do these things. But information can be powerful and revealing, and, in the case of sexual practices, it can be remarkable.

One surprise was that what people do — and what they'd like to do — depends upon their race and social class. Unlike finding a partner, which, as we showed, happened the same way no matter what a person's race, education, or religion, and unlike the frequency of sex, which, as we showed, also was independent of social networks and social distinctions, certain sexual preferences and practices turn out to vary markedly with income, religion, and race. And, since social characteristics often vary with geography, people in different parts of the country may desire different sexual practices and behave differently in bed.

The next surprise was how few sexual activities people found appealing. The myth is that whether or not they pursue an array of sexual practices, most people would like to veer somewhat, or sometimes, from vaginal intercourse. But our survey shows that most other practices are not very attractive to the vast majority of Americans. We are not a nation that seeks sexual variety. Instead, it seems, we practice the tried and true.

As with other analyses of our data, we do not separate homosexuals from heterosexuals in studying sexual practices because there were few homosexuals in our survey.

We approached our study with no preconceptions of what people ought to like. Instead, we felt that the nation had suffered from a dearth of data while, at the same time, it was saturated with opinions. Americans have strong and often clashing views of the merits, even the morality, of various sexual practices, but there is a limited amount of reliable data on whether the views so publicly expressed extend to the private world of sexuality or whether what people say and what they do are entirely different matters.

For example, some people with very traditional views of sexuality say that vaginal intercourse, in marriage, is the only sexual practice that is acceptable. They cite oral sex and anal sex, in particular, as immoral or unnatural and view most other sexual practices as evidence of moral decay. This view is reinforced by the fact that the sodomy laws of some states make oral sex and anal sex illegal, even when they occur in marriage. Other people argue that a variety of sexual practices may be important in providing pleasure to a willing partner and in any case there should not be any laws interfering with the private sexual practices of consenting adults.

In our survey, we wanted to get beyond the fantasies and the stories we tell ourselves about sex and get accurate information about sexual practices. The sexual acts that couples decide upon, or reject, are key not only to the problems of sexual misunderstanding, sexual negotiation, and sexual pleasure but also to understanding the spread of the sexually transmitted diseases, including AIDS.

We wanted to know two things: What do people actually do with each of their partners? And what would they like to do?

To learn what people do, it seemed to us that we needed to ask questions that linked specific sexual practices to specific sexual partners. Instead of asking people how many partners they had and then asking them, on average, how many of a list of sexual practices they performed and how often, we asked what individuals did with each sex partner. That is, instead of asking, "Now, thinking about all of the sexual partners you have had in the past year, how many times, on average, did you have oral sex with them: never, some of the time, most of the time, or all of the time?" we asked, in the context of talking about sex with a specific partner, and looking back over the past year, "When you had sex with that partner, how often did he or she perform oral sex on you?" and "When you had sex with that partner, how often did you perform oral sex on him or her?" The point is that a person may have no oral sex with one partner and oral sex all the time with another or may give oral sex often but receive it seldom. Averaging the two together conceals the social characteristics of a relationship that might result in oral sex in one relationship and not in another, or in giving it but not receiving it.

To our surprise, we discovered that although the sexual menu is long and varied, only one practice — vaginal intercourse — stood out as nearly universal. It is, of course, the only sexual activity that can result in the birth of a baby and it is the only practice that is universally and morally sanctioned by all religions, so its popularity almost certainly reflects more than the pleasure it can give couples. Vaginal sex also is what most people imagine when they think of sex. It is the sexual activity that defines the loss of virginity, the one that teenagers dream of when they think of "going all the way."

That special status of vaginal intercourse stands out in our data. No other genital sexual activity even approaches it in prevalence even though all these data include homosexual as well as heterosexual respondents. Ninety-five percent of our respondents told us that they had vaginal sex the last time they had sex. Eighty percent said that every time they had sex in the past year they had vaginal sex. An additional 15 percent said they usually had vaginal sex when they had sex.

But what about other practices? That is where we find powerful social influences on what happens when people have sex. Some of the data are displayed in Tables 10 and 11 (these tables exclude same-gender partners in a few instances, as described in the table notes).

Table 10
Frequency and Duration of Sex

Panel A: By Gender, Age, and Marital Status

Social Characteristics	Average Frequency of Sex Per Month	Duration of Last Sexual Event		
		15 minutes or less	15 minutes to 1 hour	1 hour or more
GENDER				
Men	7	11%	69%	20%
Women	6	15	71	15
AGE				
Men				
18–24	7	5	65	31
25–29	8	7	67	26
30–39	7	9	69	22
40–49	6	14	73	13
50–59	5	22	73	5
Women				
18–24	7	7	70	23
25–29	8	10	71	19
30–39	6	15	72	13
40–49	6	15	72	13
50–59	4	30	63	6
MARITAL/RESIDENTIAL STATUS				
Men				
Noncohabiting	6	3	60	36
Cohabiting	8	10	68	23
Married	7	16	75	9
Women				
Noncohabiting	5	11	59	30
Cohabiting	8	16	71	13
Married	7	16	76	8

Notes: Both average frequency of sex and duration of sex in last event are calculated for all respondents who engaged in any coupled sex in the last year. The frequency includes same-gender partnerships but the duration data exclude same-gender partnerships. Percentages in duration rows total 100 percent.

Panel B: By Education, Religion, and Race/Ethnicity

Social characteristics	Average frequency of sex per month	Duration of last sexual event		
		15 minutes or less	15 minutes to 1 hour	1 hour or more
EDUCATION				
Men				
Less than high school	7	19%	61%	20%
High school graduate or equivalent	7	12	69	19
Any college	6	8	72	20
Women				
Less than high school	6	26	60	14
High school graduate or equivalent	6	17	69	14
Any college	6	11	74	15
RELIGION				
Men				
None	7	9	65	26
Mainline Protestant	6	10	72	18
Conservative Protestant	7	14	67	19
Catholic	7	10	71	19
Women				
None	6	13	67	20
Mainline Protestant	6	14	74	12
Conservative Protestant	7	17	69	14
Catholic	6	14	71	16
RACE/ETHNICITY				
Men				
White	7	10	71	19
Black	6	15	60	25
Hispanic	8	13	71	16
Women				
White	6	14	72	14
Black	6	18	61	22
Hispanic	8	18	66	16

Notes: Both average frequency of sex and duration of sex in last event are calculated for all respondents who engaged in any coupled sex in the last year. Percentages in duration rows total 100 percent.

The lefthand column of numbers in Table 10 shows the average frequency of sex per month — the average for women is six times a month and for men it is 7 times a month. The second, third, and fourth columns show the percentage of people defined by that row who spent less than fifteen minutes having sex the last time they had it, the percentage who spent between fifteen minutes and an hour, and the percentage who spent an hour or more. So, for instance, looking at the eighth row in Panel A, we see that of the eighteen- to twenty-four-year-old women, 7 percent spent fifteen minutes or less the last time they had sex, 70 percent spent between fifteen minutes and an hour, and 23 percent spent an hour or more.

From Table 10, we see pronounced differences among social groups when we look at the length of time people spent having sex. Older people, who have sex less often than younger people, reported spending less time at it when they do have sex. Married men are five times more likely than single men to spend fifteen minutes or less in a sexual encounter.

These times are unlikely to be absolutely accurate, we suggest, and are more indicators of relative amounts of time spent. We gave our respondents a choice of time periods, asking, Did your last sexual event take fifteen minutes or less, fifteen minutes to thirty minutes, thirty minutes to an hour, one to two hours, or more than two hours? The psychological literature suggests that people overestimate the time that activities take, so it is likely, then, that our respondents overestimated the time they spent having sex.* Accordingly, the time estimates are more reliable as indicators of who spent more or less time than as exact measures.

Our finding that young people spend more time than older people and single people spend more time than married people may reflect the ways that people define the beginning and end of their sexual encounters. Unmarried people may be including time spent with their clothes on, hugging and kissing and caressing. Thirty percent or more of these people said their last sexual event lasted an hour or more. Married people may start counting when their clothes are off and they are in bed together. Only 9 percent of them said their last encounter

*Elizabeth Loftus, *Eyewitness Testimony* (Cambridge, Mass.: Harvard University Press, 1979).

lasted an hour or more. Of course, it also is likely that people who have been sexual partners for years do not need or always want to spend as much time on preliminaries.

But that explanation does not fully account for the data. It does not explain, for example, why a quarter of blacks said they spent at least an hour the last time they made love, but just one out of six Hispanics spent that long.

We suspect that some married people find themselves spending less time when they have sex because they often feel pressured by their responsibilities — their jobs and families. One married woman, Karen Karbo, who reviewed sexual instruction videotapes for *Redbook* magazine, wrote that that was her problem. One tape, she said, started out with couples complaining that they had no time for sex, with one woman in a videotape saying, "Sometimes I feel like we make love just so we can get back to obsessing about our work." Karbo commented that when she and her husband watched this video, "These situations seemed real to us."

Table 11 shows the percentage of people who reported engaging in particular sex acts. These acts are passive oral sex (that is, the respondent's genitals and the partner's mouth), active oral sex (that is, the respondent's mouth and the partner's genitals), and anal sex, that is, a penis in the partner's anus.

The percentages for oral and anal sex are reported both over the entire lifetime and for the last sex event. For anal sex, we also show the percentages for the past twelve months. Thus, the second row in Panel A tells us that 68 percent of all the women respondents had engaged in active oral sex at some time in their lives, that 19 percent had had active oral sex the last time they had sex, that 73 percent had engaged in passive oral sex sometime in their lives, and that 20 percent had engaged in passive oral sex the last time they had sex. Finally, the data tell us that 20 percent of these women had had anal sex in their lifetimes, 9 percent had it in the past year, and 1 percent had it the last time they had sex.

The most striking finding in Table 11 is that there is a marked effect of education and race on the practice of oral sex. This practice, it turns out, has gained its greatest popularity among young, better-educated whites. It is much less common among the less-educated and among blacks.

Table 11
Percent Engaging in Oral and Anal Sex Over the Lifetime and in the Last Sex Event

	Active oral sex		Passive oral sex		Anal sex		
Social Characteristics	*Lifetime*	*Last sex event*	*Lifetime*	*Last sex event*	*Lifetime*	*Past 12 months*	*Last sex event*
GENDER							
Men	77%	27%	79%	28%	26%	10%	2%
Women	68	19	73	20	20	9	1
AGE							
Men							
18–24	72	28	74	29	16	7	2
25–29	85	32	85	34	22	11	1
30–39	81	30	83	31	31	11	2
40–49	79	27	82	26	33	12	3
50–59	59	13	62	14	16	4	3
Women							
18–24	69	19	75	24	16	10	1
25–29	76	24	80	24	20	12	2
30–39	74	20	79	23	24	9	1
40–49	70	19	75	15	24	9	2
50–59	44	9	52	10	12	2	1
MARITAL/RESIDENTIAL STATUS							
Men							
Noncohabiting	71	29	75	33	23	9	3
Cohabiting	84	30	86	35	29	10	2
Married	80	25	80	23	27	10	2
Women							
Noncohabiting	62	23	70	26	20	11	1
Cohabiting	75	19	80	22	20	10	2
Married	71	17	74	17	21	7	1

Panel A: By Gender, Age, and Marital/Residental Status

Notes: (1) Measures of the percent engaging in anal or oral sex in the past twelve months or last sex event includes only those respondents who engaged in opposite-gender coupled sex in the past twelve months. Measures of engaging in anal or oral sex over the lifetime includes all respondents. (2) The measure of percent engaging in anal sex in the past twelve months is specific to the "primary" and "secondary" partners as defined in the survey. Respondents who had more than two partners during this period and engaged in anal sex with any partner not designated primary or secondary are not represented.

Panel B: By Education, Religion, and Race/Ethnicity

	Active oral sex		Passive oral sex		Anal sex		
	Lifetime	Last sex event	Lifetime	Last sex event	Lifetime	Past 12 months	Last sex event
EDUCATION							
Men							
Less than high school	59%	16%	61%	16%	21%	9%	1%
High school graduate or equivalent	75	30	77	25	23	8	3
Any college	81	27	84	31	28	11	2
Women							
Less than high school	41	10	50	13	13	9	1
High school graduate or equivalent	60	16	67	19	17	7	2
Any college	78	22	82	22	24	9	1
RELIGION							
Men							
None	79	34	83	35	34	9	1
Mainline Protestant	82	27	83	24	22	7	2
Conservative Protestant	67	22	70	24	21	7	2
Catholic	82	27	82	29	28	13	4
Women							
None	78	29	83	31	36	17	3
Mainline Protestant	74	20	77	19	20	8	1
Conservative Protestant	56	13	65	16	17	6	1
Catholic	74	22	77	22	20	10	1
RACE/ETHNICITY							
Men							
White	81	28	81	29	26	8	2
Black	51	17	66	18	23	8	3
Hispanic	66	25	67	15	38	15	2
Women							
White	75	21	78	22	23	8	1
Black	34	10	49	13	10	6	2
Hispanic	56	11	62	15	19	3	1

Twice as many women who went to college have given or received oral sex as compared to those who did not finish high school and twice as many of these better-educated women had or received oral sex the last time they had sex.

Much larger percentages of women under age fifty as compared to those over fifty have given or received oral sex in their lifetimes. And those in the oldest age group were less than half as likely to have had or received oral sex the last time they had sex. This is suggestive evidence that oral sex came into vogue in the 1960s. Blacks seem to have much less oral sex than whites. For example, 81 percent of white men have had oral sex performed on them, but just 66 percent of the black men have had it performed on them. And 75 percent of white women have performed oral sex on a man but just 34 percent of black women have performed it. White women were more than twice as likely as black women to have active oral sex and were nearly twice as likely as black women to have passive oral sex the last time they had sex.

Conservative Protestants were less likely to have engaged in any oral sex, as compared to other religions, for both men and women.

Why should this be? It sounds remarkable, if not implausible, for a sexual practice to be popular in some groups and shunned by others. After all, nearly everyone knows that there is such a thing as oral sex and so nearly everyone could have tried it and continued to include it in their repertoires if they wanted to.

The explanation may lie in the history of oral sex. As long ago as the 1920s, marriage manuals recommended oral sex to married couples, with one manual describing it as the "genital kiss."* It was presented as something you might do for a partner if you wanted to express physically how intimate, how emotionally close you felt. It was seen as a special gesture, not something that would normally be part of your sexual practices.

This view of oral sex as special to particular moments in particular relationships began to soften in the 1950s with the reports from the Kinsey studies that oral sex was fairly common and the resulting change in sex advice books that it was a technique that was especially satisfying for women. By the 1970s, the sex experts began saying that

*T. H. Van de Velde, *Ideal Marriage: Its Physiology and Technique* (New York: Covici-Friede Publishers, 1930; original in 1926).

oral sex could be part of the sex act for every couple, whether or not they were married. It became less of a special gesture and more a routine, expected sexual practice. Now, college textbooks discuss oral sex as a "technique" for arousing your partner, a marked transformation from the old view of it as a deeply significant emotional act by married or well-established couples.

So we might expect that the older people in our survey would have much less experience with oral sex. As for the disparities between whites and blacks and between educated and less well educated, we think that the explanation lies in social networks. As we have seen, Americans group themselves into social networks that serve as a source, and almost the sole source, of sexual partners. If others in your social network are trying oral sex, it is likely that you will have a partner who will try it with you, or that you will try it with your partner. If others in your network are willing to engage in it, you will be encouraged to try it too. But if others in your social network resist oral sex, you will be much less likely to try it and, if you do try it, less likely to say you enjoy it.

It is thought that oral sex in the sixties became a popular practice on college campuses. College students, living with and dating others in communities where oral sex was viewed as part of being sexually proficient, would be much more likely to try it and much more likely to continue with it. So, to this day, it is common among the well-educated.

But oral sex apparently did not take on the same aura in communities of less-educated people and among blacks, and it never has. Since there is little cross-racial dating and little sexual contact between better- and less-educated people, oral sex has remained a practice that is mainly popular among just one group of Americans.

Social scientists have collected little information about anal sex because they were too shy and because they assumed that it was rare. But once the AIDS epidemic began, researchers have wondered whether that assumption was true. Since anal sex is a much more efficient way to transmit HIV than vaginal sex, it suddenly became important to know how prevalent the practice is. If many heterosexuals had anal sex and they also had multiple partners, HIV could spread more rapidly among them.

Our data show that anal sex was much more prevalent than might have been expected. In Table 11, same-gender partners are not included in the information about the last event or the past twelve months, but they are included for the information about the lifetime. Nearly as many women as men report having anal sex. About a quarter of American men and women have had anal sex in their lifetimes and nearly 10 percent had anal sex in the past year. Yet only about 2 percent had anal sex the last time they had sex.

There is a slightly greater tendency to have tried anal sex among the better-educated and among people with no religion. Far fewer black women than white women have tried it, with Hispanic women reporting a rate between those of blacks and whites.

We were somewhat surprised to find that very few people said they used drugs before sex and that only a small percentage always or usually drank before or during sex. One of our myths is that many people have sex only when they have lost some control over themselves, after drinking or using drugs like cocaine. Yet even the young unmarried men and women — those most likely to fit this scenario — rarely drank or used drugs.

Only about 9 percent of men and 6 percent of women said they usually or always drank before or during sex. Moreover, it was mostly men and women in their forties who said they tended to drink before or during sex.

About 30 percent of men who drank before sex said they drank alone, and the older the men were the more likely they were to be solitary drinkers. Twenty-seven percent of the eighteen- to twenty-four-year-old men who drank before sex drank alone, but half the fifty- to fifty-four-year-old men said this was their typical behavior. We find that while marriage makes it less likely that men will regularly drink before or during sex, it also makes it more likely that if the men do drink, they do it alone.

Drug use before or during sex was so infrequent that we can draw no conclusions about who was most likely to do it. Only one man in 100 and one woman in 200 said they had ever used drugs in the past year before having sex with their partner.

But knowing what people did is only half of the picture. We also wanted to know what sexual practices people found appealing. The sexual menu is long, including not just vaginal, anal, and oral sex, but also such things as group sex or having your partner stimulate your anus or forcing sex or being forced to have sex or using a dildo or vibrator or having sex with a stranger. You may not actually do some of these things, but you may want to try them or find them attractive. We wanted to know, do people of different ages or different religions or different races want different things? Do married people want different sorts of sex than single people do?

We found, however, that although the sexual menu is long, people's selections are limited. Only three practices had a strong attraction for most people, and two of those three were still rejected by substantial proportions as unappealing.

As Table 12 shows, of all the practices on the sexual menu, only vaginal intercourse has nearly universal appeal. Nearly 80 percent of women aged eighteen to forty-four rated vaginal intercourse as very appealing and an additional 18 percent rated it somewhat appealing. Slightly fewer older women said it was very appealing and slightly more found it not at all appealing. But even among these women aged forty-five to fifty-nine, vaginal sex was rated as at least somewhat appealing by 93 percent of the respondents.

Men were even more enthusiastic about vaginal intercourse. A higher proportion — about 85 percent — of both the older and younger men said it was very appealing and small proportions said it was unappealing.

A distant second in appeal was watching a partner undress. Younger men and women liked this more than older people, a finding that might be expected since our society equates sexiness with having a young body. And men liked watching a partner undress more than women did. Yet 30 percent of women age eighteen to forty-four found it very appealing and another 51 percent said it was somewhat appealing, so young women as well as young men seemed to like watching their partner undress.

Social influences, the effects of our culture, are almost certainly the reason why. Women's bodies are our sex objects, the slow striptease is erotic, female nudity is titillating to most men. But women repeatedly claim in arenas like magazine articles that they find nude men unerotic, not particularly exciting.

Table 12
The Appeal of Selected Sexual Practices

| | Panel A: Women | | | | | | | |

	Ages 18–44				Ages 45–59			
Selected sexual practices	Very appealing	Some-what appealing	Not appealing	Not at all appealing	Very appealing	Some-what appealing	Not appealing	Not at all appealing
Vaginal intercourse	78%	18%	1%	3%	74%	19%	2%	6%
Watching partner undress	30	51	11	9	18	49	16	17
Receiving oral sex	33	35	11	21	16	24	14	45
Giving oral sex	19	38	15	28	11	20	17	52
Group sex	1	8	14	78	1	4	9	87
Anus stimulated by partner's fingers	4	14	18	65	6	12	14	68
Stimulate partner's anus with your fingers	2	11	16	70	4	12	12	73
Using dildo/vibrator	3	13	23	61	4	14	17	65
Watching others do sexual things	2	18	15	66	2	11	13	74
Same-gender sex partner	3	3	9	85	2	2	6	90
Sex with stranger	1	9	11	80	1	4	6	89
Passive anal intercourse	1	4	9	87	1	3	8	88
Forcing someone to do something sexual	0	2	7	91	0	0	5	95
Being forced to do something sexual	0	2	6	92	0	1	5	95

Panel B: Men

Selected sexual practices	Ages 18–44				Ages 45–59			
	Very appealing	Somewhat appealing	Not appealing	Not at all appealing	Very appealing	Somewhat appealing	Not appealing	Not at all appealing
Vaginal intercourse	83%	12%	1%	4%	85%	10%	1%	4%
Watching partner undress	50	43	3	4	40	47	7	5
Receiving oral sex	50	33	5	12	29	32	11	28
Giving oral sex	37	39	9	15	22	33	13	32
Group sex	14	32	20	33	10	18	22	50
Anus stimulated by partner's fingers	6	16	24	54	4	12	23	60
Stimulate partner's anus with your fingers	7	19	22	52	4	16	20	60
Active anal intercourse	5	9	13	73	1	7	9	83
Using dildo/vibrator	5	18	27	50	3	17	24	57
Watching others do sexual things	6	34	21	39	4	25	21	50
Same-gender sex partner	4	2	5	89	2	1	5	92
Sex with stranger	5	29	25	42	2	23	23	52
Passive anal intercourse	3	8	15	75	2	5	10	84
Forcing someone to do something sexual	0	2	14	84	1	2	12	86
Being forced to do something sexual	0	3	13	84	0	2	10	89

Note: Row percentages total 100 percent.

Molly Haskell, writing in *Lear's* magazine, captured the woman's view of most male nudity when she explained that naked men in movies are curiously unstimulating to most women: "But the truth is that most of us women are not that eager to see male stars in the altogether. [William] Baldwin's brother Alec shows too much of his birthday suit in *Prelude to a Kiss* and Richard Gere's seminude thrashing and prancing in *Sommersby* are about as erotic as his self-consciously lusty smile."

Holly Brubach, writing about mail-order catalogues in the *New York Times Magazine,* made a similar point. She spoke of International Male, for example, with its suggestively posed and scantily clothed models. "For me and for most of the women I know, an excursion through this catalogue is uneventful: Here's a guy with a neck like a tree trunk; there's one with nice legs. So what?" Brubach added that men obviously have a different reaction when they see photographs of women who are scantily dressed. With the Victoria's Secret catalogue, she wrote, "the pleasure this experience holds for men is obvious." She added, however, that women get pleasure from it too. "But the fact remains that for many women, looking at pictures of other women is an incitement to fantasy — not because they want to know these women but because they want in some vague way to *be* these women, to evoke in men the feelings they imagine the women in the pictures do."

With men expected to respond to nude women and women hearing that other women do not respond to most nude men, cultural forces are probably encouraging exactly the sorts of responses we saw.

The only other sexual activity on our menu that aroused any great enthusiasm from significant numbers of respondents was oral sex. But unlike watching a partner undress, which almost no one found totally offensive, oral sex definitely elicited mixed reactions, from strongly enthusiastic to extremely unenthusiastic. Both men and women were more interested in receiving it than giving it. Younger people liked it more than older people, men liked it more than women, and half the older women did not like either giving or receiving it at all. While a third of younger women found the idea of receiving oral sex very appealing and another third said it was appealing, one in five of these women aged eighteen to forty-four said it was not appealing at all to receive oral sex. Half the men in this younger age group, in contrast, said receiving oral sex was very appealing and only one in six said it was unappealing.

After vaginal sex, watching a partner undress, and oral sex, the remainder of our list of sexual behaviors appealed only to small minorities of people and were rejected as not at all appealing by most. In all instances, women seemed less enthusiastic than men, but most men did not find the practices appealing either. For example, 10 percent of the younger women said the idea of sex with a stranger was appealing or very appealing. About a third of the younger men said it was appealing or very appealing. But about eight out of ten women and almost one out of two men gave sex with a stranger the lowest rating — not at all appealing.

Lowest of all in their appeal were forcing people to have sex and being forced. More than 90 percent of women said either of these activities was not appealing at all. About 85 percent of men similarly judged forced sex and being forced not at all appealing.

One of the questions our data addressed was "Do women have different sexual preferences than men?" Certainly, there is anecdotal evidence that they do, as shown in the many examples of popular versions of erotic images. So entrenched are the stereotypical scenes that even a slight variation from them can seem aberrant. For example, writer Sallie Tisdale writing in *Harper's* magazine told of a mortifying incident that occurred in the 1970s, when she was twenty, several months pregnant, and working in a social work office. Her office held a seminar on sexuality, she said, and "we were determinedly liberal about the whole thing. I believe the point was to support clients in a variety of sexual choices. We were given a homework assignment on the first day, to make a collage that expressed our own sexuality."

Tisdale dutifully went home and fulfilled the assignment. But when she brought in her collage and compared it to her those of her colleagues, she was ashamed. "I returned the next morning and saw that my colleagues, male and female both, had all made romantic notions of candlelight and sunset. I was the youngest by several years, heavy bellied, and I had brought a wild version of masked men and women, naked torsos, skin everywhere, darkness, heat." Tisdale felt it was somehow not normal to be drawn to the more erotic images. "I knew I was struggling, distantly and through ignorance, with a deep shame," she wrote.

The problem was that Tisdale's images differed from the prevailing norms about what she ought to think about sex and, in particular, what women ought to think about sex. A variety of studies over the years have repeatedly pointed to substantial differences between the fantasies of women and those of men.

Nearly all women report fantasies that are soft, hazy, romantic, that veer far from explicit sex. Every writer of romance novels understands this and writes about love lost and love found, passionate situations, and being swept away. Most romance novels always downplay sex acts and sexual intercourse.

Most men, but, again, not all, focus on body parts and sex acts — the usual stuff of pornography. It is not that men are not attracted by romance, but, for them, they often say, romance is a means to an end and the end they are striving toward is sexual intercourse. Women, in contrast, often say that what is arousing about the sexual ending is the romantic beginning. Women and men may share the same sexual activities, but the weights that are given to the various elements are not always the same.

We have no reason to believe these differences between men and women reflect some sort of genetic imperative. They are likely instead to be cultural, reflecting what we tell boys and girls and men and women about what is a masculine vision of sexiness and what is a feminine vision. Whether we like or dislike the masculine and feminine versions of erotica, they persist and are an integral part of our culture.

For the traditional female perspective on sex, Daphne Merkin explained why certain books appeal to women: "Indeed, many of us prefer, perversely, the anticipation of sex to the thing itself. Or we have the opposite wish — which is to prolong the aftermath of love-making, avidly seeking out its physical aspect in lingering smells and rumpled sheets. There's a whole literature of erotic longing, with over-tones of bliss and undertones of pain-in-pleasure, that has sprung up to accommodate this predilection. It's a literature written by women for women — and for men intrigued by the inner life of women."

But the public world of sex, as portrayed in books and movies, increasingly is emphasizing the sort of sex that, our survey says, appeals to men. Censorship is weakening and antiromantic scenes of raw, explicit sex, without the haze of romance, are starting to proliferate. Since these movies are made with an eye to huge box-office receipts, the question arises: Are women really quite so repelled by this sort of sex as they have said they are? One of two things may have happened: Either many women decided they liked the raw sex that is now being depicted or they decided it was at least tolerable when it was packaged correctly.

We found that the most striking differences between men and women occurred when we focused on the extremes — how many people found an activity "very appealing" as opposed to just "appealing." Although most women did not find anything except vaginal intercourse "very appealing," their sexual preferences looked closer to those of men when we asked what they found simply "appealing." It may be that women who enjoy at least the idea, if not the practice, of behaviors like oral sex or group sex are less likely to desire them enough to say "very appealing." Or it may be that our society encourages men to say they are very stimulated by some of these activities but discourages women from feeling the same way.

Another way to look at women's preferences is to ask how many women, as compared to men, found various practices not at all appealing. It turns out that women are much more likely to express a strong distaste for sexual practices, with the exception of vaginal intercourse. For example, more than three-quarters of women aged eighteen to forty-four said the idea of group sex was not at all appealing. In contrast, a third of men in that age group gave the idea of group sex that lowest rating. Nearly 80 percent of women in this age group found the idea of sex with a stranger not at all appealing. But only half as many men aged eighteen to forty-four gave group sex this rating. Men, encouraged by society to say they are sexually adventurous, may be just as reticent to believe a practice is "not at all appealing" as women are to consider an uncommon sexual practice to be "very appealing."

But these possible explanations do not mean that our respondents are shading the truth in their replies. When we ask about a fact — how many partners did you have? What did you do the last time you had sex? — the answer is clear and reliable. When we ask an opinion — Is oral sex very appealing, appealing, unappealing, or not at all appealing? — there is more room for fuzziness in replies and more room for social conventions about how strongly men and women are supposed to feel about sex to push the data slightly one way of another.

Yet with these differences between men and women's stated preferences, there is certainly a potential for conflict. What if he wants oral sex and she hates it? What if she wants anal sex and he is appalled? Or what if he wants to watch her take off her clothes and she feels it makes her into a sex object to undress in a provocative way?

In most sexual partnerships, these conflicts, if they arise, show up too late in the development of a relationship to be easily corrected. Nearly everyone in our study reported that they knew their current sexual partner at least one month before having sex. Yet during this time, when the couple becomes ever more socially and emotionally committed to each other, almost no one finds out what their future sexual partner wants to do in bed. Specific sexual practices may be on people's minds but they are not in their conversations. A couple may be kissing and hugging and fondling each other. That is innocuous enough. But it is when they get to other sexual acts — vaginal sex, oral sex, anal sex — and when they get to questions of pleasure and orgasms that the problems loom and sex can turn into a series of compromises and negotiations.

In the beginning, when a relationship runs into sexual difficulties, the individuals often hope that things will get better or at least more coordinated. If it does not get better, they may be so committed to each other that they feel they cannot back out or say, "If the sex is no good, I don't want to get married."

This inability to talk about sex before actually having sex has consequences that go beyond disappointment or disillusionment with the long-awaited culmination of the courtship. Not only do we not want to ask what our partner prefers to do during the sex act but we also cannot bring ourselves to ask about our partner's sexual past. This is why it is so difficult for many people to use contraception and condoms and why the prevention of AIDS and sexually transmitted diseases rests on such shaky ground. Most people want to start a new sexual relationship without the ghosts of the past. Yet the ghosts of the past may include silent infections with bacteria or viruses that cause venereal diseases or AIDS. And, of course, there are also ghosts of sexual likes and dislikes, things learned from a previous partner and things that are distasteful because of what occurred in other relationships.

The data on how appealing various sexual practices are support our arguments about how difficult it can be to find a sexual partner who, right off the bat, has the same sexual preferences as you have. If you desire anything but vaginal sex or, perhaps, oral sex, it will be hard to find a partner with your tastes. You may be able to satisfy your tastes anyway, by finding a partner who will go along with you. But you may have to give something in return.

In the game of trading sexual favors, pleasing your partner in return for being pleased yourself, men and women are not equal. That might explain why about three-quarters of women aged eighteen to forty-four said they had performed oral sex on a man, but less than a fifth of women in this age range said giving oral sex was "very appealing." If a partnership is unequal — the man is of higher social class or the woman is more educated, for example — we might expect that the person with more power or prestige might have his or her way.

On the other hand, people might go along with sexual practices as a sort of silent barter, trading favor for favor or as a way to give pleasure to someone they love. A third of women aged eighteen to forty-four found giving oral sex somewhat appealing, indicating that a total of half the women in this age range at least are not repelled by the practice. And nearly half said they found the idea of receiving oral sex very appealing. Some may be providing oral sex to their partner so their partner would provide it to them.

As Vanessa Feltz wrote in *Redbook* magazine in an article on "Orgasm Etiquette," with oral sex, "It's one act where even the uninhibited may draw the line. Deny it if you dare, but oral sex *is* fraught with embarrassment. And, to be honest, I'm not crazy about giving it. It makes my jaw ache. But I am wild about receiving it, so a little quid pro quo makes sense."

Many people accommodate or compromise, and, as our survey showed, most are physically and emotionally satisfied with their sex lives. Our findings on preferences and practices show, however, why a man might have felt a sense of lingering dissatisfaction when the exotic sexual world of novels and movies turned out to be so different from the world of conventional sex in marriage. And it hints at why people from different walks of life might have sexual misunderstandings and conflicts.

Another source of sexual differences might be the very region where you and your partner grew up. Just as southerners, for example, tend to be more politically conservative than New Yorkers or people from Massachusetts, just as midwesterners often have a different view of social welfare than Texans, so people from different geographic regions tend to have different sexual preferences and practices as well.

But sex with a partner is only one form of sex. There is also the sex you might perform alone, stimulating yourself. In the next chapter we describe this sort of sex, asking once again whether there is a social context to the behavior, whether people of different social groups and backgrounds are more or less interested in such things as pornography and masturbation.

8

MASTURBATION AND EROTICA

SEX with a partner is the public world of sex. It is a world of stakeholders and expectations, of performances and judgments, of negotiations and problematical outcomes. It is, like all social worlds, a place in which what a person does has consequences. There is another world of sex, however, one that is partially independent of this public world. This is the world of fantasy, of the private consumption of erotic materials and self-masturbation.

In this secluded personal realm, you do not have to pay as much attention to others, and the goal of personal pleasure can become central. It is a world without the need to negotiate with others and where there is no worry about whether your partner is satisfied. It is a world largely without social constraints, although even in the world of fantasy, the demands of society can intrude. To fantasize about Julia Roberts or Richard Gere, you need the existence of Julia Roberts or Richard Gere. And there is always the worry that private behavior will be exposed, as boys, for example, worry that their mothers will discover their masturbation.

We had two reasons for wanting to explore this arena. First, it is a large domain of sexual conduct. Previous research suggested that masturbation is common among young people and that many people continue to masturbate as they grow older. Simply to learn if that suggestion is correct, we wanted to document the prevalence of masturbation.

A second reason for asking about the private world of sex was to understand the totality of American sexual behavior. Was private sex a supplement to sex with a partner, a behavior people resorted to in the absence of partners? Or was it independent of or generated by sex with partners? It did not seem to us that the answers to these questions were obvious.

And, as we found, the usual assumptions were incorrect. Those who think about sex the most and who are most likely to peruse erotic materials are not those who have little sex with a partner but those who have relatively abundant sex with a partner. The people who masturbated the most were those who are thought to masturbate the least, and vice versa. And we think we know why this is so.

We began by asking our respondents how often they thought about sex. This, of course, is a question that people cannot answer precisely, but they can locate themselves on a scale of a little to a lot.

Table 13 shows that the critical variable determining how often a person thinks about sex is whether that person is a man or a woman.

Men told us that they think about sex often — more than half said they have erotic thoughts every day or several times a day and only four out of one hundred said they think about sex less than once a month. Women, in contrast, more often report that they think about sex a few times a week to a few times a month.

Table 13
Responses to the Question:
"How Often Do You Think about Sex?"

	"Every day" or "Several times a day"	"A few times a month" or "A few times a week"	"Less than once a month" or "Never"
Men	54%	43%	4%
Women	19	67	14

Note: Row percentages total 100 percent.

Table 14
Percentage Purchasing Autoerotic Materials
in the Past Twelve Months

Materials	Men	Women
X-rated movies or videos	23%	11%
Visit to a club with nude or seminude dancers	22	4
Sexually explicit books or magazines	16	4
Vibrators or dildos	2	2
Other sex toys	1	2
Sex phone numbers	1	.
Any of the above	41	16

Note: Percentages are separate for each cell.

Likewise, as Table 14 shows, men were several times more likely than women to report seeing an X-rated movie or going to a topless club or reading a sex magazine or book. Only a tiny percent of either gender reported using a vibrator or other sex toy, and, of course, these may well have been used with a partner and not for self-stimulation. The bottom row of Table 14 emphasizes the point that men, far more than women, report using these materials: 41 percent of men but only 16 percent of women said they had in the past twelve months done any of the six things listed here.

Who are these men and women who fantasize about sex and seek out erotica? The conventional wisdom says they are people who have little sex with a partner, who have few partners and a paltry sexual experience. But we found that the men and the women who use fantasy and who use autoerotic materials are those who seem to seek out the most sex with a partner and who find the greatest number of other sexual experiences appealing. We might, in fact, say that these are the people who are most interested in sex and the most sexually active, not the sexual loners that popular imagery depicts. They are the people who find more sexual practices very appealing, are more likely to engage in oral sex, and are more likely to have multiple sexual partners. Private sexual experience, we find, goes along with sexual experience in general.

We also asked about masturbation, a subject that, of all the very

FIGURE 11:
Frequency of Masturbation

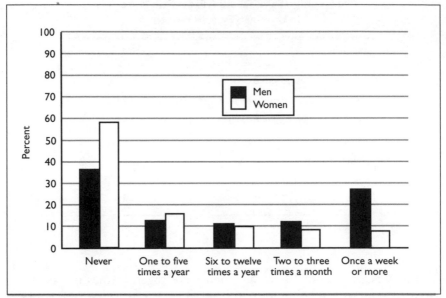

common sexual practices, remains the most problematic and the most poorly studied. People, and most magazines and books giving sexual advice, do not talk about masturbation in the same way they talk about orgasms or oral sex. Masturbation remains in the shadows, a practice that few discuss.

Yet, we find, many, if not most, people masturbate. Our data indicate, as seen in Figure 11, that, among Americans aged eighteen to fifty-nine, about 60 percent of the men and 40 percent of the women said they masturbated in the past year. About one man in four and one woman in ten reported that they masturbate at least once a week. And these are not adolescents, they are adults, most of whom have regular partners for sexual intercourse.

The large number of adults who masturbate seems puzzling, at least according to the widespread view of masturbation as a sexual outlet. If people masturbated as a substitute for sex with a partner, to release sexual tensions, then people who have partners should masturbate only very rarely or not at all. Yet not only does that hypothesis turn out to be incorrect, but, we find, exactly the opposite effect occurs. Those whom the substitute-outlet theory says are most likely to masturbate actually masturbate the least and those who are supposed to masturbate the least do it the most. In that sense, masturbation is like using erotica and having frequent thoughts of sex — not an outlet so much as a component of a sexually active lifestyle.

But, if masturbation is so common, why does it trouble so many people to talk about it? One reason is that the practice is burdened by a dramatically negative history. It is condemned by Judaism and Christianity and while it is clear that the biblical sin of Onan, an immoral spilling of one's seed on barren ground, was not only about masturbation, over the centuries the two have become identified as one and the same.

Yet while the biblical strictures on masturbation were part of the inheritance of Christianity, it was not until the eighteenth century that a true campaign against it began. The opening shot in this campaign was part of the early medicalization of sexuality. The Swiss physician S. A. D. Tissot published his volume, *Onanism, Or, A Treatise on the Disorders of Masturbation* in 1741. It was soon reprinted dozens of times and translated into all the major European languages.

In Tissot's time, doctors believed that body fluids, like blood or bile, had to be in perfect balance for a person to be in robust physical health. Tissot argued that the same is true for sexual fluids. He said that if men ejaculate too often or if women expend sexual fluids that are produced during arousal, their bodies will be depleted of these vital substances and they will fall ill. He concluded that people with tuberculosis or other diseases that caused a weakening or wasting of the body were, in fact, suffering from the consequences of masturbation. He also warned that "diseases of the nerves," many of which would now be called neuroses, were caused by too much sexual excitement, and in particular, by masturbation. He argued further that the "convulsive" effects of sex can damage the nervous system, and that women were particularly susceptible.

Tissot's theories initiated a century and a half of dire medical warnings about the consequences of masturbation. For example, toward the end of the eighteenth century, Benjamin Rush, a signer of the Declaration of Independence, warned that masturbation causes poor eyesight, epilepsy, memory loss, and pulmonary tuberculosis. He wrote that women who masturbate "are feeble and of a transient nature compared to the strain of physical and moral evils which this solitary vice fixes upon the body and mind."

Victorian doctors wrote of the sad fate that would befall masturbators. One, William Acton, described a boy with a "sallow, pasty" complexion, a face speckled with acne. "The boy shuns the society of others, creeps about alone, joins with repugnance in the amusements of his schoolfellows. He cannot look anyone in the face, and becomes careless in dress and uncleanly in person. His intellect becomes sluggish and enfeebled."

The next step was for the medical profession and self-declared experts to devise ways to prevent young people from masturbating, protecting them from themselves, as the doctors saw it. Their advice often was received with avid enthusiasm by Americans who, by the middle of the nineteenth century, had become obsessed with the idea that masturbation was evil and dangerous and must be eliminated.

One response to the supposed dangers of masturbation was the idea that certain foods could quell masturbatory urges. J. H. Kellogg said that cornflakes would do the trick. Sylvester Graham, inventor of the graham cracker, had a complete dietary plan. Men should eat grains and avoid meat. They should exercise strenuously and sleep on hard wooden beds. Kellogg and Graham became popular sexual advisers, writing best-selling books that described the dire consequences of masturbation.

Graham, for example, wrote in his 1834 book, *A Lecture to a Young Man,* that masturbation would transform a young boy into "a confirmed and degraded idiot, whose deeply sunken and vacant, glossy eye and livid shriveled countenance, and ulcerous, toothless gums, and fetid breath, and feeble, broken voice, and emaciated and dwarfish and crooked body, and almost hairless head — covered perhaps with suppurating blisters and running sores — denote a premature old age! a blighted body — and a ruined soul!" Kellogg's bestselling book, *Plain Facts for Old and Young Embracing the Natural History and Hygiene of Organic Life,* published in 1888, had a similar horrifying description of the masturbator. There were thirty-nine signs of masturbation that should alert parents, Kellogg wrote, including, rounded shoulders, weak backs, paleness, acne, heart palpitations, and epilepsy. The masturbating young people also could develop bashfulness, boldness, mock piety, and confusion. They might start using tobacco or biting their nails or wetting the bed.

To curb masturbation, Kellogg suggested that parents bandage the child's genitals, cover them with a cage, or tie the hands. Another remedy was circumcision, "without administering an anesthetic, as the brief pain attending the operation will have a salutary effect upon the mind, especially if it be connected with the idea of punishment." Kellogg suggested that older boys have their foreskins sutured shut, over the glans, to prevent an erection. His advice for parents of girls was to apply "pure carbolic acid to the clitoris."

Entrepreneurs began inventing devices that could prevent masturbation, and some even obtained patents. These included a genital cage that used springs to hold a boy's penis and scrotum in place and a device that sounded an alarm if a boy had an erection.

It is not clear how many people actually tried these frightening prescriptions or what success they had in reducing rates of masturbation among the young. They did, however, produce a reign of terror and fear that was reflected in the anxieties reported by young men as late as the Kinsey studies conducted in the 1930s and 1940s.

The sexual reformers of the twentieth century, Sigmund Freud and Henry Havelock Ellis, railed against these extreme measures, but they still thought that masturbation could cause sexual dysfunction, including impotence, premature ejaculation, and an aversion to intercourse. The medical profession gradually realized that masturbation did not cause physical disease. However, doctors, psychiatrists, psychologists, and counselors continued to believe that masturbation caused mental disorders.

We are left with a conflicted and confused heritage. Many people suspect that masturbation somehow is bad for them. Others believe that not masturbating is evidence that they have a strong will and control over a primitive drive. And our religious traditions continue to proscribe masturbation.

Even today our views of masturbation reflect this legacy. On one side are members of various religious groups who continue to condemn masturbation in traditional terms and for traditional reasons. This influences those who feel that masturbation must be bad for them or for their children or those who feel that not masturbating is a measure of willpower and triumph over a nearly overwhelming drive. On the other side are those who feel that masturbation is not a crime or a vice. But even the most liberal tend to see masturbation as an activity that is appropriate only for the young or those without partners. Among adults, masturbation has the taint of sexual failure, a practice engaged in by those without the social skills or desirability to find a sexual partner.

Because of masturbation's legacy and image, it is rarely discussed. Some adults who have spoken about masturbating say that, as adolescents, they were so ignorant about it that they did not even connect it with sex. Felicia, a wealthy New York businesswoman, said that when she was a teenager, "I knew there was this pleasurable thing you did in the bathroom alone by yourself, masturbating, but I never really connected it with intercourse in bed with a man."

Others joke about it. Comedian Jerry Seinfeld has a pet phrase to describe those who refrain from masturbating: "Master of Your Domain." He also asserts that all men do it anyway. "We all *have* to do it. It's part of our lifestyle, like shaving," he says.

The few times that masturbation has become a public issue, many people reacted to it with nervous titters or with shock and disgust. Two infamous masturbators reveal what many Americans think about the practice: the fictional character of Alexander Portnoy and the real-life actor Pee-wee Herman.

Portnoy was a creation of the novelist Philip Roth. In the book *Portnoy's Complaint,* Portnoy described himself as an inveterate and compulsive masturbator. He made the practice actually sound funny, an irresistible urge that the insatiable Alexander Portnoy indulged at the most inopportune moments. While many laughed, others were disturbed by Portnoy's tales of unbridled and incompetent lust.

James Atlas, an editor of the *New York Times Magazine,* noted, however, that even as hundreds of thousands of Americans read *Portnoy's Complaint,* the book also shocked and revolted the nation. "Twenty-five years on we tend to forget the amazement, the incredulity, the *shock,* produced by 'That Book' — as offended readers gingerly referred to *Portnoy's Complaint,*" he wrote.

The story of Pee-wee Herman is a sadder one. He was a comedian with a successful television and film career who especially appealed to children. In 1991, when he was thirty-nine, he was arrested for masturbating in a movie theater that showed X-rated films. During his trial, it turned out that the three detectives who arrested Pee-wee regularly patrolled pornographic movie houses looking for people to arrest for "exposing their sexual organs in public."

The resulting scandal cost Pee-wee Herman his television show and probably his career. He was convicted and fined and required to use his own money to make an antidrug film. Why, one might ask, was he not punished in a manner that befit his crime — required, for example, to use his own money to make an anti-public-masturbation film?

In such a climate of ignorance, anxiety, and public condemnation, we might expect that masturbation would be rare and that it would be rarest of all among people who are sexually active. After all, if masturbation is used to relieve sexual tension, why would anyone want to indulge in such a practice if they had plenty of sex with a partner? And even people without partners might try not to masturbate, considering how condemned masturbation is. But our data show that these assumptions are not at all correct.

First of all, masturbation is not rare. Although men are more likely to masturbate than women, the practice is common among both genders, as Figure 11 shows.

But even more surprising is the effect of age on a person's likelihood of masturbating, as seen in Figure 12.

When we focused on people of different ages, we noticed that the youngest people in our study masturbated *less* than any other group except people over age fifty. Previous studies by others have found that most adolescent boys masturbate. Portnoy, although a caricature, still captured a truth. Yet, in our study, many people who were just past adolescence were not masturbating. Just six out of ten men aged eighteen to twenty-four said they masturbated in the past year. Fewer than half the men over age fifty-four masturbated. But more than seven out of ten men in their late twenties masturbated, as seen in Figure 12. Among women, as well, fewer than four out of ten aged eighteen to twenty-four masturbated. Fewer than three out of ten over age fifty-four masturbated, but nearly half the women in their thirties masturbated.

What accounts for these findings?

FIGURE 12:
Frequency of Masturbation by Age and Gender

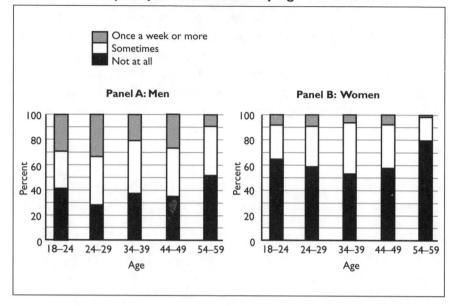

We conjecture that there are different explanations for masturbation among men and among women and among the young as compared to the old.

The low rates of masturbation among men aged eighteen to twenty-four most likely reflect their opinion of the practice as something that kids do, something that they have now outgrown. As these young men move into relationships with women, whether these involve sexual intercourse or not, masturbation becomes, for them, more taboo. The young men begin masturbating less even if they do not have another sexual "outlet." The amount of masturbation, then, is controlled more by social factors, by its image as a behavior of young boys, than by any sort of drive to release sexual tension.

The pattern among young women is different. Our study shows that women begin to masturbate at older ages than do men and that masturbation is not so strongly linked to adolescence. In fact, many women probably start to masturbate after they have begun having sexual intercourse rather than before they have had it.

The lower rates of masturbation among people older than fifty reflect very different social circumstances, we suggest. As people grow older, they usually have less sex with a partner. Although we cannot rule out effects of biology or a decline in sex hormones, social factors also loom large. Many older people, women in particular, no longer have a partner and others may respond to social conventions that tell them that sex is no longer appropriate for them. Our society tells older people that their bodies are no longer sexy and that work and caring for a family is more important than seeking sexual pleasure. We believe that our finding that fewer older people masturbate reflects a pattern of general decline in sexual behavior. Older people do not use masturbation to compensate for having less sex with their partners, as the sexual-drive theory might predict.

What about the people who are neither young nor old? These are the most sexually active people in America; they are most likely to have regular partners and are most likely to have sex of all kinds. They are also most likely to masturbate. Nearly 85 percent of men and 45 percent of women who were living with a sexual partner said they had masturbated in the past year. Married people were significantly more likely to masturbate than people who were living alone.

In fact, we discovered that the same groups that are most likely to have oral sex — white, educated liberals — are also the most likely to masturbate. For example, twice as many black men as white men did not masturbate in the past year. More than half of all men and more than three-quarters of all women with less than a high-school education did not masturbate in the past year. In contrast, when we looked at people with advanced degrees, only one out of five men and six out of ten women did not masturbate.

Our conclusion from these data is that masturbation is not a substitute for those who are sexually deprived, but rather it is an activity that stimulates and is stimulated by other sexual behavior. We do not have data that would tell us whether masturbation occurs on days when partners are absent or whether it occurs when they are present, but we do know that people having more sex with their partners are more likely to masturbate. This is a social explanation for our findings — that the more sex you have of any kind, the more you may think about sex and the more you may masturbate. It is an explanation that is consistent with our general theme that social factors influence our sexual lives.

We also looked at how often people masturbated — a different question from whether they masturbated. Here, we found that there is no obvious relationship between how often a person masturbates and how often they have sex with a partner. Frequent partnered sex tells us that a person is likely to have masturbated at some time in the past year. But it does not tell us that the person is likely to have masturbated relatively frequently.

When we asked those who said they masturbate why they do it, most said it was "to relieve sexual tension." Nearly two-thirds of the women who masturbated and more than seven out of ten men who masturbated cited this as a reason. About a third of the men and women also said that they were masturbating because they had no sexual partner available and a third of the women and about a quarter of the men who masturbated said they did it to relax. (Respondents gave more than one answer, so percentages can total more than 100 percent.) Almost no one — just 5 percent of the women and 7 percent of the men — said they masturbated because they were afraid of AIDS or sexually transmitted diseases.

We believe, however, that when our respondents said they were "relieving sexual tension," they were actually giving back to us a socially induced answer. The tensions they were feeling were the result of their being in sexually stimulating environments in which desire is experienced more frequently. Since they may share the cultural belief that they have a sex drive independent of social influences, they may interpret their desires as arising from internal sources.

The fact that we question these responses has nothing to do with our faith in the replies of our respondents when we asked them more objective questions, such as "How many sex partners have you had?" or "How often did you masturbate?" In this case, we asked them to tell us why they did something sexual, not what they did. And we elicited replies that may be interpretations rather than objective facts.

People who masturbated also were likely to feel guilty — evidence that the social condemnation of this act affects even those who practice it. About half of the men and women who masturbated said they felt guilty.

Table 15
Frequency of Masturbation and Feelings of Guilt

	Frequency of masturbation			
Feelings of guilt	One to five times a year	Six to twelve times a year	Two to three times a month	Once a week or more
Men				
Any guilt feelings*	25%	16%	18%	41%
No guilt feelings	18	18	22	43
Women				
Any guilt feelings	47	24	14	14
No guilt feelings	32	25	22	21

Notes: "Any guilt feelings" includes those who masturbated at least once last year and reported "always," "usually," "sometimes," or "rarely" feeling guilty about masturbation. Row percentages total 100 percent.

Table 15 shows the rates of masturbation for the men and for the women who said they masturbated in the past twelve months by whether the person felt any guilt about this practice. For the men, the frequency of masturbation for those who felt guilt was very similar to the frequency for those who did not. The guilt, apparently, did not alter their behavior. Of course, those who did feel guilt may have masturbated more if they had not felt as they did, but we see no indication in these data that men's feelings of guilt affected how often they masturbated. For the women, in contrast, there is some hint in the table that those who felt guilty masturbated somewhat less often. Since we did not ask people who did not masturbate questions about whether masturbation would make them feel guilty, we cannot see if guilt had anything to do with their failure to masturbate.

We also asked whether people who masturbate seek out more sexual experiences in general. We find that they do. For example, we find that there is a strong link between finding various sexual activities "very appealing" and masturbating. The list of sexual activities included, for example, vaginal sex, oral sex, anal sex, watching a partner undress, group sex, and stimulating a partner's anus. People who rarely or never masturbated found an average of 1.2 items on our list very appealing. People who masturbated frequently found an average of 2.9 activities very appealing, a two and a half–fold difference.

Data like these help explain why white, college-educated people who are living with a partner are most likely to masturbate. They are members of a group that tends to experiment with sex. Although they may be religious, they are less responsive to religious strictures.

In contrast, young women who are not masturbating are more inexperienced at sex — many are still virgins — and most are not actively experimenting with sexual techniques. Older people who are having less sex in general are also less likely to masturbate.

Many blacks are part of a social group that is conservative and conventional about sexual behavior. They, too, are less likely to masturbate.

So even without much open discussion of masturbation, even with the stigma that still hangs over the act, we find that the practice is so strongly influenced by social attitudes that it becomes more a reflection of a person's religion and social class than a hidden outlet for sexual tensions.

9

HOMOSEXUAL PARTNERS

Nᴏᴛ too long ago, many Americans could say that they never met a gay man or a lesbian and that they knew nothing about homosexuality. But that was before the gay liberation movements of the 1970s and the AIDS epidemic that first appeared in the 1980s. Homosexuals are now a visible presence in American society. Now, many Americans who would never have seen an openly gay man or lesbian see them in many places — on television, on the covers of national magazines, in the newspaper, if not in their own neighborhood or workplace. The national spotlight has been on homosexuals and homosexuality.

The AIDS epidemic reenergized the gay movements of the 1970s by forcing homosexuals to mobilize to deal with the impact of AIDS on their communities. In the process of working on issues of AIDS prevention, securing health care, and acting against AIDS discrimination, a renewed concern with gay civil rights has been generated.

Some gay men and lesbians advocated new laws to protect them from discrimination in jobs and housing. Some wanted to marry, while others argued that they and their partners be given the same benefits as married couples. Lesbian mothers and gay fathers were publicized in newsmagazines and newspapers. President Bill Clinton found that his first protracted political battle, after his inauguration, was over his promise to eliminate the ban on gays in the military.

Some Americans professed to be scandalized by the very idea of homosexuals, so numerous, so open about their sexual preference. Other Americans, confronting homosexuality for the first time, did so with compassion, horrified by the terrible epidemic that so decimated the numbers of gay men, leaving family, friends, and lovers in a state of mourning.

Yet with the emergence of homosexuality into the mainstream of society came new questions and a recasting of older ones. How many gay men and lesbians were there in society? Could the sexual behavior of gay men change (a question equally important for lesbians and heterosexual women and men)? Were gay men and lesbians good parents and how did their children turn out? Finally, was homosexuality somehow chosen or was it inborn or some combination of nurture and nature?

Some of these questions are important because of their bearing on the AIDS epidemic: how large it is, where it is going, and who is at risk of HIV infection. But others touch upon basic issues related to sexuality. They cut to the heart of questions about how malleable our sexual preferences and practices are.

Our findings do not specifically address the nature-nurture question about homosexuality. But they strongly suggest there are major social influences on the prevalence of homosexuality. And, we find, just as social networks control the search for heterosexual partners, so they control the search for homosexual partners. Gay and lesbian sex plays by many of the same rules as heterosexual sex.

We did not have enough data on gay men and lesbians to answer many of the questions we had. We could not say, for example, how many partners they had or where they met them. We could not say what their sexual preferences and practices were. But we could ask how many Americans desire sex with a person of the same gender, how many have had sex with people of the same gender, where do homosexuals live, and what are their social characteristics.

Because of the stigma that clings to homosexuals in America, we asked about homosexual behavior in a variety of nonjudgmental ways. Our aim was to allow people to answer our questions honestly, without ever making them feel they were being placed in a special social category.

In our survey, we did not mention the word *homosexual*, except when we asked people whether they identified themselves as homo- sexual, bisexual, or heterosexual. But we did ask about homosexual behavior in several ways. Early in the survey, we gave the respondents a self-administered questionnaire that asked how many partners they had had in the past year and whether these partners were all of the same sex, all of the opposite sex, or whether they had partners of both sexes. In the section where we asked for detailed information about the social characteristics of the respondent's partners for the last year, we asked whether these partners were men or women. Finally, at the very end of the questionnaire, we gave the respondents another self- administered questionnaire and asked them to tell us about specific sexual acts and the gender of the person they had sex with. For ex- ample, if the respondent was a man, we asked whether he had ever had oral sex with another man.

Taken together, our survey in conjunction with other recent sur- veys portrays a minority population, subjected to intense prejudice, that has developed a way of responding to stigma. And they reveal why it is that almost every figure or statement about homosexuality is so controversial.

One of the first and most politically charged questions that AIDS has elicited is: How many homosexuals are there? The question has taken on a life of its own, with ramifications well beyond AIDS. Some religious conservatives, for example, would like the number to be very low, so they can argue that homosexuality is a perversion and should not be tolerated, that the overwhelming majority of Americans would never dream of indulging in such behavior. Many gay groups would like the number to be large, so they can argue that homo- sexuals are a force to be reckoned with, that any politician who avoids or alienates gay voters does so at his or her peril. They have promoted the phrase "one in ten" — one American in ten is gay or lesbian, they assert.

We'd like to be able to give a clear, definite answer to the gay numbers question, but it turns out that the answer is subtle and shaded with gray, and that the answer to the question of how many homosexuals there are depends very much on what you mean by "homosexual."

It may sound like an odd response, a sort of deflection of the question. Yet, we find, there are three reasons why we cannot so simply say that a person is or is not gay.

First, people often change their sexual behavior during their lifetimes, making it impossible to state that a particular set of behaviors defines a person as gay. A man who has sex with men today, for example, might not have done so ten years ago. Does a man who has homosexual sex in prison count as a homosexual? Does a man who left his wife of twenty years for a gay lover count as homosexual or heterosexual? Do you count the number of years he spent with his wife as compared to his lover? Does the married woman who had sex with her college roommate a decade ago count? Do you assume that one homosexual experience defines someone as gay for all time? Often implicit in a figure like one in ten is the assumption that homosexuality is a characteristic like green eyes that is part of a person's identity and never changes.

A second reason is that there is no one set of sexual desires or self-identification that uniquely defines homosexuality. Is it sexual desire for a person of the same gender, is it thinking of yourself as a homosexual, or is it some combination of these behaviors that make a person a homosexual? Is a woman a lesbian if she finds it sexually arousing to look at other women, but has only heterosexual intercourse? Does it matter if she considers herself a heterosexual?

A third reason is that homosexual behavior is not easily measured. For centuries, homosexuals have been stigmatized and persecuted, a legacy that is revealed in national surveys of public opinions. From 1972 until 1991, polls showed that over 70 percent of Americans believed that homosexuality was always morally wrong. Even though the recent struggles of gay men and lesbians to gain acceptance have had an effect on the public's mood, the history of persecution has a lasting effect both on what people are willing to say about their sexual behavior and on what they actually do.

Nonetheless, many people have accepted the widely quoted figure that 10 percent of Americans are homosexual, a figure that often is attributed to Alfred Kinsey. Yet Kinsey also emphasized that there is no single measure of homosexuality and that it is impossible to divide the world into two distinct classes — homosexual and heterosexual. He argued, as we do, that the best way to discuss homosexuality is to report several numbers.

For example, Kinsey reported in 1948 that 37 percent of the non-random sample white men he interviewed had had at least one sexual experience with another man in their lifetime. This percentage included all experiences including those in adolescence. He then reported that of these same men, 10 percent had only homosexual experiences for any three-year period between ages sixteen and fifty-five (this is probably where the popularized 10 percent figure came from). This could include men who had sex with other men only a few times a year while having no sex with women during that time. And he reported that 4 percent of these men had sex only with men from adolescence on.

Kinsey did not publish quite comparable figures for women, though he did estimate that about 13 percent of women had ever had at least one homosexual experience in which they had an orgasm (this is comparable to the 37 percent figure for men).

Since Kinsey's studies, the 10 percent number has taken on a life of its own. Like many controversial numbers — the number of homeless people, the number of malnourished children in America, the number of hard drug users — the 10 percent number has been repeated more often than it has been examined.

Wherever 10 percent came from, it is clearly higher than any figures from recent studies. If it is interpreted as meaning that one in ten adults in the United States is exclusively homosexual, it is higher than Kinsey himself stated. His number for that was 4 percent. In fact, a reanalysis of the Kinsey data for college men only, showed that the proportion of men who said they had had exclusively homosexual experiences since age eighteen was 3 percent. An additional 3 percent said they had significant amounts of both homosexual and heterosexual experiences after age eighteen.*

By interviewing volunteers and people nominated by earlier re-

---

*John H. Gagnon and William Simon, *Sexual Conduct* (Chicago: Aldine Press, 1973).

spondents, Kinsey almost certainly included people who were more sexually active and more willing to discuss their sex lives. He also made it more likely that he would find homosexuals by recruiting volunteers in prisons and reform schools and by asking homosexuals who were part of social networks in large cities to bring in their friends and acquaintances to be part of his study.

In our nationwide sample of adults age eighteen to fifty-nine, we focused on three different aspects of homosexuality: being sexually attracted to persons of the same gender, having sex with persons of the same gender, and identifying oneself as a homosexual. The three categories are distinct, we found, and produce three different estimates of homosexuality in America.

To learn how many people desire people of the same gender, we looked at responses to a question asking respondents to rate having homosexual sex on a scale ranging from "very appealing" to "somewhat appealing" to "not appealing" to "not at all appealing." We defined homosexual sex for men as having anal or oral sex with another man or masturbating another man. For women, we defined it as having oral sex with another woman, using a dildo or sex toy on another woman, or masturbating another woman.

In addition, we looked at the replies to a question later in the interview that asked women if they were sexually attracted to "only men, mostly men, both men and women, mostly women, or only women" and that asked the same question of men, only for them the choices were "only women, mostly women, both men and women, mostly men, or only men."

Some of our findings are displayed in Figure 13.

The bar graph shows that estimates of the prevalence of homosexuality depend very much on what question you ask and what you think it means to be a homosexual.

We found that more people find others of the same gender sexually attractive than have homosexual sex. About 5.5 percent of the women said they found the thought of having sex with someone of the same gender very appealing or appealing. About 4 percent of the women said they were sexually attracted to individuals of the same gender.

Less than 2 percent of the women in our study, however, said they had sex with another woman in the past year, about 4 percent said

FIGURE 13:
Aspects of Same-Gender Sexuality

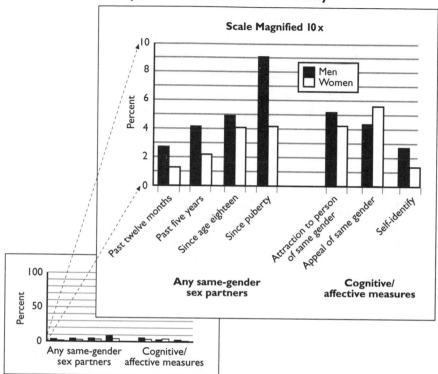

Note: Attraction measured by following question: "In general are you sexually attracted to... only women, mostly women, both men and women, mostly men, only men?" (order of answer categories reversed for women). Appeal measured by following question: "How would you rate this activity: having sex with someone of the same sex... very appealing, somewhat appealing, not appealing, not at all appealing?" Self-identification derived from following question: "Do you think of yourself as... heterosexual, homosexual, bisexual, something else?"

they had sex with another women after age eighteen, and a little more than 4 percent said they had sex with a woman at some time in their life.

About 6 percent of the men in our study said they were attracted to other men. About 2 percent of the men in our study said they had sex with a man in the past year, a little more than 5 percent said they had homosexual sex at least once since they turned eighteen, and 9 percent said they had had sex with a man at least once since puberty.

Yet 40 percent of men who say they have had sex with another man at some time in their life have that sex before they are eighteen and do not have sex with another man when they are older. Women who have sex with women, in contrast, are not so likely to have their homosexual experiences in adolescence and, in fact, are usually eighteen or older when they first have sex with someone of the same gender.

Finally, we asked respondents whether they consider themselves heterosexual, homosexual, bisexual, or something else. This question elicited the lowest rates of homosexuality. About 1.4 percent of the women said they thought of themselves as homosexual or bisexual and about 2.8 percent of the men identified themselves in this way.

The bar charts in Figure 13 show our estimates of the proportions of the population who are homosexual by the three separate measures of behavior, desire, and self-identity. We can also ask how much overlap there is in these measures and that overlap is shown in Figure 14.

Figure 14 shows, for example, how many women had sex with another woman (a behavioral measure), but did not feel any desire for other women at the time of our interview (the desire measure), nor

FIGURE 14:
Interrelationship of Three Aspects of Same-Gender Sexuality:
Desire, Behavior, and Self-Identification

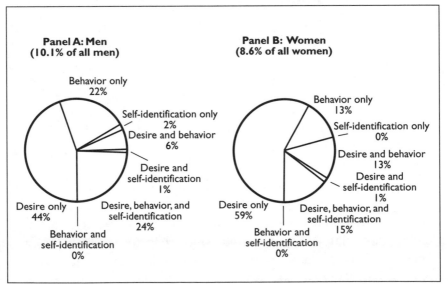

consider themselves to be homosexual (the self-identity measure). The pie chart says that 13 percent of the 150 women fell into that category.

The pie chart also shows that, for women, the number who find lesbian sex desirable but never act on that desire (59 percent) dwarfs the number who both desire other women and have had sex with them. It also shows that a substantial proportion of these women (13 percent) do not consider themselves lesbians even though they both desire other women and have had sex with women. All these proportions pertain to the 8.6 percent of women who were defined as homosexual by any of three measures.

The pie chart in Figure 14 shows that men are more likely to act upon their desire for other men. Men who desire other men and have had sex with men are also more likely than women in that situation to identify themselves as homosexuals.

Data like these illustrate how difficult it is to decide who is, and who is not, a homosexual and they show how different definitions of homosexuality can dramatically alter the estimates of its prevalence.

No matter how we define homosexuality, we come up with small percentages of people who are currently gay or lesbian. These numbers, in fact, may sound astonishingly low, especially to residents of cities like New York or San Francisco, where there are large gay and lesbian communities. But, we found, gays and lesbians are not evenly distributed across the country. They tend to live in large cities and to avoid or leave small towns and rural areas, as seen in Figure 15.

More than 9 percent of men in the nation's twelve largest cities identify themselves as gay. But just 3 or 4 percent of men living in the suburbs of these cities or in most of the larger cities of the nation say they are gay and about 1 percent of men in rural areas identify themselves as gay.

Lesbians, too, cluster in cities, but the tendency is not so pronounced as for gay men. There are several possible reasons for this. Many women with the desire to have sex with other women do not act upon their desires and as a result many cities never reach the critical mass of lesbian women that can produce an independent lesbian community. And even in the larger cities with well-developed lesbian communities, many women do not participate, preferring to live in small groups of close friends and acquaintances. If lesbians are rela-

FIGURE 15:
Percent Identifying Themselves as Homosexual or Bisexual,
by Current Place of Residence

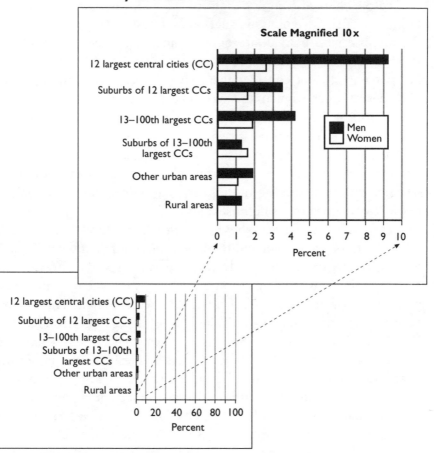

tively monogamous, they may not have constructed institutions that facilitate finding large numbers of sexual partners. Finally, if lesbian couples can successfully live more closeted lives than can gay male couples, that would make the pressure to leave small towns and suburbs less pressing.

Since there are so few women who identify themselves as lesbians, we did two other analyses to determine if the data indicating that they were more likely to live in large cities were real or spurious. First, we asked whether the General Social Survey, another large national sample that was independent of our own, found the same thing. It did.

Then we pooled our data with those of the General Social Survey, to look at the largest possible sample size, and we defined lesbians as women who had had a female partner in the years since they turned eighteen, the broadest possible definition. That made the association clear and significant. We saw that the percentage of lesbians by that measure was as high as 6.2 in the largest cities and that it was as low as 2.8 percent in rural areas.

This grouping of homosexuals in cities makes sense both economically and socially, and it helps explain what happened when a gay journalist, Neil Miller, set off one day to find what he called gay America.

To anyone who has been to New York or San Francisco or who has seen photographs of huge marches in Washington, D.C., and parades in other large cities on Gay Pride Day, Miller's journey might sound bizarre. Why should it take a journey to find gays? To anyone who has heard the chants of Queer Nation, a militant activist group, when they shout, "We're here! We're Queer! Get used to it," Miller's quest might sound superfluous. Why bother to look for gays and lesbians since, as some loudly proclaim, they are everywhere, they are one in ten in the population?

But Miller had a hunch that the newfound gay activism of the 1980s might be hiding what he thought could be another picture of gay and lesbian life. He explained why in his book, *In Search of Gay America: Men and Women in a Time of Change.* "I knew a lot about the gay neighborhoods of the urban centers and the people who lived there but I knew next to nothing about cities like Louisville and Knoxville, about small towns and rural areas," he said. "I wanted to know, twenty years after the Stonewall riots, if gay pride and progress had finally begun to trickle down to the grass roots; if the options for living, working, and being belligerently ourselves that we had won in cities like San Francisco, New York, and Boston extended to the rest of the country, to the towns where so many of us had grown up, to minority communities, to mid-sized cities." After all, Miller noted, "Moving to the suburbs, the ultimate in American conformity, might represent boldness and even vision for a gay man who thought he had no option but to live within the narrow confines of an urban gay ghetto."

It was an intriguing quest. If, as we have shown, we find our sexual partners through our social networks, and if, as we have shown, there are severe restrictions on who can choose whom, how do gays and lesbians living scattered throughout the nation fare in their search for partners? If middle-aged heterosexual women can have difficulty finding a partner, how much harder might it be for a lesbian living in a small town? Or what would it be like to be a middle-aged gay man in an isolated rural area?

Miller was looking for stories of social integration. He was searching for the gay monogamous couple, living in the suburbs and assiduously mowing their lawn on the weekend, having cookouts with the neighbors. He was searching for the lesbian mothers living in a small town, completely open about their sexual orientation, yet fitting in with the other mothers, joining the PTA. He was looking for gay men and lesbians who had become part of the larger social networks of their communities.

He found some successes. There was Gerald L. Ulrich, the mayor of Bunceton, Missouri, population 418, who was beloved by the townspeople. There were Al Philipi and John Ritter, living openly as gay men and farmers in Olgivie, Minnesota, population 374, and well accepted by their neighbors. But much more often he found a dearth of any sort of social networks.

In Fargo, North Dakota, a medium-size city with a population of more than 66,000, the sole public meeting place for gays and lesbians was a bar called My Place. When Miller visited it, he said, "I found My Place rather dismal; on both a Monday and Tuesday nights, a handful of people were sitting around, the place was dark, the music loud." He found gays and lesbians in small towns who would drive for hours to go to bars or parties in the nearest cities, the only place they could find other gays and lesbians. And he heard some poignant stories of the futile search for partners.

There was Larry, convicted of "crimes against nature" in Tennessee for having oral sex with a man. When Miller visited him, Larry lived with another man, Andy, in a small town in Virginia. "Except for contact with Larry's family, Larry and Andy lived an isolated life," Miller wrote. He explained that the men "don't do much except watch TV (they had a VCR but had gone through all the movies available in town, they said), visited Larry's mother (who had adopted

Andy as one of the family), drove to Bluefield, across the West Virginia line, to visit the minister of Larry's church, or maybe over to Charleston on weekends." Then there was Betsy, a middle-aged lesbian who lived in Rapid City, South Dakota. "Betsy said that there was very little going on for gay women in Rapid," Miller wrote.

So many of these gay men and lesbians faced an overwhelming problem in their small towns and cities: it was impossible for them to establish the sort of social network that facilitates the search for friends and sexual partners. Gays and lesbians clearly are a minority population. Added to this difficulty is the prejudice that so many face when they are public about their sexual orientation, a prejudice so severe that many gays and lesbians do not want their neighbors and colleagues to know they are homosexual. The result, as Miller discovered, is that gays and lesbians who live outside big cities can be isolated and lonely.

As we discussed in a previous chapter, heterosexuals often are introduced to their sexual partners by family members or colleagues at work, a strategy that is rarely an option for many homosexuals. Many gays and lesbians have hesitated even to tell their families that they are homosexuals. They may be more like Jill, a lesbian who lives alone in Selma, Alabama, and who told Miller that she could never tell her mother she was a lesbian. "I see her being dead on the floor, if I ever said to her, 'Guess what, mama, you've raised a queer.'"

If a man is the only gay person in a tiny town in the middle of the country, he will find it hard to meet sexual partners and, if he is open about his sexuality, he is likely to suffer prejudice and discrimination. But if he moves to New York and lives in a large community of gays and lesbians, he will find many more potential partners and will be in an environment where homosexuality is both accepted and perhaps even promoted.

By living in cities with other homosexuals, gays and lesbians also can establish their own social networks to find partners. They will have circles of close friends who can introduce them to prospective partners and who will pass judgment on some partners. In a sense, homosexual communities in large cities have become their own social worlds, allowing the formation of the same weblike networks that flourish in the heterosexual community.

But it is not just that homosexuals tend to move to large cities from the small towns and rural areas where they grew up. In our survey, we asked people where they were living when they were fourteen years old, and, with those data, we discovered that people who were raised in large cities were more likely to be homosexual than people who were raised in suburbs, towns, or the countryside. This relationship also showed up in the General Social Survey, an independent national sample. We can only speculate about why this might be so. It might be that it is easier for a person to be gay or to learn to be gay or to explore a gay lifestyle when growing up in a larger community that has other gays.

Not only do people who identify themselves as gays and lesbians tend to live in urban areas, but they tend to be more highly educated, our study shows. This supports the popular image of the sophisticated, affluent gays that has emerged with the AIDS activist movement. Many of the activist leaders or those who garner the most attention fit this mold perfectly, giving rise to a sort of gay stereotype.

Our study shows that twice as many college-educated men identify themselves as homosexual as men with high-school educations, 3 percent of college-educated men said they were gay as compared to 1.5 percent of men with high-school educations. For women, the trend is even more striking. Women with college educations are eight times more likely to identify themselves as lesbians as are women with a high-school education. Four percent of female college graduates identify themselves as lesbians as compared to less than half a percent of female high-school graduates.

It also is possible that middle-class and college-educated gays and lesbians might be more willing to report to us that they are homosexuals.

Far more women and men experimented with homosexuality than currently identify themselves as lesbians or gays. It seems likely that many try it and then go back to being heterosexuals, neither desiring others of their own gender nor finding the idea of homosexual sex very appealing. Pressure to conform and fear of discrimination may well play a role in these decisions.

At the beginning of this chapter we raised a number of questions that have become salient because of the AIDS epidemic. In terms of the numbers of gay men and lesbians, our figures are closer to the findings of AIDS surveys in the United States as well the surveys of sexuality in England and France than to the Kinsey studies of the 1940s. Because of the limitations of earlier studies, we cannot decide whether behavior has changed or whether the earlier studies were overestimates. Our suspicions are that something of both has happened. If these numbers are correct, however, the absolute numbers of men infected with HIV will be smaller than they would be if 10 percent of the population was gay. While we do not have data on behavior change in our survey it is clear from other research that dramatic changes in sexual practices among gay men have reduced the rates of new infections with HIV.

We have no direct data on the nature-nurture question, however our findings are relevant to how that debate might proceed. If any nature theory is based on a constant proportion of the population being "homosexual," our findings suggest that proportion is very small, and that the status may change for individuals from one age to another. More important, both those who have a nature as well as a nurture point of view will be required to identify more precisely what homosexuality is. Is it attraction, behavior, or identity that these theories predict or is it some combination of the three? And is the combination the same in women and men? These debates have enough politics in them to assure that no single study will settle the matter.

However, what we can conclude is the importance of community size and social networks in forming the structure of opportunities and constraints for homosexual as well as heterosexual desire. One factor is surely size; small numbers of like-minded folks are rarely found scattered across the countryside. Neither poets nor homosexuals (nor Jews, for that matter) are found equally distributed in every town and every suburb; it takes a number of poets to have a poets' society, a number of homosexuals to make a community, and a number of Jews to create a congregation. These forces tend to create communities in urban places. The reason that Miller did not find a gay or lesbian couple on every block is a combination of stigma and structure.

10

SEXUALLY TRANSMITTED DISEASES

T HE diseases spread by sex are numerous and ancient: gonorrhea, syphilis, genital warts, genital herpes, hepatitis B. The list goes on, with many of the diseases dating back to biblical times.

But our understanding of who gets these diseases, how common they are in the population, and who is at risk has been surprisingly scanty. Are they diseases of the poor or is everyone at risk? Can you tell how likely your partner is to have a sexually transmitted disease? Is there any way to recognize the most dangerous potential partners and stay away from them?

We have answers to these questions. One surprise is that the people who are most likely to be infected with sexually transmitted diseases are not the same group as those who are at risk for AIDS — they are a much larger group. We can describe who is at the greatest risk and we can say which groups in the population tend to get which diseases.

The pieces fall together to form a road map showing particular attitudes and practices that converge to make some people very likely to be infected and other attitudes and practices that lead people away from getting one of these diseases. Although we find that large numbers of Americans have had a sexually transmitted disease at least once in their lives, there is nothing random about where the diseases strike.

In this chapter, we will focus on diseases other than AIDS, leaving AIDS to a chapter of its own. That is because, for a variety of reasons, the AIDS epidemic really is different from the epidemic of all other sexually transmitted diseases.

Despite the fact that sexually transmitted diseases are always with us, there have been very few reliable facts about how many people are infected and who these people are. It's an old dilemma that has plagued the medical profession for the past century. We've seen hyperbole and clearly exaggerated estimates of the numbers of people infected and we've seen the very existence of the diseases hushed up, for, unlike infections elsewhere in the body, infections of the reproductive organs have been thought of as dirty, not a subject for polite conversation and certainly not something that should afflict good, moral people. We have seen public health officials actually state that they would hate to see the diseases eradicated because they can be used to scare people away from illicit sex. And we have seen the advent of a cure for the bacterial diseases — antibiotics that could have stamped out gonorrhea and syphilis, if only the nation had used them aggressively. Unfortunately, however, we lost the chance. The diseases are with us, with a vengeance.

The study of sexually transmitted infections has been mired in debates over the guilty and the innocent, the partner who strays, the partner betrayed, the prostitute as the pool of infection. Ever since the end of the nineteenth century, when venereal diseases began to be widely discussed, this is the scenario that has dominated public debate. Most recently, in the 1980s, an epidemic of genital herpes was viewed as the scourge of the sexual revolution. Herpes infections were called "the new scarlet letter," indelible proof, or so it was said, of profligate sex. *Time* magazine, in a 1982 article on herpes, crowed that "The herpes counterrevolution may be ushering a reluctant, grudging chastity back into fashion."

Now herpes has been replaced by HIV/AIDS as the scourge of the sexually profligate and the same morality play of the innocent and the guilty is being played out with a new infection. The viral infections have given the condom a new life and the debate over condom education is repeating the standard refrain over the morality of sex rather than the prevention of infection.

But the sexually transmitted viral infections are just a few of the large list of infections that public health officials report as being widespread. Since the viral infections cannot be cured and the bacterial infections are now developing antibiotic-resistant strains, there is considerable trouble on the horizon.

Our data are the first from a representative national survey to ascertain how many Americans have had a sexually transmitted disease. We expect that they are an underestimate because not all of our respondents who had a venereal disease would know it. But by tallying the number who told us they had been diagnosed, we could find a minimum estimate of how many people had had such a disease.

On the advice, and at the request, of the Centers for Disease Control and Prevention, we focused on nine diseases: gonorrhea, syphilis, genital herpes, chlamydia, genital warts, hepatitis, AIDS, and, for men, nongonococal urethritis and, for women, pelvic inflammatory disease. Five of these diseases — gonorrhea, syphilis, chlamydia, nongonococal urethritis, and pelvic inflammatory disease — are caused by bacteria and can usually be cured with antibiotics in their early stages; the others are caused by viruses and cannot be cured, although sometimes the symptoms can be treated.

We asked respondents in our survey if they had ever been diagnosed by a doctor with any of the sexually transmitted diseases on our list, questioning them about how many times they had had these diseases and whether they had been infected in the past year. For a variety of reasons, which we will discuss, we think our respondents generally answered honestly.

The first surprise was that a large number of Americans — one in six — said they have had a sexually transmitted disease. And a significant percentage said they had had one of the diseases in the past year — about 1.5 percent. One percent said they had a bacterial venereal disease in the past year, and half a percent said they had a viral disease. To put the numbers in perspective, nearly as many women said they had a venereal disease in the last year as said they had been pregnant in the last year.

Panel A of Figure 16 (on page 188) shows the proportions of Americans who ever were diagnosed with one of the venereal diseases we questioned them about. Men, for example, were most likely to have had gonorrhea — about nine out of a hundred had been told they had it at some time in their life. Women may have been less aware of gonorrhea infections because the tiny round bacteria that cause the disease do not always elicit symptoms in women. Instead, they can silently infect and scar a woman's fallopian tubes, leaving her infertile yet unaware that she had had an infection.

Women, however, were more likely than men to have had at least one sexually transmitted disease at some time in their lives. They were twice as likely as men to have had genital warts, more than twice as likely to have had a chlamydia infection, and three times as likely to have been infected with genital herpes. Overall, 18 percent of women and 16 percent of men have ever had one of the nine sexually transmitted diseases covered in our survey.

Panel B of Figure 16 shows the proportions of Americans who said they were diagnosed with a sexually transmitted disease in the past twelve months. This panel shows that the most common diseases of today differ from the most common diseases of years past. Chlamydia and genital warts have leaped to the number one and number two positions, pushing out gonorrhea.

Panel B also shows that the person with any sexually transmitted disease in the past year is far more likely to be a woman than a man. Nearly twice as many women as men got a chlamydia infection in the past year. They were more than four times more likely than men to have gotten gonorrhea. So few men were newly diagnosed with genital herpes in the past year that their rate does not even show up on the graph. But nearly three women in a hundred got this viral infection.

We do not interpret these findings as evidence that women are promiscuous and men are not. Instead, they reflect the medical finding that it is at least twice as easy for a man to infect a woman with virtually any sexually transmitted disease, including AIDS, than it is for a woman to infect a man.

The results are all the more revelatory because the nation has had so little information on how many Americans are infected with a sexually transmitted disease and who those people are. It is a situation

FIGURE 16:
Lifetime and Annual Rates of Sexually Transmitted Infections

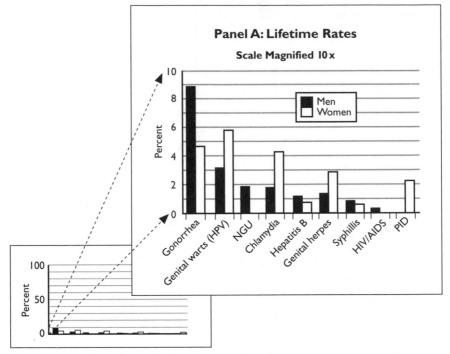

Panel A: Lifetime Rates
Scale Magnified 10x

(Men, Women)

Categories: Gonorrhea, Genital warts (HPV), NGU, Chlamydia, Hepatitis B, Genital herpes, Syphillis, HIV/AIDS, PID

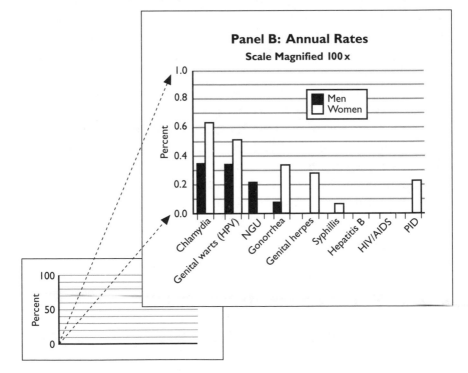

Panel B: Annual Rates
Scale Magnified 100x

(Men, Women)

Categories: Chlamydia, Genital warts (HPV), NGU, Gonorrhea, Genital herpes, Syphillis, Hepatitis B, HIV/AIDS, PID

with a long history that is tied up with America's attitudes about sex and reluctance to ask about sexual practices that, even now, has left us with scare stories, but few hard facts.

Because the diseases are spread through sex, they bring to bear all the fears and moral values and revulsion that sex so often elicits. It is a story that precedes AIDS but seems eerily prescient. As the story of attempts to control the spread of sexually transmitted diseases shows, there were no new arguments that arose with AIDS. Disease as a punishment from God, arguments over sex education, the distribution of condoms, contact tracing, mandatory testing, concern for the "innocent victims" — all were part of the battle to control syphilis and gonorrhea. The sexual arguments seem stuck in a groove, perhaps because we have had no new ways of thinking about sexual behavior.

In his book *No Magic Bullet: A Social History of Venereal Diseases in the United States Since 1880,* Harvard historian Allan M. Brandt explained the problem: "Since the late nineteenth century, venereal disease has been used as a symbol for a society characterized by a corrupt sexuality. Venereal disease has typically been used as a symbol of pollution and contamination, and cited as a sign of deep-seated sexual disorder, a liberalization of what was perceived to be a decaying social order. Venereal disease makes clear the persistent association of disease with dirt and uncleanness as well, revealing pervasive cultural attitudes and values. We have known since the late nineteenth century that venereal diseases are caused by micro-organisms, yet the persistent association of dirt and disease is remarkable."*

Because these diseases were thought to be a sort of punishment for moral looseness, and a threat to people to be faithful to their partners, some public health officials had decidedly mixed feelings when, at last, in 1943, penicillin was discovered and the bacterial diseases could be cured. Syphilis and gonorrhea seemed under control at last. Critics of the social order worried that without the fear of venereal diseases, people would fall into licentious behavior patterns.

William Snow, a leader of the nation's campaign against venereal diseases, wrote, "It is a reasonable question, whether by eliminating disease, without commensurate attention to the development of hu-

---

* (Oxford: Oxford University Press, 1987).

man idealism, self-control, and responsibility in the sexual life, we are not bringing mankind to its fall instead of fulfillment." Dr. John Stokes, a leading venereal disease expert, said that he feared that antibiotics might "inaugurate a world of accepted, universalized, safeguarded promiscuity." Philip Mather of the American Social Hygiene Association commented that "When you get into venereal diseases you get into sex, and when you get into sex you get into the most fundamental thing in the human race. We can't *cure* it." As Brandt wryly notes, "In this turn of phrase, Mather made sexuality itself into a disease."

But, of course, venereal diseases did not disappear from the land, and, in fact, by the 1960s, their rates were on the rise again. Doctors and public health officials began blaming what they called the three "p's": permissiveness, promiscuity, and the Pill. Brandt says, however, that a more important reason is that federal funds for diagnosing and treating the diseases were severely cut, high-risk populations, such as homosexuals, were not the focus of attention, condom sales often were prohibited by law, and the nation fell back on moral posturing.

In the decades following the 1960s medical scientists began recognizing more and more sexually transmitted diseases so that the roster grew to at least twenty, including genital herpes, chlamydia, human papilloma virus, which causes genital warts, hepatitis B, and, of course, AIDS. Now, we have the specter of a host of venereal diseases and an unending stream of magazine and newspaper articles warning us of their dangers. We also have a moral strain running through these scary reports: that sexually transmitted diseases are a symptom of licentiousness and that the real problem is promiscuity.

But what did we really know about the extent of the problem? Recent studies provided vastly different estimates of the number of people who become infected. For example, one well-respected non-profit organization, the Alan Guttmacher Institute, estimates that there are 200,000 to 500,000 new cases of genital herpes each year. On the other hand, Joseph D. Lossick, an epidemiologist at the Centers for Disease Control and Prevention, estimated that there are 150,000 to 200,000 new infections annually. The Guttmacher Institute estimates that a million Americans become infected with gonorrhea each year. Lossick and others suggest the number may be somewhat lower. Yet Lossick, a leading scientist at the nation's disease tracking center, is by no means trying to play down the problem. He writes that sexually transmitted diseases "have been and are currently at epidemic levels." *

The wildly varying estimates of the number of Americans who are infected with sexually transmitted diseases reflect the enormous deficiencies in the way data have been collected. The public health dilemma is that if we do not know how common the diseases are or who gets them, we cannot decide who is at risk or even what constitutes risky behavior. It is perfectly plausible, for example, that the diseases smolder in poor neighborhoods, among minority communities. It is also possible that they occur throughout the population, without regard to race or income or geographic location. Yet there has never been a systematic national study that could determine the epidemiology of these diseases.

The Centers for Disease Control and Prevention asks doctors to report sexually transmitted diseases, but few private doctors do. Public clinics report them, but as cases, not as patients. That means that if a man comes in one day with gonorrhea, is cured, and comes back the next month with a new case, the clinic reports his reinfection as another case. If he and his partner ping-pong the disease back and forth to each other, their infections will be reported by the public clinic as a sequence of separate cases, as though they involved different individuals. So if you try to guess how many people are infected, you will overestimate if you look at figures from clinics and grossly underestimate if you look at figures from private doctors.

Each sexually transmitted disease presents its own problem to epidemiologists who are trying to discern how many people are infected, and who these people are. Herpes is different from chlamydia, which in turn is different from gonorrhea, creating a veritable Gordian knot of an overall problem.

With herpes, there is no good way to estimate the number of new cases because the viral infection is not a reportable disease, meaning

---

* "Epidemiology of Sexually Transmitted Diseases: A Clinical Syndrome Approach," in Vincent A. Spagna and Richard B. Prior, eds., *Sexually Transmitted Diseases: A Clinical Syndrome Approach* (New York: Dekker, 1985).

that there is no requirement that doctors report cases to the Centers for Disease Control and Prevention and there is no national survey of how many people are infected. In addition, herpes infections tend to recur, because the virus can become dormant but usually erupts again and again over the years. This means that a certain proportion of the cases of herpes are actually cases that were diagnosed previously, in the same people.

Chlamydia infections, too, are not reportable, making it hard to know how many people are infected. Chlamydia estimates also are beset with another problem — the disease can be difficult to diagnose. Definitive laboratory tests for the bacteria are expensive and, often, unavailable in clinics.

Even a disease like gonorrhea, which is reportable, can elude epidemiologists when they try to determine its incidence. About 75 percent of the reported gonorrhea cases are from public health facilities, such as venereal disease clinics, which does not tell us how many people are diagnosed and treated by private doctors.

For all these reasons, the national statistics on the prevalence of sexually transmitted diseases have been sorely deficient. Yet, even so, it was surprising to learn that at least one American out of six has been infected.

Knowing how many people were infected, however, addresses only one question. Another is the social characteristics of these people who have had sexually transmitted diseases. And there, we could draw on answers to other questions, elsewhere in our survey. How many sex partners did the respondents with sexually transmitted diseases have? What were their attitudes about sex? Did they believe sex was a special expression of love between two people or was it also a recreation between consenting adults? Did they drink heavily? Did they have sex education in school? We put the data together to yield a risk profile of people who were more likely to get a venereal disease, and those who were comparatively safe.

The people who are most likely to be infected share one key characteristic: They have many sex partners. Individuals with many partners, especially those rarely using condoms, have as much as a tenfold greater chance of becoming infected than do those with few or only one partner. That risk is also correlated with other behaviors and at-

FIGURE 17:
Lifetime Rates of Sexually Transmitted Infections,
by Number of Partners and Gender

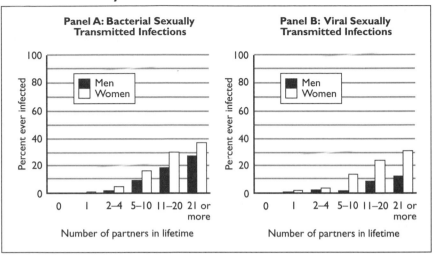

Note: Bacterial STIs include gonorrhea, chlamydia, syphilis, NGU, and PID.

Note: Viral STIs include genital warts, genital herpes, hepatitis B, and HIV/AIDS.

titudes that go along with having many sexual partners. It matters little if you are black, white, Hispanic, Asian, or Native American. It matters not at all if you had sex education in high school. It does not matter if you are rich or poor. It does not matter if you have a college degree or never finished high school. The overriding variable, the characteristic of risky behavior, is having unprotected sex with many partners.

Panel A of Figure 17 shows that if a man had two to four sexual partners in his lifetime, his chances of ever having a sexually transmitted bacterial disease are about 3 percent. As the number of partners he had increases, his risk grows until, if he had more than twenty partners, his risk is about 28 percent, a tenfold increase. The same pattern holds for women. A woman who had two to four sexual partners in her lifetime has a 5 percent chance of ever being infected with a bacterial sexually transmitted disease. If she had more than twenty partners in her lifetime, her chances of being infected soar to more than 35 percent.

The other panel of Figure 17 shows that men and women with multiple sexual partners also run comparably high risks of getting viral diseases, which, unlike bacterial ones, are incurable. With viruses, the pattern by number of sex partners is just as striking. A woman with two to four partners over her lifetime has a 4 percent chance of having a viral sexually transmitted disease. If she had more than twenty partners, her chance would be about 32 percent.

We also looked at the relationship between the number of sex partners over the past twelve months and whether the respondents said they had ever been told by a doctor that they had a sexually transmitted disease in the same time period. Just as Figure 17 shows a close relationship between the number of sex partners over a lifetime and the incidence of sexually transmitted diseases over a lifetime, so too did this relationship exist over the past twelve months.

Of those who had one sex partner in the past twelve months, 1 percent had a sexually transmitted disease and that included the recurring viral diseases, like herpes; of those who had two to four sexual partners, 4.5 percent had a sexually transmitted disease and of those who had five or more partners, 5.9 percent of them had a sexually transmitted disease within the past year. Those with more partners had more disease, over the past year and over a lifetime.

Some diseases were concentrated in particular groups of Americans. Blacks were about twice as likely as whites and Hispanics to have had gonorrhea, but less likely to have had viral diseases, particularly genital warts. One possible explanation for the lower rate of viral infections lies in the type of medical care many black Americans receive. They are more likely to be diagnosed at venereal disease clinics, which have funds to diagnose gonorrhea but do not always have money to diagnose other diseases, like genital warts. Another explanation is that there may be the lower prevalence of viral infections in the black community and, since blacks rarely have sex with people of other races or ethnicities, the viral disease rate would remain low.

The gonorrhea rates are more of a puzzle. They too might reflect the very restricted partner choices that most Americans have. An epidemic of gonorrhea could fester in black communities and not spread to other racial or ethnic groups.

Who, then, are these people who have many partners? And who

are their sexual partners? By looking at our respondents' replies to a variety of questions about their sexual behavior and partner choice, we can piece together a profile of typical people with multiple partners. We cannot analyze homosexuals separately, however, because there were too few of them. But gay men are at risk of sexually transmitted diseases for the same reasons that heterosexuals are at risk and our findings apply equally to them. Lesbians may be at risk because they have oral-to-genital contact, which also can spread infections.

We asked, for example, whether people who have many partners tend to go through a sequence of monogamous relationships or whether they are more likely to have several sexual relationships at once, none of them monogamous. The data show that the more partners a person has had, the more likely he or she is to have had non-monogamous relationships. We also found that the partners of the person with many sexual relationships are, in turn, engaged in non-monogamous relationships. This means that a man who had several partners in a year is likely to be having sex with people who also have several partners. The partners this man chooses have a greater chance than average of having a venereal disease simply because they too had multiple partners.

People have a pretty good idea of whether their partner is faithful to them. People who have only one partner want their partner to be monogamous as well and people who have several partners are much less likely to expect their partners to be faithful to them.

For example, of men and women who had only one partner in the past year, 98 percent said that to the best of their knowledge their partner was faithful to them, and the same percent said they expected their partner to be faithful. Among the respondents who had, say, three partners in the past year, however, only 78 percent reported that they thought their primary partner was faithful to them, and only 87 percent of them said they expected their primary partner to be faithful. So those who had more partners themselves expected their primary partner also to have more partners. And secondary partners are even less faithful, as one might anticipate. These secondary partners are more likely to be less faithful, to be expected to be less faithful, and to have had more partners during the past year.

The more partners people had, the more likely they were to have sex with people whom they did not know well. For example, when we asked people who had two partners in the past year whether they had known either of those partners for less than two days before having sex, one out of six said yes. But that figure jumped to one out of three people with three or more partners in the past year. About a quarter of people with two partners in the past year said they had had a one-night stand during that time — sex with someone they just met and never had sex with again. But nearly two-thirds of people with three or more partners in the past year had had a one-night stand.

The respondents with the most partners also tended to engage in risky behaviors — unprotected sex.

Figure 18 shows that although people were more likely to use condoms when they had more partners, nearly half of our high-risk respondents said they never use condoms during vaginal intercourse, with their primary or secondary partners. These people tended to be more careful with their primary partner than those who had fewer partners, perhaps wanting to protect a spouse or lover from infection. But the low frequency of their condom use suggests that they still expose themselves and their partners to infection. People with several partners are much more likely to always use condoms with their secondary partners than with their primary partner. This suggests that they perhaps seek more protection when they perceive greater risk.

We also found that people with the most partners were the respondents who were most likely to have paid for sex. About three out of every hundred people who had at least three partners in the past year said they had paid someone for sex. Essentially no one who had fewer than three partners in a year paid for sex. Those with the most partners were also more likely to have ever had group sex and anal intercourse.

The people with the most partners also were more likely to have said they were "strongly affected" by drugs or alcohol the last time they had sex, a practice that could make them more likely to have sex with someone they did not know well and less likely to use a condom.

The picture that emerges is highly consistent. The more partners an individual has, the more likely he or she is to have sex with people who themselves have many partners, the more likely he or she is to have sex with virtual strangers, the more likely he or she is to have been under the influence of drugs or alcohol during some sexual encounters, and while it is more likely that a condom was used, the rate of increased use of a condom does not seem great enough to offset the higher risks of infection.

In a way, the findings are entirely predictable. If you are looking for people who get sexually transmitted diseases, it would be expected that they would have many partners and that they would place less importance on monogamy than people who do not get these diseases. But what is remarkable is the consistency of the data. The respondents were asked questions at various times during the hour-and-a-half interview about sexual behavior and the numbers of partners they had and their attitudes about sex and whether they had ever had a sexually transmitted disease. The fact that the replies fit together to form such a coherent picture indicates to us that we really are seeing an image of the sort of behavior that puts people at risk. It shows that sexually transmitted diseases are not confined to the poor and destitute, they have nothing to do with dirt or ignorance. In fact, the at-risk person can be found on any college campus or anywhere else; it is only a matter of the number of partners and the associated behavior.

We find, however, that when we turn our attention to AIDS, the most frightening sexually transmitted disease of all, a very different picture emerges.

FIGURE 18:
Frequency of Condom Use in Past Twelve Months with Primary and Secondary Sex Partners

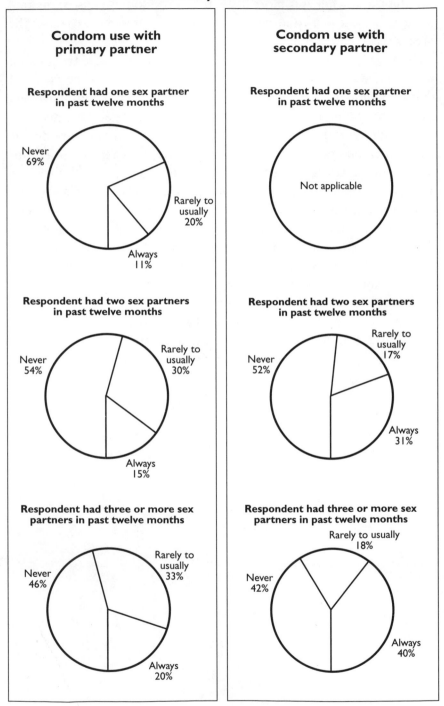

Condom use with primary partner

Respondent had one sex partner in past twelve months

Never 69%
Rarely to usually 20%
Always 11%

Respondent had two sex partners in past twelve months

Never 54%
Rarely to usually 30%
Always 15%

Respondent had three or more sex partners in past twelve months

Never 46%
Rarely to usually 33%
Always 20%

Condom use with secondary partner

Respondent had one sex partner in past twelve months

Not applicable

Respondent had two sex partners in past twelve months

Never 52%
Rarely to usually 17%
Always 31%

Respondent had three or more sex partners in past twelve months

Rarely to usually 18%
Never 42%
Always 40%

11

AIDS

As the nation edges into the second decade of the age of AIDS, the devastation the disease has wrought seems more baffling and troubling than ever. AIDS has cut a swath through America, and no one has been able to stop it. Scientists and politicians have issued deeply disturbing predictions about where the epidemic is headed, and the nation sometimes seems powerless against the virus's expected relentless spread.

And through it all, the few hard facts that accumulated were mixed with much speculation.

We cannot presume to provide definitive answers to the most pressing questions about AIDS, but we can provide a perspective, one that is gleaned from our understanding of how people choose their partners, how many partners people have, and how easily HIV is spread through sexual intercourse. From everything that our respondents told us about sex in America, we can construct a picture of where the AIDS epidemic is now and where it is going. We can give realistic estimates of who is at greatest risk of being infected with HIV, and why. We also can speak of who is at lower risk. Our image of the epidemic is at odds with many public pronouncements, but it is consistent with what many knowledgeable experts say to each other and it is consistent with national data on HIV infections.

Speculation about the directions the epidemic would take began in its early years, soon after the new disease that we now call AIDS was recognized. At the time, it was uncertain how large the epidemic might become and who was vulnerable to infection. It quickly became clear that the primary groups infected were men who had sex with men; intravenous drug users, their partners, and their children; and hemophiliacs and others who had received contaminated blood products. With proper handling of the blood supply, this final group has only a tiny risk. The pressing questions began to center on the other groups.

As the epidemic evolved, some scientists, public officials, and AIDS activists said that it was spreading in the general population or that it was inexorably moving to particular groups thought to be at risk, like high school or college students. Others countered these claims, pointing out that most of the young people who were infected with HIV were themselves from the same groups that were predominantly infected in the early phase of the epidemic — men who had sex with men and intravenous drug users and their sexual partners.

The limited consensus on the questions of who was at what level of risk meant that many individuals were unable to estimate their own risk. It also meant that national policy could not be satisfactorily determined. What is the HIV risk for a single woman in a city with few AIDS cases, like Des Moines, Iowa, if she has unprotected sex with a man she is dating? Is this the same as or different from the risk to a man who has casual unprotected sex with a woman he meets at a bar in a city like New York, where the virus has long been prevalent? Will the AIDS virus continue to spread among gay men and intravenous drug users or will it slowly decline in prevalence as more people protect themselves against infection?

The questions are layered with political implications. If AIDS remains a disease primarily of gay men and of intravenous drug users, who tend to be black or Hispanic and often desperately poor, will America care about AIDS? Do we need to think that we or our children are personally at risk in order to combat the epidemic?

On the other hand, if AIDS is a disease that is rapidly spreading to heterosexual, middle-class communities, what can be done to protect people who still think of it as a disease of gay men and drug addicts?

One answer is espoused by the National Commission on AIDS and by many advocacy groups for people with AIDS. These groups say that everyone is at risk. AIDS is a disease that does not discriminate, they say.

Mary Fisher, a former commission member, uses her own situation as an example of how anyone can get AIDS. Fisher is HIV positive. A wealthy woman who seems the most unlikely person to be infected with HIV, she was infected, she says, by her former husband, who was an intravenous drug user. And now she travels around the country speaking about the threat that the epidemic is to us all.

Fisher says that in her travels, she often meets people who tell her that they are not at risk of being infected. But, Fisher says, "we're all at risk. This is a heterosexually transmitted disease. We're all at risk and we need to protect ourselves."

"We've worked so hard to make AIDS everyone's disease," says David Rogers, vice chairman of the National Commission on AIDS. Another national committee, however, a blue-ribbon panel put together by the National Research Council, came to a different conclusion. In its report, *The Social Impact of AIDS in the United States,* it says that AIDS is not spreading into the general population. Instead, the report says, the disease is concentrating in the most marginal groups, the poor and disenfranchised, the blacks and Hispanics who already suffer from what the committee called a synergism of plagues. People at risk for getting AIDS already are a group in which "poverty, poor health and lack of health care, inadequate education, joblessness, hopelessness, and social disintegration converge to ravage personal and social life."* The group adds that, "many geographic areas and strata of the population are virtually untouched by the epidemic and probably never will be; certain confined areas and populations have been devastated and are likely to continue to be." (We note that one of us, John Gagnon, was a member of that National Research Council panel, so their views and our views are not fully independent.)

---

*Albert T. Jonsen and Jeff Stryker, eds., *The Social Impact of AIDS in the United States* (Washington, D.C.: National Academy Press, 1993).

The strategies that will best combat AIDS depend enormously on who is right. Is AIDS "everyone's disease," as David Rogers says, or is it a disease of poor people, mostly blacks and Hispanics in some inner city neighborhoods, along with gay men in some cities? The question, put another way, is: Who is being infected and how easily does the disease spread? To answer those questions, we need to know about social groups in which HIV infections occur and about the likelihood that the virus will be spread from these groups to others that so far have had few HIV infections.

In part, the debate hinges on the question of what an epidemic is. The word is used casually, sometimes to gain attention for a disease, like breast cancer, and in this sense it means simply a disease that afflicts large numbers of people. But scientists define an epidemic as a disease that is spreading rapidly, as opposed to remaining entrenched, never disappearing but not infecting large numbers of new people each year. Each winter, the nation has a flu epidemic — the virus strain of the year rapidly takes hold and engulfs the country, infecting person after person until finally it dies away. On the other hand, there is no epidemic of heart disease. Although heart disease remains a leading cause of death, the number of Americans who have heart disease has actually been declining for decades.

If there is an AIDS epidemic starting to race through the general population, if the epidemic is igniting among heterosexuals who are not drug users or their sexual partners, we can expect to see the number of infected heterosexuals soar, multiplying each year.

We know that AIDS is spread through sexual intercourse, and that it seems to spread more efficiently through anal intercourse than through vaginal intercourse. We know it also is transmitted very efficiently when an infected intravenous drug user shares needles with people who are uninfected.

But we also know something else about HIV, something that makes an epidemic difficult to sustain. Compared to other diseases, including other sexually transmitted diseases, it is very difficult for HIV to spread.

Scientists at the Centers for Disease Control and Prevention have estimated the chances that HIV will be transmitted by vaginal, oral, or anal sex. They had data from men with hemophilia who were infected at the beginning of the epidemic and from men and women who were infected early on through blood transfusions. Many of these people were married or were having sex regularly with a single partner, and so researchers could ask how often an infected person had unprotected sex, on average, before his or her partner was infected.

From these data, the researchers estimated that a man who is infected with HIV has just one chance in five hundred of transmitting the infection to a woman in a single act of unprotected intercourse.* Women are less likely — exactly how much so is uncertain — to transmit HIV to a man. Anal intercourse increases the odds of transmitting HIV, although, again, the exact risk is uncertain. But, on the whole, the chances are not very much more or less than one in five hundred that any single act of sexual intercourse, with an infected man or woman, with vaginal or anal sex, will transmit an HIV infection. Those odds go down to almost zero if the man uses a condom correctly. These estimates have a lot of uncertainty built into them, but the important point, on which there is general agreement, is that HIV is not easily transmitted in a single act of oral, anal, or vaginal intercourse. On the other hand, these odds do accumulate with frequent unprotected sex with an infected partner. After five years of regular unprotected sex with a partner who is infected with HIV, a person has a two out of three chance of becoming infected.

In contrast, other sexually transmitted diseases are easily spread. The chance that a man infected with gonorrhea will transmit it to a woman in a single act of sexual intercourse is one in two. An infected woman has one chance in five of transmitting gonorrhea to a man. Nearly as high odds hold for syphilis.

In addition to knowing that it is hard to transmit HIV, we also know that comparatively few people are infected. In our survey, we asked people whether they had been diagnosed as being infected with HIV. If there were enough people with HIV, in theory, we could have information about who gets AIDS, and how, from our own data. But we immediately faced a problem. Although AIDS is widely feared and

*Norman Hearst and Stephen B. Hulley, "Preventing the Heterosexual Spread of AIDS: Are We Giving Our Patients the Best Advice?" *Journal of the American Medical Association* (April 22/29, 1988).

widely known, only a small percentage of the general population has the disease. For example, of the 12 million new cases of sexually transmitted diseases reported to the Centers for Disease Control and Prevention in 1991, just 50,000 were AIDS cases. That means that less than one half of one percent of new sexually transmitted disease cases were AIDS.

The number of Americans, adults and children, who have ever been diagnosed with AIDS was reported to be around 340,000 by the end of September, 1993. Of these persons, about 205,000 had died. This means that about 135,000 Americans are living with AIDS at the present time.

The 135,000 figure does not totally portray the problem, however. For many years, the proportion of the population diagnosed with AIDS has been described as the tip of the iceberg, with those infected with the virus, HIV, but not yet diagnosed with the disease, AIDS, representing the portion that is underwater. The Centers for Disease Control and Prevention reported in 1989 that somewhere between 800,000 and 1,200,000 Americans had been infected with HIV, an estimate with the midpoint of about a million people. They also estimated that between 40,000 and 80,000 new infections have occurred in each of the years 1990, 1991, 1992, and 1993. Taking the middle of these estimates would mean that 240,000 new infections have occurred since 1989. If the estimate of one million persons infected with the virus (including those who have AIDS) were true, it would mean that one in 250 people in the United States is infected with the virus.

A number of observers have argued that these figures might be too high, but there were very few directly observed data to settle the issue. It was an argument over mathematical modeling, the way the estimates were derived from the numbers of AIDS cases.

A study by the National Center for Health Statistics attempted to find out directly how many Americans are infected with HIV. Researchers interviewing a randomly chosen sample of 7,992 American households for a health and nutrition survey, asked each respondent to supply a blood sample that would be tested for the presence of HIV. Neither the interviewer nor the respondent would know what the test showed, but the tests would provide an estimate of what proportion of Americans living in households are infected.

Reporting in December of 1993 at a medical meeting, the National

Conference on Human Retroviruses and Related Infections, Geraldine McQuillan, an epidemiologist with the National Center for Health Statistics said that, based on these data, anywhere from 300,000 to 1.02 million Americans were infected, but that the most likely number was around 550,000. She estimated that about half were white men and almost all the others were blacks. Women constituted about a quarter of the infected people. McQuillan also suggested that the figures might be an underestimate because the survey might have missed many drug users.

Increasingly, the consensus among scientists is that the widely cited figure of a million Americans infected with HIV may be too high. A better estimate, most scientists think, is between 600,000 and 800,000.

In our survey of 3,159 adults, we would expect to find one person with AIDS and one or two with HIV. In fact, we found five with AIDS or HIV infections, which is certainly within the expected range, especially because we excluded people over age sixty and under eighteen from our survey and AIDS is more concentrated among young adults.

With a sample the size of ours, it is not possible to make any estimate of the number of people who have AIDS or HIV infections. We could have just as easily had ten or none. In addition, there is the problem of denial — even in a questionnaire on sex with interviewers who are not judgmental, there is the possibility that persons with HIV or AIDS might not be willing to report it.

We also inquired whether respondents had ever been tested for AIDS or ever changed their sexual behavior because of risks of AIDS. It is striking that 27 percent of the sample said they had been tested. Those tested tended to be younger, more educated, and living in larger cities. Thirty percent of blacks, 26 percent of whites, and 25 percent of Hispanics said they had been tested. Of those who were currently married, 23 percent had been tested, while 37 percent of those cohabiting had. Of those who were not cohabiting, 30 percent said they had been tested. There was no difference between the poor, the middle income, and the wealthy in the percentages who had been tested.

Perhaps more importantly, those who had been tested were disproportionately those with many sex partners since age eighteen, and more partners within the past twelve months, as seen in Figure 19. Nineteen percent of those with no sex partner in the past year had been tested, 25 percent of those with one partner last year had been

FIGURE 19:
Responses to HIV/AIDS: Percent Ever Tested for HIV/AIDS and Percent Reporting Change in Sexual Behavior in Response to AIDS

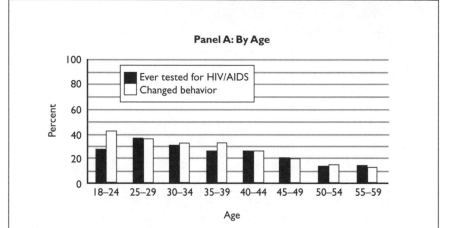

Panel A: By Age

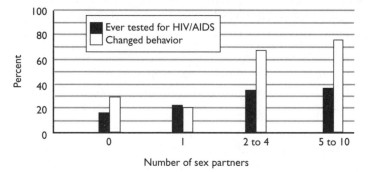

Panel B: By Number of Sex Partners in Past Twelve Months

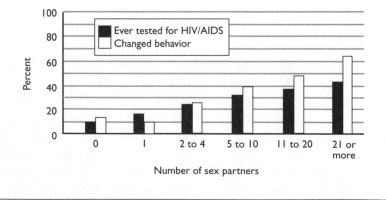

Panel C: By Number of Sex Partners Since Age Eighteen

tested, and more than 35 percent of those with two or more partners in the last year said they had been tested.

When we asked if they had changed their sexual behavior because of AIDS, 30 percent of the sample said they had. They, too, tended to be the younger respondents and those living in large cities. There was no pattern by education or income level but 46 percent of blacks, 37 percent of Hispanics, and 26 percent of whites said they had changed their behavior. While only 12 percent of the married respondents had done so, 40 percent of the cohabiting respondents had and 32 percent of the noncohabiting respondents had changed their behavior.

Again, the stronger patterns were by numbers of partners, again as seen in Figure 19. Of those with zero or one sex partner since age eighteen, only about 10 percent said they had changed their behavior, but as the number of lifetime partners rose, so did the proportion who had changed their behavior. More than 63 percent of people with more than twenty partners over their lifetime said they had changed their behavior. Of those with one partner last year, 20 percent said they changed their behavior; 68 percent of those with two to four partners over the past year did so, and 76 percent of those with five or more partners over the past year changed their behavior because of AIDS.

Clearly, the responses to the two questions about testing for AIDS and changing sexual behavior suggests purposive behavior. Those who responded are those most at risk, and this is why only 10 percent of the married respondents who are monogamous said they changed their behavior. They are not at much risk and may not have needed to change their sexual behavior. Those most at risk have taken steps to find out if they are infected and to change their behavior. Here is yet another instance in which we see choice and strategy in the sexual behavior of adults.

While these data suggest that those at highest risk for HIV transmission, simply based on their numbers of partners, are those who are most likely to have been tested and the most likely to have changed their conduct, this does not give us much purchase on the directions the epidemic is going. It does suggest that at least members of particular risk groups are aware of their risk of infection, and this is a hopeful sign. However, to understand the sexual dimensions of the epidemic we need to rely more on what we have learned from other research on transmission and from what others have learned about sexual conduct in the United States and the sexual connections between various groups.

We believe that the best way to think about the spread of AIDS is as a social behavior, one that can be analyzed like any other behavior. For example, where the virus goes depends in large part on how many Americans have sexual intercourse, when in their lives they have it, how many partners they have, and who those partners are. To understand whether HIV will spread to young gay men, we need to know how many sexual partners gay men have, how old these partners are, whether they practice safe sex, and how many men in the community are infected. To examine the spread of HIV from infected gay men to men who have sex with women and men, we need to know with whom the bisexual men will have sex as well as where they live and what their social networks are like. Is it likely that a married man in Boise, Idaho, where there is little AIDS, will have sex with a male prostitute, become infected with HIV, and then go home and infect his wife? Is it likely that a teenage boy in San Francisco will have sex with an infected gay man, become infected with HIV, then have sex with his girlfriend and transmit HIV to her?

The other piece of the picture is AIDS among intravenous drug users, the second group to be hit hard by the epidemic. In fact, although the number of new HIV infections is much lower than in the early 1980s among gay men, it does not appear to have declined among drug users and their sexual partners. To ask about the spread of AIDS, we need to know about drug and sex contacts between intravenous drug users living in urban ghettos and those living outside the inner cities. How likely is it that HIV infections among drug users will spread to people living outside their neighborhoods or, even, to someone of another race living in the same neighborhood? Do people living in poor neighborhoods routinely have sexual contacts with people living elsewhere? How many sexual partners do drug users have, and who are these partners? How likely is it that drug users will spread HIV infections by sharing needles with people outside their communities? Do middle-class Americans come into poor neighborhoods and share needles with intravenous drug users who live there?

Our survey can answer some of these questions. The answers to others can be inferred from research conducted by a wide range of scientists.

We already have an answer to one of our questions. As we discussed in chapter 9, about 3 percent of adult men define themselves as homosexual, about 2.5 percent said they had sex with another man in the past year and about 5 percent said they had sex with another man since they turned eighteen.

We also found that men who have sex with men tend to live in large cities and to shun small towns and rural areas. Our study shows that as many as 9 percent of the men in the nation's twelve largest cities say they have sex with men, but just 2 percent of men in small cities said they do. Only about 1 percent of men in rural areas said they have sex with men.

These findings have significant implications for understanding the spread of the AIDS virus. Since men who have sex with men tend to live in large cities, it can be hard for an epicenter of a sex-related AIDS epidemic to get started in any but the largest cities, where there are sufficient numbers of gay men and where, in the late 1970s and early 1980s, gay men in some social groups had enormous numbers of sexual partners, ensuring that the hard-to-transmit AIDS virus, once introduced, would take hold.

In the late 1970s and early 1980s, in gay communities in cities like New York and San Francisco, HIV silently made its inroads. It was a time when some gay men in these cities went to bathhouses, having impersonal sex with strangers and exploring their newfound sexual freedom. When the Centers for Disease Control and Prevention began questioning gay men with the new disease in 1982, its investigators found that men who had AIDS had twice as many sexual contacts as men who were uninfected, that they were twice as likely to visit bathhouses, and that their partners were far more likely to have more partners than the partners of uninfected men. Some of the men had had extremely large numbers of sexual partners. Gay men with AIDS interviewed in the early 1980s reported they had on average 1,100 partners in their lifetimes and some had had many more. These numbers may sound implausible, but with anonymous sex in bathhouses and clubs, a man could be the receptive partner for anal sex with a dozen or more partners in a weekend.

In addition, most men with AIDS reported frequent anal intercourse, which scientists have since discovered is the easiest way to transmit the AIDS virus sexually. Even if HIV is difficult to transmit in a single act of anal intercourse, such large numbers of partners guarantee exposure and the frequent anal intercourse makes the virus's transmission likely. In addition, many of these highly sexually active men traveled between large cities such as Los Angeles, New York, and San Francisco, visiting bathhouses and sex clubs when they were away from home. In this way, HIV spread to other large gay communities.

But not all gay men were part of this social scene. Those who became infected tended to be those who participated in the life of sexual bathhouses and casual sex. Other gay men living quietly and having sex with only one or a few partners escaped infection. Still others who lived outside the largest gay communities escaped infection, even though they had sex with many partners. For example, the National Research Council report told of fifty-seven black men living in Harlem and having sex with one another. None was infected with HIV although they did not use condoms. The reason was that they had no sexual partners outside their group. So even though AIDS has devastated the gay community in the largest cities, not all gay men and not all gay communities were affected. Whether a man was at risk depended in large part on his social network.

What about intravenous drug users? In the 1980s, as a great fear of drug use swept the nation, as cocaine, then crack, were introduced, the press wrote article after article about the growing drug menace. It began to seem as if drugs, even including injected drugs like heroin, were threatening everyone. No longer were drugs a problem of the poor, we were told. Now they were a problem for everyone. We saw newspaper and television reports of the middle-class or professional drug addicts. The *New York Times* put a story on page one about an anonymous professional man who managed to keep a job while remaining a secret heroin addict.

Researchers who study intravenous drug use offer an alternative view. Since the end of World War II, intravenous drug use, largely heroin, was concentrated among poor people in the inner cities, mostly blacks and Hispanics. Such people, most of whom were men, were soon caught up in cycles of addiction that usually culminated in a loss of work, unemployment, the continual search for drugs, arrest, conviction, imprisonment, and then a return to the cycle of addiction. Intravenous drug users often married and had children, but frequently separated from their families as a result of their drug use. They were isolated in the city, often coming into contact with non-drug users only when they were engaged in theft or when they were arrested and in contact with the police and other law enforcement personnel.

Given the relative social isolation of these populations, what role could they play in spreading the epidemic to other social groups?

John Gagnon and Shirley Lindenbaum, an anthropologist at the City University of New York, who studied the AIDS epidemic in New York City as members of the National Research Council's Committee on AIDS Research, think the role of these drug users in spreading AIDS outside their social group is small. In the report "The Social Impact of AIDS in the United States," they wrote that "intravenous drug users appear to be a relatively immobile population that depends on a strong network of neighborhood residential and social ties to maintain contacts with 'running buddies' and drug suppliers. This population's sexual partners are also relatively immobile and often they and their children share common households with the drug users."

If drug users stay in small areas of cities, sharing needles with each other, the situation is ripe for HIV to take hold but to be walled in by the neighborhood barriers. All that is needed is for one member of the group to be infected and soon most of the others will be. By sharing needles on a daily basis with infected people, a drug user has a high probability of becoming infected. In many inner-city neighborhoods of cities like New York, 50 to 75 percent of heroin users are infected with HIV. The virus is likely to spread to the sexual partners of the drug users because even though it is hard to transmit in a single act of sexual intercourse, transmission becomes increasingly likely if a couple repeatedly have unprotected sex.

For example, a woman who is the regular sexual partner of an infected drug user who does not use a condom may have about one chance in five hundred of being infected if she has sex with him just one time. But if she has sex with him ten times, her risk rises to one in fifty. If she has sex with him a hundred times, the likelihood that she will be infected rises to a little more than one in six. And if she is infected, her newborn children have about a 20 percent chance of being infected by her, during pregnancy.

On the other hand, if HIV does not enter a drug-using network, the people will be safe from AIDS even if they share needles.

But if AIDS is to spread to the general population, more is needed than simply large numbers of infected people in big cities where gay men congregate and where intravenous drug users live in the poorest sections of town. Two other conditions must be met. First there would need to be a permanent bridge, a way for the rest of the population to have continuing, frequent, sexual or needle-sharing contact with these groups. And, second, there would need to be frequent sex or needle-sharing among members of the general population to sustain and feed the epidemic.

Our data strongly suggest that neither of these conditions is, or is going to be, met. We are not denying that some people who are neither gay nor drug users nor the inner-city partners of drug users become infected. Of course there will be people like Mary Fisher, infected by her husband who, she says, injected drugs and shared needles. Of course there will be people like a bisexual man living on Long Island who secretly traveled to New York City and had sex with men. He became infected with HIV and infected his wife. But cases like these do not constitute evidence of a burgeoning epidemic among the non-drug-using heterosexuals. In the case of Mary Fisher and in the case of the wife of the Long Island man, the transmission chain has come to a screeching halt. The virus broke out of its usual groups but was transmitted no farther. The only way these people could have been a bridge to the general heterosexual population was if each had transmitted HIV to one or more others, who in turn had spread it to others and so on. That did not happen.

All of our data on sexual networks and sexual behavior argue strongly that these sporadic aborted breakouts of the AIDS virus into the general population are the exception, not the rule, in the AIDS epidemic.

The first necessary condition for the virus to spread is regular and frequent sexual contacts between infected and uninfected groups. The largest infected group is gay men. To spread the virus to the heterosexual population, the gay men would either have to have frequent sex with bisexual men, who would then have to have frequent sex with many women, or the gay men would themselves have to have frequent sex with many female partners. But then those women who are infected would have to have frequent sex with many other men to take the epidemic one more step into the general population.

None of our data suggest the existence of a large number of such men and none of our data suggest that the many infected women have sufficient numbers of male partners to spread the epidemic further in the United States.

With intravenous drug users, the likelihood of infecting sexual partners is clearly restricted to women or men who are like them socially. This is what our data show, that people have sex with people who are like them.

Men and women who are intravenous drug users are most likely to infect those who are closest to them, since heterosexual transmission usually requires repeated exposure. Since their partners have sexual partners who share their social characteristics, the infection will spread, if it does, to people who are like the drug users. Even in this case the epidemic will spread differentially, with women more likely to get infected from men than men from women. Since most black and Hispanic women have few partners, they are unlikely to spread the epidemic much further even in their own communities and even more rarely to those who are socially unlike them.

It is unlikely that a woman from the non-drug-using middle class will meet and have sex with an inner-city drug user who has shared needles with his neighborhood friends who are HIV positive. Few men in the general population inject drugs, so it is also unlikely that a woman would meet and have sex with a middle-class drug-using man who shared needles with a person with HIV. It can happen, but it is very unusual. Far fewer women than men inject drugs, and it is twice as difficult for a man to contract HIV from sex with a woman as it is for a woman to get an HIV infection from sex with a man. So if the genders are reversed in these scenarios, the transmissions become even more unlikely.

Another possibility is that men who visit prostitutes will become infected and will bring the infection back to their heterosexual communities. But we found that very few men — just six in a thousand — visit prostitutes each year. And the Centers for Disease Control and

Prevention estimate that the chance that a single act of sexual intercourse with a prostitute will result in an HIV infection is about 1 in 10,000 if the man does not use an condom and 1 in 100,000 if he does.

Even when these rare transmissions from members of high-risk groups to members of low-risk groups occur, it is all but inconceivable that infected members of middle-class Americans will start an epidemic going in the general population. For that to occur, the second condition must be met — frequent sex with multiple partners or sharing of needles among large numbers of middle-class Americans.

Our study has shown quite clearly that the vast majority of Americans have very few sexual partners, making it difficult for the AIDS virus to take hold. A disease, like gonorrhea, that is easily transmitted by only a few sexual encounters is likely to break out of groups where it began. Even gonorrhea, however, is contained among the minority of Americans who have multiple sexual partners in a limited period of time and whose partners also have multiple partners. But it is much harder to transmit AIDS than gonorrhea, requiring, on average, many more contacts between infected and uninfected people. Yet our data indicate that most of the population has sex relatively infrequently, has very few sexual partners, and has one partner or none for most of their adult life. We found, as we reported in chapter 5, that 83 percent of adult Americans either had no sexual partner or had just one in the past year and were faithful to their partner. It is extremely rare for a heterosexual who is not a prostitute to have 1,100 lifetime sex partners, as the average gay men infected with HIV had in the beginning of the epidemic. Even if the epidemic requires a far more modest number of sexual partners, one hundred, say, or even fifty per person on average, HIV will not make inroads in heterosexual America. The second of the necessary conditions for an HIV epidemic to take hold — multiple partners who themselves have multiple partners — is not fulfilled.

To see this, we have drawn a sexual network, showing the contacts between a group of people in the past year. Figure 20 is made up of data from our survey and it shows how very few sexual contacts people have.

The figure is drawn to represent our data. Every set of connected dots represents individuals who are having sex together. We find that 73 percent of Americans have just one sex partner, which is why most of the network consists of isolated pairs of dots. Eleven percent have no partner, which is represented by the single dots. The rest have more than one partner and these people with more than one partner tend to have partners with more than one partner.

A typical social network, in contrast, would have many lines connecting each person to several others, who would, in turn, be connected to several others as well. In that densely connected web of connections, transmission from one person to another is easy and is likely to happen, whether the item being spread is a rumor, an idea, a point of view about a political candidate, or an infection spread through coughing or sneezing, for example. But transmitting HIV infections requires not the connections of social proximity or a conversation, but rather the connection of sexual intercourse or sharing an unsterile needle, and those networks are not dense.

We conclude that sexual contacts between infected and uninfected groups are too infrequent, and the few people who do become infected in this way have too few partners and their partners have too few partners to start an epidemic. With a virus that is as difficult to

FIGURE 20:
An Illustrative Sexual Network

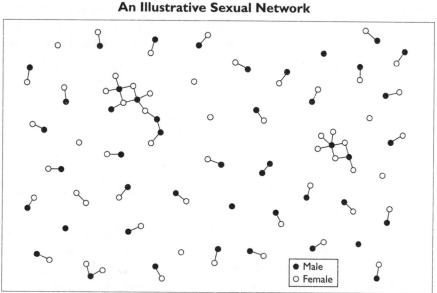

Each dot represents a person, and each line represents a sexual relationship during the past year.

transmit as HIV, this means that the disease is hard-pressed to spread beyond the groups that are now afflicted.

We believe, therefore, that AIDS is, and is likely to remain, confined to exactly the risk groups where it began: gay men and intravenous drug users and their sexual partners. We are convinced that there is not and very unlikely ever will be a heterosexual AIDS epidemic in this country.

And, in fact, that is what has happened so far. Despite a decade of dire warnings that everyone is at risk, the epidemic has not spread but instead has stayed exactly where it began. Yet, as our data show, very few people have changed their behavior to protect themselves from HIV infections. As the National Research Council report concluded, AIDS remains highly concentrated among geographically isolated groups of drug users and their sexual partners, on one hand, and gay men, on the other. Even in New York, one of the hardest-hit states, AIDS is concentrated in New York City. About 87 percent of people with AIDS in the state live in New York City. And in New York City, the pattern continues. AIDS is concentrated in six to ten neighborhoods. These are neighborhoods where gay men live and the very different neighborhoods where intravenous drug users live.

What about the statement, made by AIDS activists and even by President Bill Clinton, that HIV has spread so far and so fast that now every American knows someone with AIDS? That, it turns out, is not true, even though each American knows an enormous number of people. Social network analysts have calculated that each of us knows anywhere from 2,000 to 6,000 other Americans, a figure that may sound ludicrously high but that is not so unreasonable when you think of all the people you have known in your life. There are your neighbors when you were a child, your schoolteachers and classmates, the people you met in your summer job, salespeople in your neighborhood stores, your family and your extended family. The numbers mount quickly. Yet, still, when we asked respondents if they knew someone with AIDS, only 25 percent said they did.

As might be expected, since, as we have shown, gay men tend to be more educated and educated people tend to be part of the same social networks, the more education people had, the more likely they were to know someone with AIDS. People in our survey with college educations were three and a half times more likely than those with high-school educations to know someone with AIDS.

Yet while the epidemic is not expanding, it is changing. It is starting to concentrate even more in poor neighborhoods and less among gay men. This is because, with the realization of the consequences of frequent, unprotected sex, many gay men have changed their behavior. The old days of risky sex are gone. The bathhouses are not nearly as popular as they once were, and although HIV infections continue to spread in some gay neighborhoods, most cities report that the number of new HIV infections among gay men has flattened out or decreased. The epidemic seems to be on the wane. At the same time, however, AIDS is becoming endemic in poor neighborhoods, among drug users and their sexual partners, where behavior has changed little and where society has averted its eyes from the multiple problems of these populations.

The National Research Council report said: "A constant theme of this report and of the AIDS literature is the stigma, discrimination, and inequalities of the AIDS epidemic. At its outset, HIV disease settled among socially disvalued groups, and as the epidemic has progressed, AIDS has increasingly been an affliction of people who have little economic, political, or social power." The committee report added that as the trend continues, as HIV infections wane among educated gay men and wax in the poorest inner-city neighborhoods, HIV may become a disease that society feels it can ignore. "If the current pattern of the epidemic holds, U.S. society at large will have been able to wait out the primary impact of the epidemic, even though the crisis period will have stretched out over 15 years. HIV/AIDS will 'disappear,' not because, like smallpox, it has been eliminated, but because those who continue to be affected by it are socially invisible, beyond the sight and attention of the majority population." The committee members pleaded, in the name of compassion and decency, that the nation not allow this to happen. We wholeheartedly concur.

The data showing that HIV infections are not spreading throughout the population and the data strongly implying that HIV is not going to spread have profound implications for our efforts to quell the spread of AIDS in this country. It means, for one, that our public education campaigns focused on the general population, the "everybody is at risk" warnings, are unlikely to be effective. We should not continue to spread money around in a Johnny Appleseed way but instead should focus our efforts on the people who are suffering and dying with this disease and on those who are most at risk of getting it.

It also means that it is unrealistic to expect that a fear of AIDS will prevent adolescents from having sex. If we want to convince them that sex is undesirable at such an early age, we will fail by telling them that sex will kill them. In fact, for all the arguments of just this sort that have been going on for a decade, there is no evidence that teenagers, or young adults, have stopped having sex, but there is some evidence that they are taking more precautions than do older adults.

This does not mean that we think the nation can, or should, ignore AIDS. We think that compassion demands that we fight the disease just as aggressively when it strikes the poorest of the poor as when it strikes the rich and powerful. We also recognize that it can be more difficult to raise research funds for a disease that is not a threat to most Americans. But we strongly believe that it is better to tell the truth than to behave like scaremongers, telling the country that a disaster will soon strike us all, no matter what the data say.

12

FORCED SEX

I F there is a single issue that signals the changed relationship between men and women, it is forced sex. In the past, it was narrowly defined — a violent assault, a rape, usually by a stranger, in which a woman was penetrated sexually. If such an event became a matter for the police and courts, the outcome was often determined by a consideration of the moral character of the individual offender and the individual victim. To argue convincingly that she was raped, a woman had to demonstrate that she was socially and sexually respectable and that she in no way encouraged the offender. This meant that official rape statistics primarily represented rapes by strangers. And a woman who could not demonstrate that she was entirely virtuous need not report the crime.

Over the last two decades, the notion of forced sex has been entirely recast. Its domain has expanded, from a provable act of violent vaginal penetration to unwanted sexual approaches, from attacks by strangers to forced sex by husbands, lovers, and acquaintances, from an aberration to a common result of sexual encounters between men and women. While the days of blaming the woman are not over, it is no longer an unquestioned assumption that women bring forced sex upon themselves.

To see how conflicts arise and persist, consider two statements about sexual codes. The first is from a young working-class man, who is telling about the differences between good girls and bad girls and what is necessary to have sex with them:

"There's girls that, you know, that you have respect for and that you'll romance, you know, you'll take them out and it's like the romance scene, it's not like, you know — and then there's these other girls, you know, you're going to drive over there, you already know what's going to happen, you know, it's just no romance, you know, it's just — wham. You know, three and out."

In contrast, here is a statement of the rules that now govern sexual interactions at Antioch College, as they are explained to young men as part of their orientation:

"Each step along the way you have to ask. . . . If you want to take her blouse off, you have to ask. If you want to touch her breast, you have to ask. If you want to move your hand down to her genitals, you have to ask her. If you want to put your finger inside her, you have to ask."

In the first example, the boy romances a good girl and pushes for as much sex as he can get until she clearly says, "No." The boy assumes that he will have sex with a bad girl and if she says, "No," there is no reason to pay heed. Given her reputation, it would be difficult for this girl to demonstrate that she was forced to have sex.

In the Antioch example, it is assumed that "no" is always a possibility and the appearance of passion or silent assent is not enough to signal that the next step is permissible. Here, power is in the hands of the woman and the man must ask. Such a system, while reducing what appear to be playful and spontaneous sexual interactions, also makes the responsibility for sex more egalitarian. No woman can say under this system that she was "swept away." And no man can say that he misunderstood the signals, mistaking a "no" for a "maybe" or even a "yes."

Are the Antioch rules an exaggerated response to a minor problem of interpretation? Is there a forced-sex crisis or is it a nonissue, whose perceived incidence is inflated beyond all bounds?

What we can offer to this debate are reliable data. As has so often happened with other sexual issues, the nation has been having its acrid disputes about rape and forced sex with limited information on its frequency. Many widely cited studies had all the problems of previous sex surveys that we discussed in chapter 2. They used samples of convenience rather than randomly selected representative groups of Americans. They had abysmal response rates, raising questions of how representative their respondents were. Finally, they asked questions in misleading or confusing ways. For example, the National Crime Survey, a survey by the Bureau of Justice that is frequently cited for sexual assault figures, until recently asked about rape with the question: "Did anyone try to attack you in some other way?"

As a result of the wide variety of definitions of rape and forced sex and of the differing and, sometimes, unreliable methodologies of previous studies, we have estimates of the number of women raped that range from 5 to 25 percent.

We purposely did not use the term *rape* in asking about forced sex, reasoning that there is a fundamental difference between what most people mean when they use the word and what police, prosecutors, and judges will accept in court as legal rape. In addition, the word has strong emotional connotations that may make some women reluctant to apply it to situations they were in, although they may have felt that they were forced to have sex.

Our data reveal that the Antioch rules, much as they were ridiculed by pundits and comics, may have arisen from a valid problem. Although, clearly, sexual interactions between men and women are fraught with ambiguity and potential conflicts, there is something more going on than a few misunderstandings. There seems to be not just a gender gap but a gender chasm in perceptions of when sex was forced.

We find that large numbers of women say they have been forced by men to do something sexually that they did not want to do. But very few men report ever forcing a woman. The differences that men and women bring to the sexual situation and the differences in their experiences of sex sometimes suggest that there are two separate sexual worlds, his and hers.

There is surely some underreporting in these figures, on the part of both women and men. Some women who recognize that they have been forced to have sex may be unwilling to report it and some women who we might believe were forced might not describe the sex that way. Men who have forced women also have an incentive not to report it. But the findings are so stark that they cry out for a national dialogue. How could men and women perceive sex so differently?

We asked about forced sex in the context of a set of questions that made it clear to our respondents that we wanted to know about times when they did something against their will, because they were threatened or because they felt they had no choice. We also asked whether they had ever made someone else do something sexually that they did not want to do.

We began by asking about early sexual experiences. We asked if the respondent had ever been touched sexually during his or her childhood, before puberty. With those who had been touched, we asked more about it. Who touched them? Did it happen more than once? Did anyone know about it and, if so, who?

After a series of detailed questions about sexual experiences in childhood, we moved on to ask about sexual behavior after the respondent reached puberty. We asked about the first time the person had vaginal intercourse. Was it something you were forced to do against your will? If it was, we asked: In what ways were you forced? Did the person threaten you with physical force or with a weapon or with threats or intimidation?

Finally, after asking about the first time the respondent had sexual intercourse, we asked a more general question about forced sex: After puberty, did a person of the same or opposite sex ever force you to do anything sexually that you did not want to do? We also asked a specific question of people who had been forced the first time they had sex: Other than the first time, have you ever been forced by someone of the opposite sex to do anything sexually that you did not want to do?

People who said they had been forced were asked how many times it had happened, what their relationship was to the person doing the forcing, and what happened when the sex was forced. We also asked how many different people had forced the respondent.

In our study, we started with the advantages of having a randomly selected representative group of Americans to question and of having a very high response rate. And, from their replies to questions about other sensitive behaviors, we have confidence that our respondents are answering us honestly.

The most striking finding was how many women said they had been forced at some time in their lives after age thirteen. Almost every time, the woman was forced by a man — almost no women were forced by other women. Very few men were ever forced, either by women or by other men.

We find that 22 percent of women were forced to do something sexually at some time, but that just 2 percent of men were forced. One-third of the men who reported being forced were forced by another man, and nearly all the women who were forced were forced by men. Just six out of a thousand women said they were forced to do something sexually by another woman.

Table 16 (on page 224) shows our findings on women who were forced to do something sexually by a man.

The table shows quite large differences (on the order of 10 percentage points) across ages, education levels, and religions. The differences, however, do not seem to fall into an easily discernible pattern and they are not easily interpreted. There is a suggestion in the pattern by age that older women report a somewhat lower rate of ever having been forced. We know that the older women married at younger ages and had fewer lifetime sex partners putting them at risk with fewer lovers, but older women have also been exposed to risks for more years. It may also be that incidents that are hard to interpret, that may or may not be considered forced sex, have shifted over time. For example, a twenty-five-year-old woman in 1962 might not have thought it was forced sex if she had sex with a man who plied her with drinks first. An older woman might not consider it forced sex if her husband held her down and had sexual intercourse with her after she had made it clear that she was uninterested. Today, a young woman in either of these situations might say she was forced. This means that the differences by age in the reporting of these events, over the lifetime of individuals in different historical periods are particularly difficult to interpret.

Although there is a popular notion that women who live in large cities are more likely to be raped or have forced sex, our data show no

Table 16
**Percentage of Women Ever Forced to Do Something Sexual
by a Man, by Social Characteristics**

	Ever forced	Never forced	No answer
ALL WOMEN	22%	77%	0%
AGE			
18–24	25	75	0
25–29	22	78	0
30–39	25	74	1
40–49	21	79	0
50–59	18	81	1
MARITAL/RESIDENTIAL STATUS			
Noncohabiting	25	75	1
Cohabiting	29	71	0
Married	20	80	0
EDUCATION			
Less than high school	26	74	0
High school graduate or equivalent	17	83	0
Any college	24	75	0
CURRENT RELIGION			
None	31	68	1
Mainline Protestant	21	79	0
Conservative Protestant	25	74	1
Catholic	17	83	0
RACE/ETHNICITY			
White	23	76	0
Black	19	80	1
Hispanic	14	86	0
Asian	17	83	0
SIZE OF PLACE			
12 largest central cities (CC)	16	82	2
13–100th largest CCs	29	71	0
Suburb of 12 largest CCs	19	80	1
Suburb of 13–100th largest CCs	19	81	0
Other urban places	25	74	0
Rural	18	81	1

Note: Row percentages total 100 percent.

FIGURE 21:
**Relationship of Women Respondents to Man Who Forced Them
to Do Something Sexual**

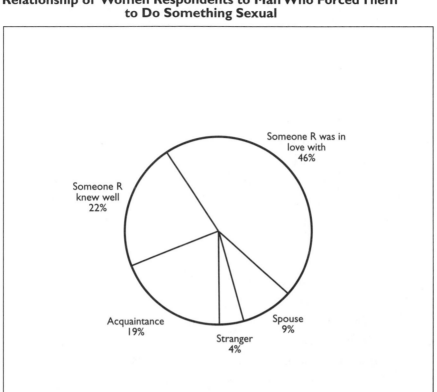

Note: Sample size = 204. Includes female respondents who reported that they had ever been "forced to do something sexual that they did not want to do by a man." Eighty-six women (or about 30 percent of all women who reported ever being forced) reported that they had been forced sexually by more than one person; they are not represented in the figure but the distribution of relationships to persons forcing is similar.

clear-cut relationship to city size. The explanation may be related to our finding that nearly all women were well acquainted with the man who was forcing them, and the majority were either in love with the man who forced them or married to him.

Figure 21 shows the relationship of the women to the men who forced them to have sex. The figure shows just how uncommon it was for a stranger to force a woman to have sex. All but 4 percent of the women knew the man who was forcing them and nearly half said they were in love with him. Even forced sex by acquaintances is unlikely —

Table 17
Comparison of Selected Features of Adult Women's Sexual and Nonsexual Experiences by Forced Sex Status

	Percent not forced	Percent forced
Not happy last year	12	20
More than ten lifetime sex partners	6	21
Ever performed oral sex	59	86
Ever received oral sex	64	91
Ever had anal sex with opposite gender	15	38
Ever had group sex	2	10
Often think about sex, last year	18	25
Lacked interest in sex, last year	31	41
Unable to orgasm, last year	22	33
Pain during sex, last year	13	20
Sex not pleasurable, last year	18	34
Anxious about sexual performance, last year	10	17
Difficulty lubricating, last year	17	26
Masturbated in the last year	37	60
Emotional problems interfered with sex, last year	42	57
N	1,285	326

Note: Cell percentages.

just 19 percent of the women said the man who forced them was an acquaintance.

We also looked at how women who had been forced responded to other questions elsewhere in the survey about sexual difficulties and about their health and happiness, and from that, we asked whether the women who had been forced differed from those who had not in any of these measures.

Table 17 allows us to compare the answers to questions about happiness, about the number of lifetime sex partners, about specific sexual acts experienced ever or within the past year, and about several sexual problems as they were reported by the women who had been forced sexually and by those who had not been forced. We see there, for instance, that in response to our question "Generally, how happy have you been with your personal life during the past twelve months?" 20 percent of the 326 women who had been forced sexually said they were sometimes fairly unhappy or unhappy most of the time, while 12 percent of the 1,285 women who had never been forced sexually said they were unhappy. That difference between 20 percent and 12 percent is statistically significant and it is a substantial difference. We cannot say if the experience of being forced in fact had caused them to be unhappy, but the fact is that those who said they were forced do differ in their response to the question about happiness from those who said they were not forced.

Looking at the several features listed here (incidentally, we have only shown those we found to be statistically significant here), we see that the women who had been forced were much more likely to have had ten or more lifetime sex partners, to have had oral sex, anal sex, and group sex, and to have masturbated in the past year. Also, they are systematically more likely to have reported one or another of the sexual problems about which we asked.

We cannot tell from our survey whether the problems experienced by the women who were forced were caused by the forced sex. For example, the problems may have been part of an unhappy sexual relationship that included what the woman perceived as forced sex. A woman who is in love with a man who treats her badly may experience forced sex and, at the same time, say she did not find sex pleasurable, that her emotional problems interfered with sex, that she was unhappy, and that she had trouble lubricating. Or a woman may not enjoy sex and may often feel that when she has it, it is against her will. We caution that interpretation of these preliminary findings is quite difficult. More study is clearly needed here.

Although many women report that they had been forced to do something sexually at some time, very few men say they ever forced a woman, and almost none say that they ever forced a man; only a minuscule proportion of women say they ever forced a woman or a man. Three percent of men report having forced a woman and two-tenths of a percent say they forced a man.

How can we reconcile the different reports of men and women about forcing women to have sex? One way to interpret these figures is to say that our respondents are not telling us the truth, that men who forced women are denying it. But, for the reasons we explained in chapter 2 and throughout the book, we do not think that is happening. Our respondents gave every indication of answering even the most sensitive questions honestly, and every cross-check we performed confirmed our belief that if there is dissembling, there is not very much.

Moreover, men overwhelmingly said they did not think the idea of forced sex is very appealing. Just two out of a thousand men aged eighteen to forty-four said the idea of forcing someone to have sex was very appealing, and six out of a thousand older men said it was very appealing. Even when we loosen the category and ask whether men found the idea of forced sex simply "appealing," very few say they do. Among younger men, 2.1 percent said the idea of forced sex was appealing. About 1.8 percent of older men found it appealing. In fact, if we add together the percentages of men, old and young, who say they found the idea of forced sex appealing with those who find it very appealing, we come up with almost exactly the number who said they have forced someone to have sex, about 3 percent.

We asked about the appeal of various sexual practices at a very different time in the interview from when we asked men if they had ever forced anyone to do something sexually, so it would be hard to imagine that the men concocted their answers to make the percentages who liked the idea of forced sex equal the number who have ever forced someone. Of course, the men who found forced sex appealing and those who said they have forced someone are not necessarily the same people. When we looked more closely at the men's replies, we discovered that about a quarter of the men who said that the idea of forced sex appealed to them also said they had forced someone.

Almost no women liked the idea of being forced to do something sexually — just one out of a thousand women aged eighteen to forty-four thought that was very appealing and no older women found the idea of forced sex very appealing. So we cannot reason that many men were forcing women because the women wanted them to.

Another possibility is that a very few men are responsible for all the forced sex that women report — perhaps those three out of a hundred men who said they had forced someone. These men would have to have multiple partners — about seven apiece — since so many women were forced, and they would have to revert to forcing sex with each of them. But that is unlikely because women who were forced usually were in love with the men or married to them, indicating that these were not short-term sexual liaisons. The women's descriptions of their partners were inconsistent with the notion that these men were having many partners. As we discussed in previous chapters, the minority of Americans who have many partners tend to have partners who have many partners and tend not to form long-term relationships.

We think that a more likely explanation is that most men who forced sex did not recognize how coercive the women thought their behavior was. Some men may have thought they were negotiating for sex, while the women who were their partners thought that they were being forced.

It could happen between a husband and a wife, with the beery man coming home from a night out with the guys, wanting sex and wanting it now. Meanwhile, his resentful wife cringes when he comes near. She does not want sex. He does. He has his way, but he does not think it was forced. She does.

Or it could happen between two young people on a date. He thinks she's really hot, that she's let him know all night how much she wants it. Her dress is so sexy. She touches his hand, then his arm, then lightly touches his thigh while they're talking at dinner. She thinks she's having an engaging conversation, just starting to get to know him. Later, when she asks him in for a cup of coffee, he makes his move. She says no. He thinks she means yes. He thinks the sex they have was consensual. She thinks it was forced.

Most people see events through a narrow lens. We suggest that our findings illustrate once again how sex can have different meanings to different people. Although we speculate that men and women can have very different interpretations of what forced sex means, the findings do not provide a way to resolve this particular war between the sexes. Instead, they show why the arguments over sexual assault are so heated.

The expanded definition of what constitutes consent in sexual matters and whether consent has been or can be freely given in any particular sexual relationship is the tip of the iceberg in a much larger debate over the relations between women and men in America. Sex is just one of the battlefields in the gender wars.

13

SEX AND SOCIETY

IN private and in public, within our families and among our friends, most of us are living the sexual lives that society has urged upon us. Social networks match up couples, sexual preferences are learned or mimicked within networks, social forces push Americans toward marriage and so richly reward wedded couples that marriage turns out to be the best way to have regular sex and the best way to have a happy sex life.

But there is more to social forces than social networks, social scripts, and a widespread conviction that marriage is the ultimate goal for nearly everyone. There also are social attitudes and beliefs, the very beliefs that show up in many of the contradictory messages that we all hear about the power and the pleasure — and the shame — of sexuality.

These attitudes and beliefs underlie some of the bitter social debates of our day. Should there be limits on a woman's right to an abortion? Should sex education be taught in schools? Should we treat homosexuality as just another lifestyle or should we consider it a sin or abnormality?

One way to look at the roots of these arguments is to ask whether there is any relationship between sexual behavior and deep-seated feelings about sexual morality. And if there is a relationship between behavior and beliefs, who is likely to hold which attitudes? Are highly educated people more likely to be libertarians? Do religious people have fewer sexual partners? Do people who view sex as a form of recreation do different things in bed than people who say their sexual behavior is guided by their religious beliefs?

In a broader sense, looking for such a relationship tests our entire thesis that sexual behavior is a social behavior, determined, shaped, and molded by society like other more visible behaviors — religious practices or recreational habits, for example. If sexual behavior were a completely independent force, not subject to conscious thoughts but controlled instead by hormones, or whipped up by drives, then it should matter little what a person's attitudes are.

We asked our respondents about their attitudes and beliefs about sexual behavior, and, separately, we asked them what appealed to them sexually and what they did. This enabled us to put the pieces together. We found that there is a strong, robust link between attitudes and sexual behavior, and that it suggests why so many social issues related to sex are so contentious. Not only do people's underlying attitudes about questions of sexual morality predict what sort of sex they have in the privacy of their bedrooms, but they even predict how often people *think* about sex.

From the different attitudes and, correspondingly, different behavior of men and women, of older and younger people, and of people of different religions, we can suggest why it is that there is a war between the sexes, why it is that many women complain that men will not commit themselves to marriage, and why it is that many older people are dismayed by the sexual practices of the young.

To learn about attitudes and beliefs, we asked several questions about opinions regarding sexual behavior and other related topics, nine of which we discuss below. For example, we asked respondents to tell us how they felt about premarital sex. Was it always wrong, almost always wrong, sometimes wrong, or not wrong at all? We asked about sex between people of the same gender. Was it always, almost always, sometimes, or never wrong? We asked respondents if their religious beliefs guided their behavior. Then, with the replies to

nine such questions in hand, we used a method called cluster analysis
to divide the population into groups according to their opinions about
those nine issues. Although people in each group varied, overall they
had a general set of similar beliefs about key issues.

Cluster analysis is a frequently used tool of social scientists who
often need to find patterns in masses of data and are not aided by
strong theory in their quest. In our case, we did not know ahead of
time how people would sort themselves out by their answers to these
questions and we knew, at the outset, that there were a large number
of possible combinations of answers to our nine questions. Since each
person answered all nine questions about his or her attitudes and
beliefs, and since we are focusing here on whether the respondents
agreed or disagreed with each statement, there are a total of 2^9 or 512
ways to answer the set of nine questions. But, we reasoned, if there
are logical or belief-driven patterns to the answers, there should be
certain clusters of replies among all these possibilities. A man, for example, who says his religious convictions guide his views toward
sexuality might also say that sex outside of marriage is always wrong,
that teenage sex is always wrong, that extramarital sex is always
wrong, and that abortions should be prohibited.

Cluster analysis underlies many studies in which people are categorized according to their replies to an array of questions rather than
a single one. For example, a cluster analysis looking for voting patterns might group people according to their replies to such questions
as: Should capital punishment be abolished? Should all companies
be required to practice affirmative action? Should handguns be out-
lawed? Should women have the right to an abortion for any reason?
Should states provide vouchers for parents who choose to send their
children to private schools? People in each group would have similar
answers to the questions. While no one question characterizes a person's political views, and while each person in a cluster will not give
exactly the same answers as every other person in the cluster, the
pattern of their replies could be a good indication of their political
leanings.

In this particular analysis, we divided the respondents into three
broad categories on the basis of their attitudes. First is the *traditional*
category, which includes about one-third of our sample. These people

say that their religious beliefs always guide their sexual behavior. In addition, they say that homosexuality is always wrong, that there should be restrictions on legal abortions, that premarital sex, teenage sex, and extramarital sex are wrong.

Second is what we call the *relational* category, whose members believe that sex should be part of a loving relationship, but that it need not always be reserved for marriage. These people, who make up nearly half of our sample, disagree with the statement that premarital sex is always wrong, for example. Most, however, say that marital infidelity is always wrong and that they would not have sex with someone they did not love. The third group is the *recreational* category, who constitute a little more than a quarter of the sample. Their defining feature is their view that sex need not have anything to do with love. In addition, most of those in this third group oppose laws to prohibit the sale of pornography to adults.

Within each of these categories, however, people varied in their attitudes, and so we subdivided the categories to further characterize our respondents. A man would be part of the relational group, for example, if he thinks extramarital sex is always wrong and that he would not have sex with anyone unless he loved her. But he might also say that same-gender sex is always wrong. A woman who is in a different group in that category might agree with him about extramarital sex and sex with a partner she loved, but disagree about same-gender sex being wrong.

Table 18 shows how the groups are categorized, according to people's replies to the nine questions on attitudes.

The columns show the percentages of our population who agree with the statements in the column on the left. We divided the traditional category into "conservative" and "pro-choice" groups essentially according to their opinions on abortion. Although people in this category nearly all believe that premarital sex among teenagers, same-gender sex, and extramarital sex are always wrong, they split on whether a woman should be able to have an abortion.

The relational category breaks down into three groups, which we have labeled as religious, conventional, and contemporary religious. Those in the religious group said that religious beliefs shape their sexual behavior and tended to say that they oppose sex between

Table 18
Description of Seven Normative Orientations toward Sexuality

	Traditional		Relational			Recreational		Total sample
	Conservative	Pro-choice	Religious	Conventional	Contemporary religious	Pro-life	Libertarian	
1. Premarital sex is always wrong	100.0†	23.6	0.0	0.4	0.8	6.5	0.0	19.7
2. Premarital sex among teenagers is always wrong	99.5	90.3	78.6	29.1	33.6	65.7	19.7	60.8
3. Extramarital sex is always wrong	98.2	91.0	92.1	94.2	52.1	59.3	32.0	76.7
4. Same-gender sex is always wrong	96.4	94.4	81.9	65.4	6.4	85.9	9.0	64.8
5. There should be laws against the sale of pornography to adults	70.6	47.2	53.1	12.2	11.7	14.9	6.4	33.6
6. I would not have sex with someone unless I was in love with them	87.5	66.0	98.0	83.8	65.3	10.1	19.5	65.7
7. My religious beliefs have guided my sexual behavior	91.3	72.9	74.7	8.7	100.0	25.0	0.0	52.3
8. A woman should be able to obtain a legal abortion if she was raped	56.3	98.6	82.3	99.1	99.3	84.3	99.8	88.0
9. A woman should be able to obtain a legal abortion if she wants it for any reason	0.5	100.0	0.0	87.4	84.9	9.3	88.6	52.4
N = 2,843	15.4%	15.2%	19.1%	15.9%	9.3%	8.7%	16.4%	100.0%

Oversample was excluded from analysis, as were respondents who had missing values for one or more items. Clusters were derived by minimizing the squared Euclidean distance between members within each cluster. All items were dichotomized before clustering. Column percentages.
†Indicates the percentage of persons in the "Conservative Traditional" cluster who believe that premarital sex is always wrong.

people of the same gender and they oppose abortions. The conventional group is more tolerant than the religious group toward teenage sex, pornography, and abortion and are far less likely to say they are influenced by religious beliefs. But most think that same-gender sex and extramarital sex are always wrong. The contemporary religious group is much more tolerant of homosexuality but people in this group say that they are guided by their religious beliefs.

In the recreational category, there are two groups. One, which we call pro-life, consists of people who oppose both homosexuality and abortion for any reason but who are more accepting of teenage sex, extramarital sex, and pornography. The second group is the libertarian group. They have the most accepting position on all the items. None of this libertarian group considers religion as a guide to their sexual behavior.

Just dividing the respondents into these groupings on the basis of their opinions, however, tells only part of the story. We also want to know how the groups differ by social characteristics. Men and women gravitate to different groups, as seen in Table 19. So do older and younger people and so do blacks and whites. The distribution of people into groups reveals why the formation of social policy regarding sexual issues is so contentious and so complex.

The top rows of Table 19 tell us that women are more likely to have the opinions we labeled "traditional" and are much less likely to have the views we called "recreational." By age, we see that the older men and women are disproportionately "traditional" and much less likely to hold the "recreational" views.

With distributions like this, it is no wonder that the battle between the sexes rages. Lance Morrow, a columnist for *Time* magazine, bemoaned men's fate. Women, he complained, have a particularly pejorative view of hapless men, thinking and saying something like "Men-are-animals-I-don't-care-if-they're-not-doing-anything-at-the-moment-they're-thinking-about-it-and-they-will-when-they-have-a-chance." Some women, on the other hand, have sniped that men are not so blameless, pointing out that many men still leer at women when they walk down the street, and some men act like they have to be dragged kicking and screaming into marriage, behaving as if marriage is a ball and chain.

Table 19
Distribution of Normative Orientations within Demographic Groups

Social characteristics	Normative orientation		
	Traditional	Relational	Recreational
GENDER			
Men	26.9%	40.1%	33.0%
Women	33.7	47.6	18.7
AGE			
Men			
18–24	17.4	46.9	35.7
25–29	21.0	46.2	32.9
30–39	26.2	38.6	35.2
40–49	31.2	38.2	30.5
50–59	40.1	31.3	28.6
Women			
18–24	23.0	51.8	25.3
25–29	27.5	54.6	17.9
30–39	34.6	46.6	18.8
40–49	34.5	44.9	20.6
50–59	47.0	43.4	9.6
MARITAL/RESIDENTIAL STATUS			
Men			
Noncohabiting	18.4	39.7	42.0
Cohabiting	8.6	48.4	43.0
Married	36.4	39.0	24.5
Women			
Noncohabiting	31.9	46.8	21.3
Cohabiting	23.9	50.4	25.6
Married	36.2	48.1	15.8
EDUCATION			
Men			
Less than high school	31.6	39.5	28.8
High school graduate or equivalent	28.3	40.9	30.8
Any college	25.0	39.8	35.2
Women			
Less than high school	36.6	47.6	15.9
High school graduate or equivalent	38.3	46.0	15.7
Any college	30.4	48.7	20.9

Table 19

(*continued*)

Social characteristics	Normative orientation		
	Traditional	Relational	Recreational
RELIGION			
Men			
None	11.7	39.1	49.2
Mainline Protestant	24.2	43.8	32.0
Conservative Protestant	44.5	30.1	25.3
Catholic	17.8	49.6	32.6
Women			
None	10.4	44.4	45.2
Mainline Protestant	30.9	51.4	17.7
Conservative Protestant	50.5	38.4	11.2
Catholic	22.2	58.0	19.8
RACE/ETHNICITY			
Men			
White	26.1	41.6	32.3
Black	32.4	25.4	42.3
Hispanic	25.3	45.1	29.7
Women			
White	30.5	48.3	21.2
Black	45.3	45.8	8.9
Hispanic	40.7	43.2	16.1

Note: Percentages in rows total 100 percent.

The distribution of men and women in the attitude clusters tells us, at least, that many more women than men are looking for love and consider marriage to be a prerequisite for sex. When women bitterly complain that the men they meet are not interested in long-term commitments, their laments have a ring of truth. Many more men than women are looking for sexual play and pleasure, with marriage or even love not necessarily a part of it. After all, men in the recreational category may be unlikely to feel that linking sex with marriage is high on their list of priorities. When men note that their girlfriends are always trying to lure them into a making a commitment to exclusivity or that their relationships seem to end with an ultimatum — marry me or get out — there is a good reason for it.

The conflicting goals of men and women — and particularly young men and young women — are played out in the lines the men may use when they meet women. And at no time is this more true than in adolescence and young adulthood, the very time that men are most likely to be part of all-male groups who have recreational attitudes toward sex.

Elijah Anderson, a sociologist at the University of Pennsylvania, tells how black teenagers in an inner-city neighborhood take on these roles: "The lore of the streets says there is a contest going on between the boy and girl before they even meet. To the young man, the woman becomes, in the most profound sense, a sexual object. Her body and mind are the object of a sexual game, to be won for his personal aggrandizement." And to win a young woman, Anderson says, the young man devises a rap, "whose object is to inspire sexual interest." *

The young women, on the other hand, want "a boyfriend, a fiancé, a husband, and the fairy-tale prospect of living happily ever after with one's children in a good house in a nice neighborhood," Anderson says. So the young man, trying to have sex with a woman, "shows her the side of himself that he knows she wants to see, that represents what she wants in a man." He may take the young woman to church, visit her family, help her with chores. But after the young man has sex with the young woman, he often leaves her for a new conquest.

The teenage woman "may know she is being played but given the effectiveness of his rap, his presentation of self, his looks, his age, his wit, his dancing ability, and his general popularity, infatuation often rules," Anderson notes.

Put differently, we see in this typical script the competitive marketplace for sexual partners. The young man is emphasizing those of his attributes that he thinks will attract the young woman. He engages in negotiations and interchanges designed, with all his strategic skills, to persuade her that a friendship that includes sex will be to her liking. She, similarly, emphasizes her attributes that she thinks might attract

---

*Elijah Anderson, *Streetwise: Race, Class, and Change in an Urban Community* (Chicago: University of Chicago Press, 1990).

the most appealing guy. She carefully calibrates her encouragement and insists on behavior that wraps sex into the bundle of activities that she desires.

Whether the outcome is a single sex episode or a more steady dating relationship or even a longer-term sexual partnership, each of these young people offers and withholds, explores and considers, and reaches agreement about the sex. The strategic behavior by each, designed to attract the partner and achieve the objective that each seeks, embeds the individual's endeavor in a social context that typically involves competition.

The table also shows us that the married men and women are least likely to hold the recreational view of sexuality, while the not-married men are far more likely to hold that set of views. The cohabiting men and women, on the other hand, are least likely to hold the traditional views of sexuality. Of course, these unmarried men and women are also likely to be younger than those who are married, so the pattern by marital status partly just mirrors the pattern we noted above that older (and married) people hold more traditional views while the younger (unmarried) people are more likely to be in the recreational category. This contributes to the battle of the generations. Older people, often the parents of teenagers or of people in their twenties, tend to have a very different view of the purpose of sex.

The age distribution also suggests the possibility that people change their attitudes over the years (though our data cannot confirm this), moving from times, in their youth, when they thought love need have nothing to do with sex to times, when they grow older, when loving relationships become more central to sexuality. People seem to move along the spectrum from libertarian toward conservative as they age. This could be one reason why 58 percent of our respondents who said premarital sex is always wrong also told us that they themselves had had sex before they were married. And it could explain why 26 percent of our respondents who told us that teenage sex is always wrong also said that they had had sex when they were teenagers. These differences by age might, on the other hand, reflect lifelong held differences of opinion of those born in the 1930s, the 1940s, and so on, but we speculate that these opinions change with age.

When we look at the relationship between race, religion, and education and attitudes about sex, we can see why people tend to feel more comfortable when they choose partners like themselves. The table shows, for example, that few who are not religious are part of the traditional category, but 48 percent of conservative Protestants are traditionalists. People with no religion are most likely to be part of the recreational category — nearly half are found here.

Our findings also show that the clichéd strife between black men and black women may, in fact, reflect fundamentally different attitudes about sex. Black women are more likely than white or Hispanic women to be traditionalists and are noticeably less likely than other women to be in the recreational category — fewer than 10 percent of black women have recreational views toward sex. But black men are noticeably more likely than other men to be in the recreational group — more than 40 percent have recreational views.

The pattern seen in Table 19 by education level is not dramatic, but it is quite systematic. Those with less than a high school level of education are more likely to hold traditional views about sexuality and less likely to hold recreational views; those with college education are just the opposite: they are more likely to hold the recreational views and least likely to hold the traditional views.

We did not have strong expectations or theories about how people's views of sexuality might be related to their social characteristics. But our findings seem to confirm the notion that people's beliefs about sexual morality are part of a much broader social and religious outlook that helps define who they are. Their orientations are reinforced by their friends and family and others in their social networks.

The next question is whether what people believe about sexual behavior is linked to what they actually do sexually. It is one thing to have a certain set of attitudes, but it is another thing to have those attitudes determine your most private acts, wishes, and thoughts. Yet that is what we find, as seen in Table 20 (on page 242). Membership in a particular attitudinal group is closely associated with what their sexual practices are. It is even correlated with how often people think about sex and how often they have sex.

The top portion of both panels of Table 20 shows the number of sex partners in the past year for the men and women who are not living with a partner. We see there that those who have traditional views about sexuality mostly have zero or one partner and only a relatively small percentage had two or more sex partners in the past year: about 30 percent of the men and about 14 percent of the women have that many. But of those who held recreational views of sexuality, about 60 percent of the men and nearly 50 percent of the women had two or more sex partners in the past year. Their attitudes and opinions, as characterized by the three categories of traditional, relational, and recreational, do in fact distinguish these unmarried and noncohabiting respondents quite effectively in terms of their number of sex partners in the past year.

To be sure, there are a few of those with a traditionalist view who have several sex partners, and a few of those with a recreationalist's view who have no sex partner or one partner, but in the main, the views they held are very consistent with the number of partners they had in the past year.

The same is true of those who are married, as seen in the second set of rows in Table 20. For the men who were traditionalists or relationalists, only 3 or 4 percent had more than one sex partner in the past year, but as many as 15 percent of those who were recreationalists had more than one. The same pattern is seen for the married women where only 1 or 2 percent of the traditionalists and relationalists had more than one partner but more than 7 percent of the recreationalists had more than one. The tremendous influence of marital status on the number of sex partners is seen here, with a vast majority of the married men and women having zero or one sex partner in the past year, and the unmarried much more likely to have several, but within both marital statuses the influence of these opinions shines through.

In contrast, people's views about sex had little bearing on how often they had sex. Roughly half of those in each of the three categories report having sex once a week or more. Although somewhat fewer recreationalists said they did not have sex at all last year, the difference between them and those in other groups was not very great. We suspect it reflects the fact that people in the recreational group are more likely to be young and may not have yet found a sexual partner, however much they may want to.

Whether they are actually having sex or not, people who are recreationalists are much more likely than traditionalists to think about

Table 20
Selected Sexual Behaviors within Normative Groups

Panel A: Men

	Normative orientation		
Sexual behaviors	*Traditional*	*Relational*	*Recreational*
PARTNERS LAST YEAR: NONCOHABITING			
None	40.6%	22.4%	12.8%
One	30.2	41.0	27.9
Two or more	29.2	36.6	59.4
PARTNERS LAST YEAR: MARRIED			
Zero or one	97.0	96.0	84.9
Two or more	3.0	4.0	15.1
LAST YEAR SEX FREQUENCY			
None	12.5	8.8	8.4
Three times a month or less	31.4	34.2	35.9
Once a week or more	56.1	57.1	55.7
THINK ABOUT SEX			
Twice a month or less	13.4	14.1	7.1
Twice a week or less	40.8	35.3	27.0
Daily or more	45.8	50.6	65.9
MASTURBATE			
Never	50.2	35.5	25.6
Three times a month or less	32.1	38.5	39.4
Once a week or more	17.7	26.0	35.0
HAD ORAL SEX (ACTIVE OR PASSIVE) WITH PRIMARY PARTNER IN LAST YEAR			
Yes	56.4	78.2	80.7
HAD ANAL SEX DURING LIFETIME			
Yes	18.7	23.1	32.3
EVER HAD SAME-GENDER PARTNER SINCE AGE 18			
Yes	2.6	4.5	7.8

Table 20

(continued)

Panel B: Women

Sexual behaviors	Normative orientation		
	Traditional	Relational	Recreational
PARTNERS LAST YEAR: NONCOHABITING			
None	46.7	25.2	14.6
One	39.1	52.6	36.6
Two or more	14.1	22.2	48.8
PARTNERS LAST YEAR: MARRIED			
Zero or one	98.0	98.5	92.5
Two or more	2.0	1.5	7.5
LAST YEAR SEX FREQUENCY			
None	18.5	10.8	8.0
Three times a month or less	31.5	34.0	39.6
Once a week or more	50.0	55.1	52.4
THINK ABOUT SEX			
Twice a month or less	45.0	36.8	30.1
Twice a week or less	40.6	44.0	39.0
Daily or more	14.3	19.2	30.8
MASTURBATE			
Never	69.0	56.6	37.5
Three times a month or less	26.0	35.4	50.2
Once a week or more	5.0	8.1	12.3
HAD ORAL SEX (ACTIVE OR PASSIVE) WITH PRIMARY PARTNER IN LAST YEAR			
Yes	55.9	73.9	83.6
HAD ANAL SEX DURING LIFETIME			
Yes	13.2	19.5	37.5
EVER HAD SAME-GENDER PARTNER SINCE AGE 18			
Yes	0.8	3.0	8.6

Note: Percentages in columns total 100 percent within the categories; the "no" percentages are omitted in the last three.

sex every day and are much more likely to masturbate. Those in the recreational group are twice as likely as those in the traditionalist group to report that they masturbated once a week or more.

Oral and anal sex and sex with someone of the same gender follow the same patterns, as is seen in the bottom three rows of Table 20. Recreationalists are more likely than traditionalists to have had oral sex in the last year with their partner. They also are more likely to have had anal sex. And they are more likely to have had same-gender sex. In fact, as we move along the scale from traditionalist to recreationalist, the frequency of oral sex, anal sex, and same-gender sex increases.

Overall, people's sexual opinions and their behavior mesh quite closely. We cannot tell whether the opinions prompted the behavior or whether the behavior prompted the opinions, or both, but the relationship is clear.

From these findings on attitudes, beliefs, and sexual behavior along with our findings on sexual networks and choices of sexual partners, we can start to see why America has such heated social policy debates about sexual issues such as abortion, public nudity, gay rights, and pornography.

As Table 19 showed, opinions and social characteristics seem to go hand in hand. The young have one set of opinions about sexuality while older adults have another; conservative Protestants have one set of views while those without religious affiliations have another; the less educated tend to have different views than the well educated. Table 20 showed that people's attitudes are reflected in their behavior, so different groups really do act differently.

In chapter 3, we saw that people tend to choose sexual partners who are just like themselves in education, religion, and race or ethnicity. Now we see that we have probably paired off with someone who has many of our own opinions about sexuality. That is, in fact, probably a key reason why we choose partners from our own social group. Of course, opinions also may shift and become more similar as the partnership continues, but when that happens, it only makes the partnership stronger. It can be very difficult to maintain a sexual relationship with someone who strongly disagrees with you about such matters as whether abortion or extramarital sex is always wrong or whether religious beliefs always guide sexual behavior.

Our friends and families, the members of our social networks, also tend to be like us in social characteristics, and so they are likely to share many of our opinions about sexual behavior. Consequently, when we have discussions with our friends we tend to be speaking to people who are like us and who agree with us about sex. So we tend to get reinforcement for our views. That is probably one of the main reasons why our opinions are so internally consistent and so well reflected in our sexual behavior.

But all this reinforcement and consistency makes it very threatening to change our views, to become convinced by an outside argument or to change an opinion about one aspect of sexual behavior, such as whether extramarital sex is always wrong, without changing any other opinions. Our opinions, behavior, and social networks all tend to encourage us to hold to those views that help tie all these opinions, beliefs, and behavior together. And when we see these sets of behaviors as woven together by our religious beliefs and our ethical principles, we are, quite understandably, reluctant to give ground. So the national debates on so many of these sexual issues become heated and all sides become entrenched. No wonder we are a nation that is deeply conflicted about sexual matters and that the disputes seem to go on forever, with no compromises in sight.

And with this we have traveled full circle, going from an investigation of what people do and who they are to who they are and what they do and what they believe about sex. We began our study by asking whether sexual behavior could be studied in the same way as other social behaviors and, if so, whether it followed any social rules. We asked whether the privateness of sexual behavior and the powerful myths put it in a class apart from other social behaviors or whether, when we drew back the curtain and looked at what really happens, sexual behavior would turn out to be not so mysterious after all.

In every instance, our data have shown that social forces are powerful and persistent in determining sexual behavior. We have found that our society constrains us, nudging us toward partners who are like ourselves. But, at the same time, it frees us, putting us together with people who have the same sorts of general understandings about sex that we do and so easing our way into sexual intimacies and revelations. We also found that although America may not be as sexy a place as it is often portrayed, most people are satisfied with the sexual lives they have chosen or that were imposed upon them.

America is not the golden land of eroticism where everybody who is young and beautiful has a hot sex life. Nor is it a land where vast hordes of miserable people, kicked out of the sexual banquet, lick their wounds in silence and resentment. Instead, it is a nation that uses social forces to encourage sexual norms and whose sexual behavior is, in large measure, socially determined. It is a nation of people who are for the most part content, or at least not highly dissatisfied, with the sexual lots they have drawn.

And, for those who feel the status quo is far from ideal, we have found that the costs of breaching the social pressures may be high, and the rewards of going along may be great. But by seeing where and how the pressures are brought to bear, we can break away from the myths and magical thinking that have captured us in the past. With unclouded eyes, we can ask whether we really want changes in sexual behavior and, if so, what the benefits and costs of these changes might be.

APPENDIX A

A Graphic Representation of
Survey Participants

**The following graphs show the makeup of the 3,159 participants
in the National Health and Social Life Survey**

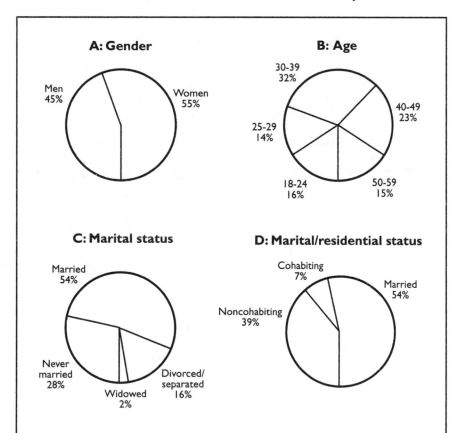

A: Gender

Men 45%   Women 55%

B: Age

30-39 32%
40-49 23%
25-29 14%
18-24 16%
50-59 15%

C: Marital status

Married 54%
Never married 28%
Widowed 2%
Divorced/ separated 16%

D: Marital/residential status

Cohabiting 7%
Married 54%
Noncohabiting 39%

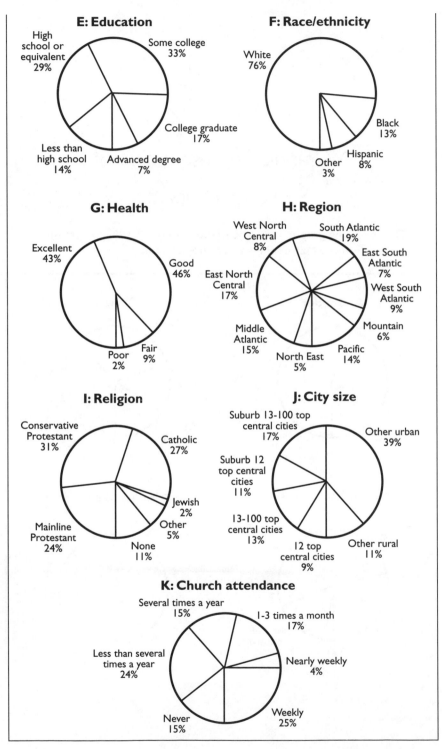

E: Education

High school or equivalent 29%
Some college 33%
College graduate 17%
Advanced degree 7%
Less than high school 14%

F: Race/ethnicity

White 76%
Black 13%
Hispanic 8%
Other 3%

G: Health

Excellent 43%
Good 46%
Fair 9%
Poor 2%

H: Region

West North Central 8%
South Atlantic 19%
East South Atlantic 7%
West South Atlantic 9%
Mountain 6%
Pacific 14%
North East 5%
Middle Atlantic 15%
East North Central 17%

I: Religion

Conservative Protestant 31%
Catholic 27%
Jewish 2%
Other 5%
None 11%
Mainline Protestant 24%

J: City size

Suburb 13-100 top central cities 17%
Other urban 39%
Suburb 12 top central cities 11%
13-100 top central cities 13%
12 top central cities 9%
Other rural 11%

K: Church attendance

Several times a year 15%
1-3 times a month 17%
Nearly weekly 4%
Less than several times a year 24%
Weekly 25%
Never 15%

APPENDIX B

The Sex Questionnaire

As administered to the respondents in the National Health and Social Life Survey by experienced professional interviewers, the questionnaire was over 120 pages in length and was supplemented by sixteen hand cards, four smaller "confidential" self-administered questionnaires, a big "life history calendar," and other survey paraphernalia.

The following questionnaire is a condensation of all that, excluding several more routine sections on background characteristics and fertility, eliminating much of the initial explanation for each section that was read to the respondents, eliminating repetition and skipping patterns, and rewritten in a third-person voice. What is left is the essence of the sex questionnaire. We note that the questions that ask for the name of a partner were used only to keep track of which person the respondent was referring to; we have no identifying information in our data set. The full questionnaire is reproduced in the companion volume, *The Social Organization of Sexuality*.

SECTION ONE: PRELIMINARY SHORT SEX QUESTIONNAIRE

The Past Twelve Months

1. How many sex partners have you had in the last twelve months? ☐☐☐ If no partners, skip to Question 5.

2. Was one of the partners your husband or wife or regular sexual partner? ☐ Yes ☐ No

3. If you had NO other partners beside your husband or wife or regular sexual partner, please go to Question 4.
   If you had other partners, please indicate all categories that apply to them.
   CIRCLE *ALL THE ANSWERS* THAT APPLY.

Close personal friend	1
Neighbor, coworker, or long-term acquaintance	2
Casual date or pickup	3
Person you paid or paid you for sex	4
Other (PLEASE SPECIFY)	
_____	5

4. Have your sex partners in the last twelve months been . . .
   PLEASE CIRCLE *ONE* ANSWER.

Exclusively male	1
Both male and female	2
Exclusively female	3

5. About how often did you have sex during the past twelve months?

Not at all	0
Once or twice	1
About once a month	2
Two or three times a month	3
About once a week	4
Two or three times a week	5
Four or more times a week	6

The Past Five Years

6. Now, think about the past five years — the time since February/March/April 1987, and including the past twelve months — how many sex partners have you had in that five-year period?

No partners (Skip to Question 8)	00
1 partner	01
2 partners	02
3 partners	03
4 partners	04
5–10 partners	05
11–20 partners	06
21–100 partners	07
More than 100 partners	08

7. Have your sex partners in the last five years been . . .
   PLEASE CIRCLE *ONE* ANSWER.
Exclusively male	1
Both male and female	2
Exclusively female	3

Since Your Eighteenth Birthday

8. Now, thinking about the time since your eighteenth birthday (again, including the recent past that you have already told us about), how many **female** partners have you ever had sex with? ☐☐☐

9. Again, thinking about the time since your eighteenth birthday (including the recent past that you have already told us about), how many **male** partners have you ever had sex with? ☐☐☐

10. Thinking about the time since your eighteenth birthday, have you ever had sex with a person you paid or who paid you for sex? ☐ Yes ☐ No

While Married

11. Have you ever had sex with someone other than your husband or wife while you were married? ☐ Yes ☐ No ☐ Never married

SECTION TWO: MARRIAGE AND COHABITATION

1. Have you ever been married or lived with someone in a sexual relationship for a month or more? We will refer to this as a Spouse/Cohab (S/C) relationship. ☐ Yes ☐ No If your answer is **No**, go to Section Three.

2. How many different people have you been married to or lived in a sexual relationship with for a month or more? Please do not include any living arrangements that lasted less than one month, unless it's someone you are currently living with. ☐☐☐
   A. Please start with the first time that you got married or lived in a sexual relationship. What is that person's first name? ENTER NAME: _____.
   B. What is the name of your next spouse or cohab? ENTER NAME(S):
   _____.
   _____.

Now, some questions about your first spouse or cohabitation partner:

3. What is (S/C's) sex? ☐ Male ☐ Female

4. What is (S/C's) ethnic/racial background? _____

5. What (is/was) the highest level of education that (S/C) completed? ☐☐

6. How many years older or younger than you is (S/C)? ☐☐ older; ☐☐ younger

7. When did you begin living with (S/C)? _ _ / _ _ / _ _ (month/day/year)

8. Were you married to (S/C) when you started living together? ☐ Yes ☐ No If **Yes,** go to Question 10. If **No,** go to Question 9. If **Male/Male or Female/Female** couple, go to Question 12.

9. Did you and (S/C) ever marry? ☐ Yes ☐ No If **Yes,** when did you get married? _ _ / _ _ / _ _ If **No,** go to Question 12.

10. Did this marriage end? ☐ Yes ☐ No If **Yes,** when did you stop living with (S/C)? _ _ / _ _ / _ _ If **No,** do you still live with (S/C)? ☐ Yes ☐ No (Go to Question 13)

11. How did this marriage end? _ _ _ _ _ _ _ _ _ _ If **Divorced,** when was your divorce finalized? _ _ / _ _ / _ _ If **Widowed,** go to Question 13. If **Separated,** go to Question 12.

12. Did you stop living with (S/C)? ☐ Yes ☐ No If **Yes,** when did you stop living with (S/C)? _ _ / _ _ / _ _

13. If you listed additional S/Cs under Question 2B, on a separate sheet answer Questions 3 – 12 for all of them.

14. Have you missed any times where you lived in a sexual relationship with someone for a month or longer? ☐ Yes ☐ No

15. What (has/did) (S/C) (done/do) most of the period you lived together?
    Work full time   1
    Work part-time   2
    Unemployed, laid off, looking for work   3
    Retired   4
    In school   5 (Go to Question 17)
    Keeping house   6 (Go to Question 17)
    Don't know   8 (Go to Question 17)

16. (When you were living together), what kind of work (does/did) (S/C) do? That is, what (is/was) (his/her) job called?
    OCCUPATION: _____
    A. What (does/did) (S/C) actually do in that job? Tell me what (are/were) some of (his/her) main duties?

    _____
    _____

    B. What kind of place (does/did) (S/C) work for?
    INDUSTRY _____

17. What (is/was) (S/C's) religious preference? Circle One
    Protestant (Christian)   01 (Go to A)
    Roman Catholic   02 (Go to B)
    Jewish   03 (Go to B)
    Orthodox (such as Greek or Russian)   04 (Go to B)
    Hindu, Muslim, or other Eastern Religion   05 (Go to B)

Other religion (SPECIFY) _____	06 (Go to B)
None	00 (Go to B)
Don't know	98 (Go to B)

A. What specific denomination is that, if any?

Baptist	01
Methodist	02
Lutheran	03
Presbyterian	04
Episcopalian	05
Other (SPECIFY) _____	06

B. How often (does/did) (S/C) attend religious services?

Never	00
Less than once a year	01
About once or twice a year	02
Several times a year	03
About once a month	04
Two or three times a month	05
Nearly every week	06
Every week	07
Several times a week	08

18. On a scale of 1 to 4, with 1 being a lot and 4 being not at all, tell me how much you (enjoy/enjoyed) spending time with (S/C)'s . . .

	A lot	Some	A little	Not at all	Does not apply
Family	1	2	3	4	7
Friends	1	2	3	4	7

19. On a scale of 1 to 4, with 1 being a lot and 4 being not at all, tell me how much (S/C) (enjoys/enjoyed) spending time with your . . .

	A lot	Some	A little	Not at all	Does not apply
Family	1	2	3	4	7
Friends	1	2	3	4	7

IF 2 OR MORE S/Cs, REPEAT QUESTIONS 15 THROUGH 19 FOR EACH.
IF *ONLY* 1 S/C, GO ON TO SECTION 3.

SECTION THREE: PARTNER IDENTIFICATION AND ONE-YEAR SEXUAL ACTIVITY

Now I am going to be asking some questions about your sexual activity during the *last twelve months*. People mean different things by sex or sexual activity, but in answering these questions, we need everyone to use the same definition. Here, by "sex" or "sexual activity," we mean any mutually voluntary activity with another person that involves genital contact and sexual excitement or arousal, that is, feeling really turned on, even if intercourse or orgasm did not occur.

In answering these questions, please include all persons or times in the *last twelve months* where you had direct physical contact with the genitals (the sex organs) of someone else and sexual excitement or arousal occurred. Certain activities such as close dancing or kissing without genital contact should NOT be included. Also, this set of questions does NOT refer to occasions where force was used and activity was against someone's will.

1. Thinking back over the past twelve months, how many people, including men and women, have you had sexual activity with, even if only one time? ☐☐☐ If **None**, skip to Box 4A, Section 4.

2. Partner name: _____ (You may refer to your partner (P) in any way you want — first name, initials, nicknames. We just need some way to refer to these partners so that when we ask you some follow-up questions we know whom we are talking about.)

3. What is (P's) sex? ☐ Male ☐ Female If partner is both "P" and "S/C," go to Question 7.

4. What is (P's) ethnic/racial background? _____

5. What (is/was) the highest level of education that (P) completed? _____

6. How may years older or younger than you is (P)? ☐☐ older; ☐☐ younger

7. Was the first time you had sex with (P) in the last twelve months? ☐ Yes ☐ No If **Yes**, go to Question 8A. If **No**, go to Question 8B.

8A. When did you first have sex with (P)? _ _ / _ _ / _ _ (Go to Question 9A)

8B. When did you first have sex with (P)? _ _ / _ _ / _ _ (Go to Question 9B)

9A. How many times did you have sex with (P) in the last twelve months? ☐☐ If only once, go to Question 11. If two or more, go to Question 10.

9B. How many times did you have sex with (P) in the last twelve months? ☐☐ If only once, go to Question 11. If two or more, go to Question 10.

10. In the past twelve months, when did you (most recently) have sex with (P)? _ _ / _ _ / _ _

11. Are there any more partners? ☐ Yes ☐ No If **Yes**, on a separate sheet, answer Questions 3–10 for next partner. If **No**, go to Question 12.

12. **IF ONLY ONE PARTNER:** RECORD NAME: _____.
    A. Is this person an S/C? ☐ Yes ☐ No If **Yes**, go to Question 17. If **No**, go to Question 14.

13. **IF MORE THAN ONE PARTNER:**
    A. Is any sex partner for the past year a S/C (that is, both "S/C" and "P")? ☐ Yes ☐ No
       If **Yes**, go to Question 17. If **No**, go to Question 13B.
    B. Which of the people that you mentioned do you consider to have been your most important or primary sexual partner during the last twelve months?
       RECORD NAME: _____. (Go to Question 14)
       If no primary partner, go to Question 13C.
    C. Of the people that you mentioned, who did you have sex with most recently?
       RECORD NAME: _____. (Go to 14)

14. What (is/was) (P's) religious preference? (Circle one)
Protestant	01 (Go to 14A)
Roman Catholic	02 (Go to 15)
Jewish	03 (Go to 15)
Orthodox (such as Greek or Russian)	04 (Go to 15)
Hindu, Muslim, or other Eastern religion	05 (Go to 15)
Other religion (SPECIFY) _____	06 (Go to 15)
None	00 (Go to 15)
Don't know	98 (Go to 15)

    A. What specific denomination is that, if any? (Circle one)
Baptist	01
Methodist	02
Lutheran	03
Presbyterian	04
Episcopalian	05
Other (SPECIFY) _____	06

15. How often (does/did) (P) attend religious services; (is/was) it . . . (Circle one)
Never	00
Less than once a year	01
About once or twice a year	02
Several times a year	03
About once a month	04
Two or three times a month	05
Nearly every week	06
Every week	07
Several times a week	08

16. What (does/did) (P) do most of the time (while you were involved)? (Is/Was) that . . .
    (Circle one)
Work full time	1 (Go to 16A)
Work part-time	2 (Go to 16A)
Unemployed, laid off, looking for work	3 (Go to 16A)
Retired	4 (Go to 16A)
In school	5 (Go to 18)
Keeping house	6 (Go to 18)
Don't know	8 (Go to 18)

A. (When you were involved,) what kind of work (does/did) (P) do? That is, what (is/was) (his/her) job called?
OCCUPATION: _____

B. What (does/did) (P) actually do in that job? Tell me what (are/were) some of (his/her) main duties?

_____

_____

C. What kind of place (does/did) (P) work for?
INDUSTRY _____. (Go to Question 18)

17. RECORD S/C NAME _____.

18. Where did you meet (P)? Circle all that apply.
Work	01
School	02
Church/church activity	03
Personal ads/dating service	04
Vacation/business trip	05
Bar/nightclub/dance club	06
Social organization/health club/gym/ volunteer-service activity	07
Private party	08
Other (SPECIFY) _____	09

19. Who introduced you to (P)? Circle all that apply.
Family	01
Mutual friends or acquaintances	02
Coworkers	03
Classmates	04
Neighbors	05
Introduced self or partner introduced self	06
Other (SPECIFY) _____	07

20. (Is/Was) (P) married, living with someone else in a sexual relationship, separated, divorced, or in a steady relationship with someone else when you first became sexually involved? (Circle one)
Married	1
Living with someone else	2
Separated	3
In a steady relationship	4
Divorced	5
None of these	6
Don't know	8

21. How long did you know (P) prior to having sexual activity for the first time? Was that . . .
Less than one day	1
One or two days	2

More than two days but less than a month	3
More than one month but less than a year	4
Or more than one year	5

BOX 3.1 DURING THE LAST TWELVE MONTHS, HOW MANY TIMES DID YOU
HAVE SEXUAL ACTIVITY WITH (P)? □□

ONLY ONCE	1 (Go to Question 23)
2–10 TIMES	2 (Go to Question 23)
MORE THAN 10 TIMES	4 (Go to Question 22)

---

22. During the last 12 months, (while you were sexually involved), about how often did you have sex with (P)? (Circle one)

Once a day or more	1
3 to 6 times a week	2
Once or twice a week	3
2 to 3 times a month	4
Once a month or less	5

A. (Did/Do) you expect (P) to have sexual activity only with you during the time you (were/are) sexually involved?

Yes	1
No	2
Not at first, but later I did	3
I did at first, but not later	4

B. (Did/Does) (P) expect you to have sex only with (him/her) during the time you (were/are) sexually involved?

Yes	1
No	2
Not at first, but later (she/he) did	3
(She/he) did at first, but not later	4

23. **(IF YOU CURRENTLY HAVE A SPOUSE/COHAB, GO TO QUESTION 27.)** Do you expect to have sex with (P) again? □ Yes □ No □ Don't know. If **No**, go to Question 25.

24. How much longer do you expect the relationship with (P) to last?

A few more days	1
A few more weeks	2
More than one month but less than one year	3
Several years	4
Lifetime	5

25. Did (P) get to know your family, that is your parents or brothers and sisters, during the relationship? □ Yes □ No

26. Did (P) get to know your close friends during the relationship? □ Yes □ No

27. Now I would like to ask you some questions about alcohol use. How often (did/do) you or your partner drink alcohol before or during sex? If **Never**, go to Question 28. (Circle one)

Always	1
Usually	2
Sometimes	3
Rarely	4
Never	5

A. Was that usually you, your partner, or both? (Circle one)

Respondent only	1 (Answer B ONLY)
Partner only	2 (Answer C ONLY)
Respondent and partner	3 (Answer both B AND C)

B. On average, how strongly were you affected by the alcohol, very strongly, somewhat, not at all? (Circle one)

Very strongly	1
Somewhat	2
Not at all	3
Don't know	8

C. On average, how strongly was (P) affected by the alcohol, very strongly, somewhat, not at all?

Very strongly	1
Somewhat	2
Not at all	3
Don't know	8

28. How often (do/did) either you or (P) use any drugs to get high or intoxicated before or during sex? If **Never**, go to Question 29.

Always	1
Usually	2
Sometimes	3
Rarely	4
Never	5

A. Was that usually you, your partner, or both?

Respondent only	1 (Answer B ONLY)
Partner only	2 (Answer C ONLY)
Respondent and partner	3 (Answer both B AND C)

B. On average, how strongly were you affected by the drugs, very strongly, somewhat, not at all?

Very strongly	1
Somewhat	2
Not at all	3
Don't know	8

C. On average, how strongly was (P) affected by the drugs, very strongly, somewhat, not at all?

Very strongly	1
Somewhat	2
Not at all	3
Don't know	8

29. Think about the times you had sex with (P) *during the past twelve months.* If you were not sexually involved the whole time, please think only about the period of time when you were involved.

    First, some questions about oral sex. By **oral sex** we mean stimulating the genitals with the mouth, that is licking or kissing your partner's genitals or when your partner does this to you.

    When you had sex with (P), how often did (he/she) perform oral sex on you? Was it . . .

Always	1
Usually	2
Sometimes	3
Rarely	4
Never	5

30. When you had sex with (P), how often did you perform oral sex on (him/her)?

Always	1
Usually	2
Sometimes	3
Rarely	4
Never	5

MALE/FEMALE COUPLES ONLY:

31. When you had sex with (P), how often did you have vaginal intercourse? By **vaginal intercourse,** we mean when a man's penis is inside a woman's vagina. If **Never,** go to Question 32. Was it . . .

Always	1
Usually	2
Sometimes	3
Rarely	4
Never	5

    A. When you had vaginal intercourse with (P), how often did you use condoms?

Always	1
Usually	2
Sometimes	3
Rarely	4
Never	5

    B. When you had vaginal intercourse with (P), how often did you use any other methods of birth control?

Always	1
Usually	2
Sometimes	3
Rarely	4
Never	5

MALE/FEMALE AND MALE/MALE ONLY:

32. When you had sex with (P), how often did you have anal intercourse with (P)? By **anal intercourse,** we mean when a man's penis is inside his partner's anus or rectum. If Never, go to Question 33. Was it . . .

Always	1
Usually	2
Sometimes	3
Rarely	4
Never	5

   A. When you had anal intercourse with (P), how often did you use condoms?

Always	1
Usually	2
Sometimes	3
Rarely	4
Never	5

MALE/MALE COUPLE ONLY:

   B. When you had anal intercourse, were you always the active (inserting) partner, the passive (receiving) partner, or sometimes both?

Active exclusively	1
Passive exclusively	2
Both	3

33. When you and (P) had sex during the past twelve months, did *you* always, usually, sometimes, rarely, or never have an orgasm, that is come or come to climax?

Always	1
Usually	2
Sometimes	3
Rarely	4
Never	5

34. When you and (P) had sex during the past twelve months, did (P) always, usually, sometimes, rarely, or never have an orgasm, that is come or come to climax?

Always	1
Usually	2
Sometimes	3
Rarely	4
Never	5

35. Now I would like to ask you how sex with (P) made you feel. Please, tell me if sex with (P) made you feel:

a. Satisfied	Yes	No
b. Sad	Yes	No
c. Loved	Yes	No
d. Anxious or worried	Yes	No

e. Wanted or needed	Yes	No
f. Taken care of	Yes	No
g. Scared or afraid	Yes	No
h. Thrilled or excited	Yes	No
i. Guilty	Yes	No
j. Other (SPECIFY) _____	Yes	No

36. How physically pleasurable did you find your relationship with (P) to be: extremely pleasurable, very pleasurable, moderately pleasurable, slightly pleasurable, or not at all pleasurable?

Extremely	1
Very	2
Moderately	3
Slightly	4
Not at all	5

37. How emotionally satisfying did you find your relationship with (P) to be: extremely satisfying, very satisfying, moderately satisfying, slightly satisfying, or not at all satisfying?

Extremely	1
Very	2
Moderately	3
Slightly	4
Not at all	5

38. People engage in sexual activities for a variety of reasons. What were your reasons for having sex with (P) during the past twelve months?

a. To make up after a fight or misunderstanding	Yes	No
b. To relieve sexual tension (arousal)	Yes	No
c. Because your partner wanted you to	Yes	No
d. MALE/FEMALE ONLY:		
To get pregnant	Yes	No
e. To express love or affection	Yes	No
f. To express or experience something else	Yes	No

(If Yes) What was that? _____

39. As far as you know, during the past twelve months has (P) had other sexual partners?
☐ Yes ☐ No If **No**, go to Question 40.
A. About how many partners was that? ☐☐
B. Were these partners all men, all women, or both? (Circle one)

Men	1
Women	2
Both	3
Don't know	4

C. Did (P) have sex with any of these people during the time you and (P) were sexually involved?

Yes	1
No	2

MALE/FEMALE COUPLES ONLY:

40. Now, some questions about vaginal intercourse. By **vaginal intercourse,** we mean when a man's penis is inside a woman's vagina. When you had sex with (P), did you have vaginal intercourse? ☐ Yes ☐ No If **No,** go to Question 41.
   A. When you had vaginal intercourse with (P), did you use condoms? ☐ Yes ☐ No
   B. When you had vaginal intercourse with (P), did you use any other methods of birth control? ☐ Yes ☐ No

MALE/FEMALE AND MALE/MALE ONLY:

41. Now, some questions about anal intercourse. By **anal intercourse,** we mean when a man's penis is inside his partner's anus or rectum. When you had sex with (P), did you have anal intercourse with (P)? ☐ Yes ☐ No If **No,** go to Section Four.
   A. When you had anal intercourse with (P), did you use condoms? ☐ Yes ☐ No
   MALE/MALE COUPLE ONLY:
   B. When you had anal intercourse, were you the active (inserting) partner, the passive (receiving) partner, or both?

Active exclusively	1
Passive exclusively	2
Both	3

SECTION FOUR: LAST EVENT

Now some questions about the very last time you had sex, that is, the most recent time you had sex in the last twelve months. These questions focus on that one time, not on any other time that you had sex with this partner.

1. Who did you have sex with most recently? ENTER NAME: _____

2. When did you last have sex? _ _ / _ _ / _ _

3. Where did you last have sex?

Your home	1
Partner's home	2
Someone else's home	3
Hotel or motel	4
Car or van	5
At work	6
A public place like a park	7
Somewhere else (SPECIFY)	8

   _____

   _____

   _____

Don't know	98
Refuse to answer	97

4. How long did this sexual activity last — from the time physical (sexual) contact began to when it ended.

15 minutes or less	1
More than 15 but less than 30 minutes	2
More than 30 minutes but less than 1 hour	3
More than 1 hour but less than 2 hours	4
2 hours or longer	5

IF YOU HAD SEX WITH THIS PARTNER MORE THAN ONE TIME (BASED ON HOW YOU ANSWERED QUESTION 9.A./9.B. IN THE PREVIOUS SECTION), GO TO QUESTION 5.

IF YOU AND YOUR PARTNER ONLY HAD SEX ONE TIME, GO TO NEXT SECTION: LIFETIME SEXUAL ACTIVITY.

5. Now some questions about alcohol use. During the most recent time you had sex, did you or (P) drink alcohol before or during sex? ☐ Yes ☐ No If **No,** go to Question 6.

    A. Was that you, (P), or both of you?

Respondent only	1 (Answer B ONLY)
Partner only	2 (Answer C ONLY)
Respondent and partner	3 (Answer both B AND C)

    B. How strongly were you affected by the alcohol: very strongly, somewhat, not at all?

Very strongly	1
Somewhat	2
Not at all	3
Don't know	8

    C. How strongly was (P) affected by the alcohol: very strongly, somewhat, not at all?

Very strongly	1
Somewhat	2
Not at all	3
Don't know	8

6. This most recent time you had sex, did either you or (P) use drugs to get high or intoxicated before or during sex? ☐ Yes ☐ No If **No,** go to Question 7.

    A. Was that you, (P), or both?

Respondent only	1 (Answer B ONLY)
Partner only	2 (Answer C ONLY)
Respondent and partner	3 (Answer both B AND C)

    B. How strongly were you affected by the drugs: very strongly, somewhat, not at all?

Very strongly	1
Somewhat	2
Not at all	3
Don't know	8

    C. How strongly was (P) affected by the drugs: very strongly, somewhat, not at all?

Very strongly	1
Somewhat	2
Not at all	3
Don't know	8

7. During the most recent time you had sex, did (P) perform oral sex on you? ☐ Yes ☐ No

8. When you had sex this time with (P), did you perform oral sex on (him/her)? ☐ Yes ☐ No

MALE/FEMALE COUPLES ONLY:

9. When you had sex with (P) this most recent time, did you have vaginal intercourse? ☐ Yes ☐ No If **No,** go to Question 10.
   A. When you had vaginal intercourse this time with (P), did you use condoms? ☐ Yes ☐ No
   B. When you had vaginal intercourse this time with (P), did you use any other methods of disease prevention or birth control? ☐ Yes ☐ No

MALE/FEMALE AND MALE/MALE ONLY:

10. When you had sex with (P) this most recent time, did you have anal intercourse? ☐ Yes ☐ No If **Yes,** go to Question 10A. If **No,** go to Question 11.
    A. This most recent time, when you had anal intercourse with (P), did you use condoms? ☐ Yes ☐ No
    MALE/MALE COUPLE ONLY:
    B. On this occasion, when you had anal intercourse, were you the active (inserting) partner, the passive (receiving) partner, or both?
Active exclusively	1
Passive exclusively	2
Both	3

11. When you and (P) had sex this most recent time, did *you* have an orgasm, that is come or come to climax? ☐ Yes ☐ No If **No,** go to Question 12.
    A. How many times did you have an orgasm? ☐☐

12. When you and (P) had sex this most recent time, did (P) have an orgasm, that is come or come to climax? ☐ Yes ☐ No

13. People engage in sexual activities for a variety of reasons. What were your reasons for having sex with (P) on this occasion?
a. To make up after a fight or misunderstanding	Yes	No
b. To relieve sexual tension (arousal)	Yes	No
c. Because your partner wanted you to	Yes	No
d. MALE/FEMALE ONLY:		
To get pregnant	Yes	No
e. To express love or affection	Yes	No
f. To express or experience something else	Yes	No
If Yes: What was that? _____		

SECTION FIVE: LIFETIME SEXUAL PARTNERS

BOX 5A   Are you eighteen or nineteen years old?
IF YES, GO TO SECTION 6.
IF NO, FOLLOW THE INSTRUCTIONS BELOW.

You have already answered questions about some of your sexual partners. Now, the following questions ask you about any *other* sexual partners you may have had since your eighteenth birthday.

In answering these questions, please count only those people who you had sex with for the first time *after you were age eighteen* and do not include anybody already listed.

Again, this section is only interested in the partners not already mentioned in the earlier sections who you had sex with for the first time between age eighteen and twelve months ago.

BOX 5B
BEFORE   IF YOU HAD *NO* S/C BETWEEN AGE EIGHTEEN AND TWELVE
MONTHS AGO, GO TO BOX 5G.
IF YOU HAD A S/C BEFORE AGE EIGHTEEN, GO TO BOX 5C.
IF YOU HAD *ONE* OR *MORE* S/Cs BETWEEN AGE EIGHTEEN AND
TWELVE MONTHS AGO, GO TO QUESTION 1, BELOW.

1. Thinking back, since you were age eighteen and during the time before you started living with (1st S/C), how many people, including men and women, did you begin having sex with, even if only one time? **Please remember, *only* tell about those persons that you have *not* discussed already.** ☐☐☐ If none, go to Box 6C. If one, go to Question 2. If two or more, go to Question 6.

2. Was this partner male or female? ☐ Male ☐ Female

3. What would you say best describes (his/her) racial background?
   White   1
   Black   2
   Hispanic   3
   Asian   4
   Other   5

4. What was the highest level of education this person received?
   Less than twelfth grade   1
   High school graduate   2
   Some college or vocational school   3
   College graduate   4
   More than college graduate   5

5. How many times did you have sex with this partner? ☐☐☐ Go to Box 5C.

6. How many of these partners were . . .
   Male   ☐☐☐
   Female   ☐☐☐

7. How many of these partners would you describe as . . .
   White   ☐☐☐
   Black   ☐☐☐
   Hispanic   ☐☐☐
   Asian   ☐☐☐
   Other   ☐☐☐

8. How many of these people had as their highest level of education . . .
   Less than twelfth grade   1
   High school graduate   2
   Some college or vocational school   3
   College graduate   4
   More than college graduate   5

9. How many of these partners did you have sex with . . .
   Only one time   ☐☐☐
   2 to 10 times   ☐☐☐
   More than 10 times   ☐☐☐

10. During this time, did you ever have sex with one partner while still involved in a sexual relationship with another partner? ☐ Yes ☐ No

---

BOX 5C
DURING IF YOUR FIRST S/C RELATIONSHIP ENDED MORE THAN TWELVE MONTHS AGO, GO TO QUESTION 11 BELOW.
IF YOUR FIRST S/C IS *CURRENT* S/C OR ENDED *LESS* THAN TWELVE MONTHS AGO, GO TO BOX 5H.

---

11. Now, some questions about any *other* sexual partners you may have had *during* the time you were living with (1st S/C). While living with (1st S/C), how many people, including men and women, did you begin having sex with, even if only one time? **Again, please count *only* those persons that you have *not* told about already and who you had sex with for the first time after you were *age eighteen.* ☐☐☐** If none, go to Box 5D. If one, go back to Question 2 under Box 5B, after answering Question 12 below. If two or more, go back to Question 6 under Box 5B, after answering Question 12 below.

12. During this time, did you also continue to have sex with any of the partners you were sexually involved with *before* the time you started living with (1st S/C)? ☐ Yes ☐ No

BOX 5D
BETWEEN IF YOU LISTED 2 OR MORE S/C RELATIONSHIPS, GO TO
QUESTION 13 BELOW.
OTHERWISE SKIP TO BOX 5I.

13. Now, some questions about any *other* sexual partners between the time you were living with (1st S/C) and (2nd S/C). During this period, how many people, including men and women, did you begin having sex with, even if only one time? **Please remember, do *not* include any persons that you have already told me about.** ☐☐☐ If none, go to Box 5E. If one, go to Question 2. If two or more, go to Question 6, after answering Question 14 below.

14. During this time, did you also continue to have sex with any of the partners you discussed earlier? ☐ Yes ☐ No

BOX 5E
DURING IF YOUR 2ND S/C ENDED *MORE* THAN TWELVE MONTHS AGO, GO
TO QUESTION 15 BELOW.
IF YOUR 2ND S/C IS *CURRENT* OR ENDED *LESS* THAN TWELVE
MONTHS AGO, GO TO BOX 5H.

15. Now, some questions about any *other* sexual partners you may have had *during* the time you were living with (2nd S/C). While living with (2nd S/C), how many people, including men and women, did you begin having sex with, even if only one time? **Please remember, *only* include those persons that you have *not* told about before.** ☐☐☐ If none, go to Box 5F. If one, go to Question 2. If two or more, go to Question 6.

BOX 5F
BETWEEN IF YOU HAVE HAD THREE OR MORE S/Cs, GO TO QUESTION 16
BELOW. OTHERWISE SKIP TO BOX 5I.

16. Now, some questions about any *other* sexual partners since the time you stopped living with (2nd S/C) and up until twelve months ago. During this period, how many people, including men and women, did you begin having sex with, even if only one time? **Please remember, *only* discuss those persons that you have *not* told about already.** ☐☐☐ If none, go to Box 5G. If one, go to Question 2. If two or more, go to Question 6.

BOX 5G
NO S/Cs IF *NEVER* HAD S/C IN LIFETIME, GO TO QUESTION 17 BELOW.

17. Now, some questions about your sexual partners since you were eighteen years old. Thinking back, during the time since you were *age eighteen* and *not* including the partners you already discussed, how many people, including men and women, did you engage in sexual activity with, even if only one time? **Please remember, *only* include those persons that you have *not* told about before.** ☐☐☐ If none, go to Section 6. If one, go to Question 2, after answering Question 18 below. If two or more, go to Question 6, after answering Question 18 below.

18. During this time, did you ever have sex with one of these people while still involved in a sexual relationship with another person? ☐ Yes ☐ No

---

BOX 5H

CURRENT S/C IF YOU HAVE A *CURRENT* S/C OR A S/C THAT ENDED *LESS*
                 THAN TWELVE MONTHS AGO, GO TO QUESTION 19 BELOW.

---

19. Now, some questions about any *other* sexual partners you may have had *during* the time you were living with (CURRENT S/C) but *not* including the people you had sex with during the last twelve months. How many people, including men and women, did you engage in sexual activity with, even if only one time? **Please remember, *only* include those persons that you have *not* told about before.** ☐☐☐ If none, go to Section 6. If one, go to Question 2, after answering Question 20 below. If two or more, go to Question 6, after answering Question 20 below.

20. During this time, did you also continue to have sex with any of the partners you discussed earlier? ☐ Yes ☐ No

---

BOX 5I

LESS THAN 3 S/Cs IF YOUR *LAST* S/C ENDED MORE THAN TWELVE MONTHS
                     AGO, GO TO QUESTION 21 BELOW.

---

21. Now, some questions about any *other* sexual partners you had *after* the time you stopped living with (LAST S/C). How many people, including men and women, did you engage in sexual activity with, even if only one time? **Please remember, *only* include those persons that you have not discussed before.** ☐☐☐ If none, go to Section 6. If one, go to Question 2, after answering Question 22 below. If two or more, go to Question 6, after answering Question 22 below.

22. During this time, did you also continue to have sex with any of the partners you discussed earlier? ☐ Yes ☐ No

SECTION SIX: MASTURBATION AND FANTASY

Part I

Masturbation is a very common practice. In order to understand the full range of sexual behavior, we need to know the answers to a few questions about your experiences with masturbation. By masturbation, we mean self-sex or self-stimulation, that is, stimulating your genitals (sex organs) to the point of arousal, but not necessarily to orgasm or climax. The following questions are *not* about activity with a sexual partner, but about times when you were alone or when other people were not aware of what you were doing.

1. On average, in the past twelve months how often did you masturbate? CIRCLE ONE NUMBER ONLY.

More than once a day	01
Every day	02
Several times a week	03
Once a week	04
Two or three times a month	05
Once a month	06
Every other month	07
Three to five times a year	08
Once or twice a year	09
Not at all this year (Go to Part II)	10

2. When masturbating in the past twelve months, how often did you reach orgasm, that is come or come to climax?

Always	1
Usually	2
Sometimes	3
Rarely	4
Never	5

3. People masturbate for many reasons. Thinking about the past twelve months, please circle the number beside all the reasons why you usually masturbated. CIRCLE ALL THAT APPLY.

To relax	1
To relieve sexual tension	2
Because of unavailability of partners	3
Because you wanted physical pleasure	4
Because you were bored	5
Because your partner did not want to have sex	6
To get to sleep	7
Because you are afraid of getting AIDS or another disease	8
Other (PLEASE SPECIFY)	9

_____

_____

4. Do you feel guilty after you masturbate?

Always	1
Usually	2
Sometimes	3
Rarely	4
Never	5

Part II

People think about sex in different ways and find some activities more appealing than others. In order to better understand how people think about sex, now some questions concerning your feelings about sex.

1. On the average, how often do you think about sex? If Never, go to Question 3.

Less than once a month	1
One to a few times a month	2
One to a few times a week	3
Every day	4
Several times a day	5
Never think about sex	6

2. How often does thinking about sex make you feel guilty?

Never	1
Rarely	2
Occasionally	3
Often	4
Nearly always	5

3. Do your thoughts or fantasies about sex usually involve a story or are they more like images or pictures?

Story	1
Pictures	2
Both	3

4. On a scale of 1 to 4, where 1 is very appealing and 4 is not at all appealing, how would you rate each of these activities:

	Very appealing	Some-what appealing	Not appealing	Not at all appealing
a. Having sex with more than one person at the same time	1	2	3	4
b. Having sex with someone of the same sex	1	2.	3	4
c. Forcing someone to do something sexual that he/she doesn't want to do	1	2	3	4
d. Being forced into doing something sexual that you don't want to do	1	2	3	4

e. Seeing other people doing sexual things	1	2	3	4
f. Having sex with someone you don't personally know	1	2	3	4

5. On a scale of 1 to 4, where 1 is very appealing and 4 is not at all appealing, how would you rate each of these activities:

	Very appealing	Some-what appealing	Not appealing	Not at all appealing
a. Watching partner undress/strip	1	2	3	4
b. Vaginal intercourse	1	2	3	4
c. Using a dildo or vibrator	1	2	3	4
d. A partner performing oral sex on you	1	2	3	4
e. Performing oral sex on a partner	1	2	3	4
f. Partner stimulating your anus with his/her fingers	1	2	3	4
g. Stimulating partner's anus with your fingers	1	2	3	4
h. Passive anal intercourse *ASK MALES ONLY*	1	2	3	4
i. Active anal intercourse	1	2	3	4

Many materials are sold for the enhancement of sexual enjoyment.

6. In the last twelve months did you . . .

Buy or rent any x-rated movies or videos	Yes	No
Buy any sexually explicit magazines or books	Yes	No
Buy any vibrators or dildos	Yes	No
Buy any other sex toys	Yes	No
Call any "pay by the minute" sex phone numbers	Yes	No
Buy anything else for sex (SPECIFY) _____	Yes	No

7. (If Yes to any of Question 6:) About how much money would you estimate you spent on these kinds of things over the past twelve months? $□,□□□.□□

There are many activities that people participate in to enhance their sexual experiences or to give an outlet to their sexual feelings. I am going to ask you about your participation in some of these activities.

8. In the last twelve months did you . . .

Go to nightclubs with nude or seminude dancers	Yes	No
Hire a prostitute or pay anyone to have sex with you	Yes	No
Attend a public gathering in which you were nude	Yes	No
Have your picture taken in the nude	Yes	No

9. (If Yes to any of Question 8:) About how many times in the last twelve months did you do (this/these)? □□□

SECTION SEVEN: CHILDHOOD, ADOLESCENCE, AND SEXUAL VICTIMIZATION

Now, some questions about your early sexual experience. This series of questions is intended to help understand the importance of various events that occur during sexual development.

1. How old were you when you reached puberty?
   FEMALE
   By puberty I mean when you had your first menstrual period? □□
   MALE
   By puberty I mean when your voice changed or when you began to grow pubic hair. □□

2. When you were growing up, in which of the following ways did you learn about sexual matters? From: (CIRCLE ALL THAT APPLY). If Can't Remember, go to Question 3.

Mother	01
Father	02
Brother(s)	03
Sister(s)	04
Other relative(s)	05
Lessons at school	06
Friends of about my own age	07
MEN: First girlfriend or sexual partner	08
WOMEN: First boyfriend or sexual partner	08
Doctor, nurse, or clinic	09
Television	10
Radio	11
Books	12
Magazines or newspapers	13
Other (SPECIFY) _____	14
Can't remember at all	98

IF YOU CIRCLED TWO OR MORE PROCEED TO QUESTION 2A. OTHERWISE GO TO Q. 3

A. From which *one* of those did you learn the most?

Mother	01
Father	02
Brother(s)	03
Sister(s)	04
Other relative(s)	05
Lessons at school	06
Friends of about my own age	07

MEN: First girlfriend or sexual partner	08
WOMEN: First boyfriend or sexual partner	08
Doctor, nurse, or clinic	09
Television	10
Radio	11
Books	12
Magazines or newspapers	13
Other (SPECIFY) _____	14
Can't choose just one (state main ones)	96
Don't know/can't remember at all	98

3. Before you were the age you identified in Question 1, did anyone touch you sexually? □ Yes □ No If **No,** go to Question 13.
   A. Before you were the age you identified in Question 1, what happened sexually? (Circle one)

Kissing	01
Touching/fondling the genitals	02
Oral sex	03
Vaginal intercourse	04
Anal intercourse	05

Now, talk about those individuals that touched you sexually . . .

4. With how many persons did this happen? □□ If one, answer these questions in the singular. If two or more, answer as presented.

5. Thinking about these persons, how many were . . .

Male	□□
Female	□□

   A. How many of these people were . . .

13 years old or younger	□□
14 to 17 years old	□□
18 years or older	□□

   B. Thinking about these persons, what were their relationships to you? How many were . . .

	Number of persons
Stranger	□□
Teacher	□□
Family friend/acquaintance	□□
Relative (uncle/cousin)	□□
Mother's boyfriend	□□
Respondent's older friend	□□
Older brother	□□
Stepfather	□□
Father	□□
Other	□□

6. With how many of these people, did this happen . . .
   Just one time   □□
   A few more times   □□
   Many more times   □□

7. How old were you when this started? □□

8. How old were you when this ended? □□

9. While you were a child, did anyone else know about these events? □ Yes □ No If **Yes**, go to Question 10. If **No**, go to Question 12.

10. Who knew? (CIRCLE ALL THAT APPLY)
    Mother   01
    Father   02
    Stepparent   03
    Brother/sister   04
    Other relative   05
    Other child   06
    Adult friend   07
    Minister/clergy   08
    Teacher   09
    Other   10
    Don't know   98

11. Did you tell them or did they discover some other way?
    I told them   1
    Some other way   2

12. Do you think that these experiences have had any effect on your life since then? □ Yes □ No If **Yes**, go to 12A. If **No**, go to Question 13.
    A. In what ways (i.e., affected your sex life, relationships with men or women, etc.)

    _____

    _____

13. Now, some questions about what you did sexually after you were twelve or thirteen, that is after puberty. How old were you the *first* time you had vaginal intercourse with a member of the opposite sex?
    □□ If **never**, indicate Never and go to Question 20.

14. Was this first intercourse . . .
    Something you wanted to happen at the time   1 (Go to C)
    Something you went along with, but did not want to happen 2 (Go to D)
    Something that you were forced to do against your will   3 (Go to A)
    A. What was your relationship to this person? (Circle one) If Spouse, go to Question 17.
       Spouse   1
       Someone you were in love with but not married to   2
       Someone you knew well but were not in love with   3

Someone you knew but not well   4
Someone you just met   5
Someone you paid to have sex   6
Someone who paid you to have sex   7
Someone you didn't know, a stranger   8
Someone else (SPECIFY) _____   9

B. In what ways were you forced to have sex? (CIRCLE ALL THAT APPLY)
Threats of or use of physical force   1
Threats to use or use of weapon, such as a knife or gun   2
Other threats or intimidation (coercion, blackmail, threats to others) 3

GO TO QUESTION 16

C. There are many different reasons why people decide to have vaginal intercourse for the first time. What was the main reason you chose to have vaginal intercourse for the first time? (CIRCLE ONE)
Affection for partner   1
Peer pressure   2
Curious/ready for sex   3
Wanted to have a baby   4
Physical pleasure   5
Under the influence of drugs or alcohol   6
Wedding night   7
Other (SPECIFY) _____   8
Don't know/don't remember   9

GO TO QUESTION 15

D. There are many different reasons why people go along with having vaginal intercourse for the first time, even when they don't want to. What was the main reason you decided to go along with having sexual intercourse this first time? (CIRCLE ONE)
Affection for partner   1
Peer pressure   2
Curious/ready for sex   3
Wanted to have a baby   4
Physical pleasure   5
Under the influence of drugs or alcohol   6
Wedding night   7
Other (SPECIFY) _____   8
Don't know/don't remember   9

GO TO QUESTION 15

15. The *first* time you had vaginal intercourse with this person, what was your relationship? If Spouse, go to Question 17.
Spouse   1
Someone you were in love with but not married to   2
Someone you knew well but were not in love with   3
Someone you knew but not well   4
Someone you just met   5
Someone you paid to have sex   6
Someone who paid you to have sex   7
Someone you didn't know, a stranger   8
Someone else (SPECIFY) _____   9

16. Was this person a relative? ☐ Yes ☐ No If **Yes,** go to 16A. If **No,** go to Question 17.
    A. What was their relationship to you?

Father	1
Mother	2
Brother	3
Sister	4
Uncle	5
Aunt	6
Cousin	7
Other (SPECIFY) _____	8

17. Did you or your partner use birth control this first time? ☐ Yes ☐ No ☐ Don't know

18. What happened sexually? (CIRCLE ALL THAT APPLY)

Kissing	01
Touching/fondling the genitals	02
Oral sex	03
Vaginal intercourse	04
Anal intercourse	05

19. How many times did you have vaginal intercourse with that person?

Just one time	1
Two to ten times	2
More than ten times	3
Still having intercourse	4

BOX 7-A WAS FIRST SEX FORCED? ☐ Yes ☐ No If **Yes,** go to Question 21. If **No,** go to Question 20.

---

20. After puberty, that is after you were the age you identified in Question 1, did a member of the opposite sex force you to do anything sexually that you did not want to do? ☐ Yes ☐ No If **Yes,** go to Question 22. If **No,** go to Question 29.

21. Other than the first time, have you ever been forced by a member of the opposite sex to do anything sexually that you did not want to do? ☐ Yes ☐ No If **Yes,** go to Question 22. If **No,** go to Question 29.

22. With how many different persons did this happen? ☐☐ If one, go to Question 23. If two or more, edit questions 23–25 appropriately.

23. What was your relationship to that person? (CIRCLE ONE)

Spouse	1
Someone you were in love with but not married to	2
Someone you knew well but were not in love with	3
Someone you knew but not well	4
Someone you just met	5
Someone you paid to have sex	6

Someone who paid you to have sex	7
Someone you didn't know, a stranger	8
Someone else (SPECIFY) _____	9

24. How many times did this happen? ☐☐

25. What happened sexually? (CIRCLE ALL THAT APPLY)

Kissing	01
Touching/fondling the genitals	02
Oral sex	03
Vaginal intercourse	04
Anal intercourse	05

BOX 7-B WAS FIRST VAGINAL INTERCOURSE BEFORE AGE EIGHTEEN? ☐ Yes
☐ No If **Yes,** go to Question 26. If **No,** go to Question 29. If never had vaginal
intercourse, go to Question 29.

---

26. Other than this first person, how many different members of the opposite sex did you have
    vaginal intercourse with before you were eighteen? ☐☐ If None, go to Question 29. If
    one, go to Question 27. If more than one, edit questions 27–28 appropriately.

None	00
One	01
More than one	02

27. How many times did you have vaginal intercourse with that person?

One time	1
Two to ten times	2
More than ten times	3
Still having intercourse	4

28. What was your relationship to that person?

Spouse	1
Someone you were in love with but not married to	2
Someone you knew well but were not in love with	3
Someone you knew but not well	4
Someone you just met	5
Someone you paid to have sex	6
Someone who paid you to have sex	7
Someone you didn't know, a stranger	8
Someone else (SPECIFY) _____	9

29. Now, some questions about your sexual experience with a member of the same sex after
    you were twelve or thirteen, that is, after puberty. How old were you the first time that
    you had sex with a member of the same sex? ☐☐ If never, indicate Never and go to
    Question 36.

30. Was this . . .

    Something you wanted to happen at the time   1 (Go to C)

    Something you went along with, but did not strongly desire   2 (Go to D)

    Something that you were forced to do against your will   3 (Go to A)

  A. What was your relationship to this person?

Someone you were in love with	1
Someone you knew well but were not in love with	2
Someone you knew but not well	3
Someone you just met	4
Someone you paid to have sex	5
Someone who paid you to have sex	6
Someone you didn't know, a stranger	7
A relative	8
Someone else (SPECIFY) _____	9

  B. In what ways were you forced to have sex? (CIRCLE ALL THAT APPLY)

_____

_____

Threats of or use of physical force	1
Threats to use or use of weapon, such as a knife or gun	2
Other threats or intimidation (coercion, blackmail, threats to others)	3

GO TO QUESTION 32

  C. There are many reasons why people decide to have sexual activity for the first time with a person of the same sex. What was the main reason you chose to have sexual contact for the first time? (CIRCLE ONE)

Affection for partner	1
Peer pressure	2
Curious/ready for sex	3
Physical pleasure	5
Under the influence of drugs or alcohol	6
Other (SPECIFY) _____	8
Don't know/don't remember	9

GO TO QUESTION 31

  D. There are many reasons why people go along with having sexual activity for the first time with a person of the same sex, even when they don't want to. What was the main reason you decided to go along with having sexual contact this first time? (CIRCLE ONE)

Affection for partner	1
Peer pressure	2
Curious/ready for sex	3
Physical pleasure	5
Under the influence of drugs or alcohol	6
Other (SPECIFY) _____	8
Don't know/don't remember	9

GO TO QUESTION 31

31. What was your relationship to the person at the time that you had sexual activity for the first time?

Someone you were in love with	1
Someone you knew well but were not in love with	2
Someone you knew but not well	3
Someone you just met	4
Someone you paid to have sex	5
Someone who paid you to have sex	6
Someone you didn't know, a stranger	7
A relative	8
Someone else (SPECIFY) _____	9

32. Was your first same sex partner older, younger, or the same age as you?

Older	1 (Answer A)
Younger	2 (Answer A)
Same age	3 (Go to Question 33)

A. How many years (older/younger) than you? ☐☐

33. What did this involve? (CIRCLE ALL THAT APPLY)

MALE/MALE ACTIVITY

Your partner stimulating your genitals with his hand	01
You stimulating your partner's genitals with your hand	02
Passive oral sex: Partner stimulating your genitals with his mouth	03
Active oral sex: You stimulating your partner's genitals with your mouth	04
Active anal intercourse: You inserting your penis in your partner's anus	05
Passive anal intercourse: Your partner inserting his penis in your anus	06
Something else	07

FEMALE/FEMALE ACTIVITY

You rubbing your genitals on your partner's body	11
Partner rubbing her genitals on your body	12
Partner stimulating your genitals with her hand	13
You stimulating your partner's genitals with your hand	14
Passive oral sex: Partner stimulating your genitals with her mouth	15
Active oral sex: You stimulating your partner's genitals with your mouth	16
Something else	17

34. How many times did you have sex with that person after the first time?

Never again	1
Just one time	2
Two to ten times	3
More than ten times	4
Still having sex	5

BOX 7-C WAS YOUR FIRST SAME-SEX ACTIVITY FORCED? ☐ Yes ☐ No If **Yes,** go to Question B. If **No,** go to Question A

A. Have you ever been forced to do anything sexual that you did not want to do by a person of the same sex? ☐ Yes ☐ No If **Yes,** go to C. If **No,** go to Box 7-D.
B. Other than this first time, have you ever been forced to do anything sexual that you did not want to do by a person of the same sex? ☐ Yes ☐ No If **Yes,** go to C. If **No,** go to Box 7-D.
C. How many times has this happened? ☐☐
D. What kind(s) of sexual activity happened? (CIRCLE ALL THAT APPLY)

Kissing	01
Touching/fondling the genitals	02
Oral sex	03
Vaginal intercourse	04
Anal intercourse	05

BOX 7-D WAS YOUR FIRST SAME-SEX PARTNER BEFORE AGE EIGHTEEN? ☐ Yes ☐ No If **Yes,** go to Question 35. If **No,** go to Question 36.

35. Other than this first person, how many different same-sex partners did you have sex with before you were eighteen? ☐☐ If None, go to Question 36. If One, answer both A and B. If more than one, edit A and B appropriately.

None	00
One	01
More than one	02

A. How many times did you have sex with that person?

Just one time	1
Two to ten times	2
More than ten times	3
Still having sex	4

B. What was your relationship to that person?

Someone you were in love with	1
Someone you knew well but were not in love with	2
Someone you knew but not well	3
Someone you just met	4
Someone you paid to have sex	5
Someone who paid you to have sex	6
Someone you didn't know, a stranger	7
A relative	8
Someone else (SPECIFY) _____	9

FEMALE ONLY:
36. In general, are you sexually attracted to . . .
    Only men   01
    Mostly men   02
    Both men and women   03
    Mostly women   04
    Only women   05

MALE ONLY:
37. In general, are you sexually attracted to . . .
    Only women   01
    Mostly women   02
    Both women and men   03
    Mostly men   04
    Only men   05

38. Do you think of yourself as . . .
    Heterosexual   01
    Homosexual   02
    Bisexual   03
    Something else (SPECIFY) _____ 04
    Normal/straight   05
    Don't know   98

SECTION EIGHT: PHYSICAL HEALTH

Now I would like to ask you a few questions about your health and some health-related topics.

1. In general, would you say your health is . . .
    Excellent   1
    Good   2
    Fair   3
    Poor   4

2. **MALES ONLY:** Are you circumcised? ☐ Yes ☐ No

3. Have you ever received a blood transfusion? ☐ Yes ☐ No If **Yes,** in what month and year?
_____

4. Generally, how happy have you been with your personal life during the past twelve months? Have you been . . .
    Extremely happy   1
    Very happy most of the time   2
    Generally satisfied, pleased   3
    Sometimes fairly unhappy   4
    Unhappy most of the time   5

5. During the past twelve months, about how regularly did you drink alcoholic beverages? Would you say that it was . . .

Daily	1
Several times a week	2
Several times a month	3
Once a month or less	4
Not at all	5

6. On a typical day when you drank, about how many drinks did you usually have? ☐☐

7. During the past twelve months, how much of the time has your physical health interfered with your sexual activities? Would you say that it was . . .

All of the time	1
Most of the time	2
Some of the time	3
A little of the time	4
None of the time	5

8. During the past twelve months, how much of the time have emotional problems interfered with your sexual activities? Would you say that it was . . .

All of the time	1
Most of the time	2
Some of the time	3
A little of the time	4
None of the time	5

9. During the past twelve months, how much of the time has stress or pressure in your life interfered with your sexual activities? Would you say that it was . . .

All of the time	1
Most of the time	2
Some of the time	3
A little of the time	4
None of the time	5

Sometimes people go through periods in which they are not interested in sex or are having trouble achieving sexual gratification. Below are just a few questions about whether you have experienced this in the past twelve months.

10. During the last twelve months has there ever been a period of several months or more when you . . . (Circle Yes or No for each question)

A. Lacked interest in having sex	Yes	No
B. Were unable to come to a climax (experience an orgasm)	Yes	No
C. Came to a climax (experienced an orgasm) too quickly	Yes	No
D. Experienced physical pain *during* intercourse	Yes	No
E. Did not find sex pleasurable (even if it was not painful)	Yes	No
F. Felt anxious just before having sex about your ability to perform sexually	Yes	No

MALE ONLY:
    G. Had trouble achieving or maintaining an erection   Yes No
FEMALE ONLY:
    H. Had trouble lubricating   Yes No

IF YOU ANSWERED **NO** TO ALL OF THE ABOVE, SKIP TO INTRODUCTION TO QUESTION 13. OTHERWISE, GO TO QUESTION 11.

11. During the past twelve months, have you ever avoided sex because of the problem(s) you mentioned? ☐ Yes ☐ No

12. Sometimes when people have problems like this, they go to someone such as a doctor or a counselor of some sort for help. In the past twelve months, have you gone to any of the following people for help with the sexual problem(s) you have experienced:

A private psychiatrist or psychologist	Yes	No
A psychiatrist or psychologist in a clinic	Yes	No
Another type of private doctor	Yes	No
Another type of doctor in a clinic	Yes	No
A marriage counselor	Yes	No
A clergy person	Yes	No
Someone else (SPECIFY) _____	Yes	No

There are several diseases or infections that can be transmitted during sex. These are sometimes called venereal diseases or VD. We will be using the term *sexually transmitted diseases* or STDs to refer to them.

13. Please answer a few questions about these diseases.

If you answered "YES" in Section A to any of the below diseases please complete B and C. If you answered all "NO" go to Question 14.	A. Circle "YES" or "NO" to whether you have *ever* been told by a doctor that you had any of these diseases.	B. How many times have you *ever* been told by a doctor you had (STD)?	C. Have you been told by a doctor you had (STD) in the past twelve months?
	YES NO		YES NO
a. Gonorrhea (clap, drip)	1 2	☐☐	1 2
b. Syphilis (bad blood)	1 2	☐☐	1 2
c. Herpes (genital herpes)	1 2	☐☐	1 2
d. Chlamydia	1 2	☐☐	1 2
e. Genital warts (venereal warts, human papilloma virus or HPV)	1 2	☐☐	1 2
f. Hepatitis	1 2	☐☐	1 2
g. AIDS, HIV	1 2	☐☐	1 2

FEMALE ONLY
h. Vaginitis — such as yeast infection or candidiasis, trich
or trichomonas
(Trichomoniasis)   1 2   ☐☐   1 2
FEMALE ONLY
i. Pelvic inflammatory disease
(PID)   1 2   ☐☐   1 2
MALE ONLY
j. NGU (nongonococcal
urethritis)   1 2   ☐☐   1 2
k. Other (SPECIFY:) _____   1 2   ☐☐   1 2

IF YOU ANSWERED **NO** TO ALL THE QUESTIONS IN COLUMN C, GO TO **BOX 8-A**, OTHERWISE, ANSWER D AND E FOR EACH QUESTION IN COLUMN C THAT YOU ANSWERED **YES.**

D. Where did you go for treatment?
CIRCLE FOR EACH **YES** IN COLUMN D.
Was it . . .

Private or group practice	1
A hospital emergency room	2
Family planning clinic	3
An STD clinic	4
Some other clinic	5
Somewhere else	6

a. 1 2 3 4 5 6
b. 1 2 3 4 5 6
c. 1 2 3 4 5 6
d. 1 2 3 4 5 6
e. 1 2 3 4 5 6
f. 1 2 3 4 5 6
g. 1 2 3 4 5 6
h. 1 2 3 4 5 6

i. 1 2 3 4 5 6
j. 1 2 3 4 5 6
k. 1 2 3 4 5 6

E. Which partner do you think may have given you (STD)?
RECORD NAME IN SPACE BELOW (nick-names, abbreviations, etc. are allowed).

a. _____
b. _____
c. _____
d. _____
e. _____
f. _____
g. _____
h. Or not partner-related (such as yeast infection)?
_____
i. _____
j. _____
k. _____

GO TO BOX 8-A

14. Have you ever wondered if you had a sexually transmitted disease? ☐ Yes ☐ No

---

BOX 8-A If you circled any "4s" in section D above, have you gone to an STD clinic?
☐ Yes ☐ No If **Yes**, go to Question 16. If **No**, go to Question 15.

15. Have you ever gone to a sexually transmitted disease or STD clinic for any reason? ☐ Yes ☐ No If **No**, go to Question 18.

16. When was the most recent time you visited an STD clinic?

☐☐　　☐☐
MONTH　YEAR

17. What was your *main* reason for going to the STD clinic? RECORD VERBATIM.

Referred by a sexual partner	1
Contacted by the clinic as a contact to an STD case	2
Experiencing symptoms	3
Going for an STD follow-up	4
For a check-up	5
Going for some other reason	6

18. During the past twelve months, have you ever experienced any of the following symptoms:

Painful or difficult urination	Yes	No
Painful intercourse	Yes	No
Lesions or sores in the genital area	Yes	No
Intense chronic itching of genital area	Yes	No
(FEMALE ONLY) Vaginal discharge	Yes	No

19. Next, I am going to read you some methods that people use to prevent getting the AIDS virus through sexual activity. For each one, please tell me whether you think it is *very effective, somewhat effective,* or *not at all effective* in preventing someone from getting the AIDS virus through sexual activity.

	Very effective	Somewhat effective	Not at all effective
A. Using a diaphragm	3	2	1
B. Using a condom	3	2	1
C. Using a spermicidal jelly, foam, or cream	3	2	1
D. Using a condom with a spermicidal jelly, foam, or cream	3	2	1
E. Having a vasectomy	3	2	1
F. Two people who do not have the AIDS virus having sex *only* with each other	3	2	1

20. Have you made any kind of changes in your sexual behavior because of AIDS? ☐ Yes ☐ No If **Yes,** go to Question 21. If **No,** go to Question 22.

21. What have you changed? RECORD VERBATIM.

_____
_____
_____
_____

22. How many people have you known personally, either living or dead, who came down with the disease called AIDS?

NUMBER □□

None   00 (GO TO SECTION 9)

23. Think about the person you have known best, living or dead, who came down with AIDS. Please tell me which best describes your relationship to that person.

A.	Husband or wife	01
B.	Partner or lover	02
C.	Son or daughter	03
D.	Other relative	04
E.	Friend	05
F.	Neighbor	06
G.	Coworker	07
H.	Acquaintance	08
I.	Patient	09
J.	Other	10

24. We would like to know a few other things about that person.
    A. Is that person currently living, or has that person died? □ Living □ Dead
    B. (Is/Was) that person male or female? □ Male □ Female
    C. How old (is/was) that person? (Is/Was) (he/she) . . .

10 years or under	1
11–20	2
21–40	3
41 years or older	4

    D. What (is/was) that person's race? (Is/Was) it black, white, Hispanic, or other?

Black	1
White	2
Hispanic	3
Other	4

    E. What state (does/did) this person live in?
    State _____

BOX 8-B IF QUESTION 22 EQUALS 1 GO TO SECTION NINE.
                IF QUESTION 22 EQUALS 2 OR MORE ANSWER QUESTIONS 23–24
                FOR EACH PERSON.

SECTION NINE: ATTITUDES

1. There's been a lot of discussion about the way morals and attitudes about sex are changing in this country. If a man and a woman have sex relations before marriage, do you think it is always wrong, almost always wrong, wrong only sometimes, or not wrong at all?

Always wrong	1
Almost always wrong	2
Wrong only sometimes	3
Not wrong at all	4

2. What if they are in their teens, say fourteen to sixteen years old? In that case, do you think sex relations before marriage are always wrong, almost always wrong, wrong only sometimes, or not wrong at all?

Always wrong	1
Almost always wrong	2
Wrong only sometimes	3
Not wrong at all	4

3. What is your opinion about a married person having sexual relations with someone other than the marriage partner — is it always wrong, almost always wrong, sometimes wrong, or not wrong at all?

Always wrong	1
Almost always wrong	2
Wrong only sometimes	3
Not wrong at all	4

4. What is your opinion about sexual relations between two adults of the same sex — do you think it is always wrong, almost always wrong, wrong only sometimes, or not wrong at all?

Always wrong	1
Almost always wrong	2
Wrong only sometimes	3
Not wrong at all	4

5. When do you think a woman is most likely to become pregnant? Is it . . .

Right before her period	1
During her period	2
Right after her period	3
About 2 weeks after her period begins	4
Anytime during the cycle	5
Don't know	8

Please tell if you strongly agree, agree, disagree, or strongly disagree with the following statements.

6. Men have greater sexual needs than women.

Strongly agree	1
Agree	2
Disagree	3
Strongly disagree	4

7. Any kind of sexual activity between adults is okay as long as both persons freely agree to it.
   Strongly agree   1
   Agree   2
   Disagree   3
   Strongly disagree   4

8. There should be laws against the sale of pornography to persons over eighteen.
   Strongly agree   1
   Agree   2
   Disagree   3
   Strongly disagree   4

9. I am a better lover after a drink or two.
   Strongly agree   1
   Agree   2
   Disagree   3
   Strongly disagree   4

10. I feel guilty when I think about someone else when I am having sex with my partner.
    Strongly agree   1
    Agree   2
    Disagree   3
    Strongly disagree   4

11. You don't need to use a condom if you know your partner well.
    Strongly agree   1
    Agree   2
    Disagree   3
    Strongly disagree   4

12. I would not have sex with someone unless I was in love with them.
    Strongly agree   1
    Agree   2
    Disagree   3
    Strongly disagree   4

13. My religious beliefs have shaped and guided my sexual behavior.
    Strongly agree   1
    Agree   2
    Disagree   3
    Strongly disagree   4

14. I try to make sure that my partner has an orgasm when we have sex.
    Strongly agree   1
    Agree   2
    Disagree   3
    Strongly disagree   4

15. Please tell whether or not you think it should be possible for a pregnant woman to obtain a *legal* abortion . . .
    A. If she became pregnant as a result of rape
        Yes   1
        No   2
        Don't know   8
        Not applicable   9
    B. If the woman wants it for any reason
        Yes   1
        No   2
        Don't know   8
        Not applicable   9

16. Who do you think usually enjoys sex more — men, women, or do they both enjoy it the same amount?
        Men   1
        Women   2
        Both the same   3
        Don't know   8

Thank you very much for participating in this study. We greatly appreciate your time. Your help on this survey will have influence on how we as a nation deal with sexual issues and diseases like AIDS.

INDEX

Abie's Irish Rose, 60
abortion, 230, 232, 233, 234, 235, 244, 245, 289
abuse, sexual. *See* children, abuse of; forced sex
acquaintance, length of, 74–77, 79
activity, sexual: masturbation and, 159, 165, 167–168; questions about, 253–262; *see also* behavior; practices, sexual
Acton, William, 160
adolescence, questions about, 272—281
adolescents, 5, 8, 9, 14, 48; AIDS and, 200, 218; sexual activity of, 94–95, 232, 233, 234, 235, 239, 287; in sexual market-place, 63, 64; sexual practices of, 27, 89–92; social networks of, 80–81; *see also* children
affection. *See* love
age: AIDS and, 205; alcohol and, 144; attitudes by, 231, 235, 236, 238, 239, 244; choice of partner and, 44, 46, 47, 48, 56, 84–85; duration of sex and, 136, 138; finding partner and, 81, 82, 83, 85–87; at first intercourse, 89–93; forced sex and, 223; frequency of sex and, 114,

115, 116, 118, 120, 121–122, 136; at marriage, 92, 96–99, 101; masturbation and, 156, 162, 163–165, 168; in NHSLS, 37, 38, 39; number of partners and, 101, 102, 104, 108–109; oral sex and, 140, 142, 143, 148; orgasms and, 126–127; sexual preferences by, 140, 144, 146–147, 176
AIDS, 4, 5, 199–218; data on, 26–27, 28, 41, 183, 188; fear of, 5, 8, 95, 110, 217–218; homosexuality and, 169, 170, 171–172; other diseases and, 184, 185, 186, 187, 189, 190, 198; politics and, 182, 200, 217; prevention of, 152–153, 189; questions about, 285–286; risks of contracting, 214; sexual partners and, 43, 44, 69, 89, 109; sexual practices and, 134, 143, 166; speculation about, 14, 199, 200, 202, 217–218; testing, 205–207
alcohol: forced sex and, 223; influence of, 93, 144, 196, 198; questions about, 258, 263, 282, 288
ambivalence about sex, 8, 9, 132; *see also* fear